"It's truly amazing what you can accomplish if no one cares who gets the credit. Pat Williams's new book on teamwork helps reaffirm that conviction for me. The content and style are truly compelling, and I found it to be a remarkable, educating, entertaining, and right-to-the-point delight to read. This book is a real winner."

—Marv Levy, former coach
and general manager, Buffalo Bills

"The Twins organization builds everything around the concept of teamwork. There is no substitute for it in any field of endeavor. My friend Pat Williams has written the textbook on this important topic."

—Ron Gardenhire, manager, Minnesota Twins

"As I read Pat Williams's new book on team building, I thought this man was preaching to the choir. Everything I believe in and have practiced as a college and pro football player, college coach, and TV analyst is nailed down tightly in these well-crafted chapters. Read, apply—and get ready for great results."

—Bill Curry, head football coach,
Georgia State University

"Pat Williams and I first crossed paths over forty years ago when he was a young baseball executive and I was an even younger ball player. Pat was a team builder then and still is today. His new book will teach all of us how to do it. This is the best team-building book you will ever read."

—Dusty Baker, manager, Cincinnati Reds

"Pat Williams has been an inspiration to me for over thirty-five years because he dreams big and achieves those dreams through a love of sports and teamwork. In this book, Pat gives you his blueprint for living out your dreams and the importance of making it a team effort."
—Doug Collins, NBA TV Analyst, Turner Network Television, and former NBA player and coach

"Pat Williams is clear, compelling, and interesting in laying out his principles of team building. *Extreme Dreams Depend on Teams* is the best book Pat has written and is a great read for all of us who want to grow as leaders."
—Steve Reinemund, dean of business, Wake Forest University, and retired chairman/CEO, PepsiCo

"As one who has devoted his life to principles of faith, learning, caring for our brothers and sisters in the human race, defending human rights, and living out good sportsmanship, I have always believed in the power of teamwork. Pat Williams has written a book that embraces the breadth and scope of teamwork as it applies in all of these areas of life. His new book teaches us to dream extreme dreams of making the world a better place—then building teams to make those dreams come true."
—Father Theodore Hesburgh, president emeritus, University of Notre Dame

"This is *the* playbook on teamwork. Through historical examples and personal experiences, Pat Williams inspires new levels of aspiration and performance. This is one of those treasured books that, after you've marked up every page, you find yourself buying for all your friends."
—Howard Schnellenberger, head football coach, Florida Atlantic University

"Written by a master who learned from the masters, this is the required textbook for any course in building successful teams. Pat Williams tells how to write the music, craft the instruments, unify the orchestra, and conduct a championship symphony."
—Gary Bettman,
commissioner, National Hockey League

"Even though baseball is a sport built around individual accomplishments, you cannot win championships unless you do it as a team. Pat Williams's new book captures *everything* I believe and teach about team building. You will be educated, inspired, and motivated to take action by reading EXTREME DREAMS DEPEND ON TEAMS."
Mike Scioscia,
manager, Los Angeles Angels of Anaheim

"Whether on the playing field or in the corporate field or on the battlefield, winning is the result of teamwork. History has shown again and again that a disciplined, cohesive team can prevail against overwhelming odds and obstacles. In EXTREME DREAMS DEPEND ON TEAMS, Pat Williams reveals the inner workings of winning teams and shows us how to achieve 'impossible dreams' through the power of teamwork. Whatever field you compete in, you must read this book."
—Gen. Tommy Franks,
United States Army (Ret.)

"The facets and essence of teams and teamwork are vividly illustrated. I read this with great interest."
—Bill Parcells, executive vice president, Miami Dolphins

"EXTREME DREAMS DEPEND ON TEAMS captures everything I taught and believed in during my career as a manager with the Reds and Tigers. This book will soon be a classic on team-building."
—Sparky Anderson, MLB Hall of Fame manager

"Baseball fans remember the Oriole way of playing that I taught for years in the minor and Major Leagues. It was all based on playing as a team. Pat Williams's excellent new book will tell you exactly how to do it."
—Earl Weaver, MLB Hall of Fame manager

"Everything I believe about teamwork in sports and life is contained in the pages of this important book. Read, apply, and watch your team soar to the top."
—Chuck Tanner, former MLB manager

"This is the best book on teamwork, leadership, and the human spirit that I have ever read!"
—Sean Payton, head coach, New Orleans Saints

"I've been around teams my whole life—playing football at Notre Dame and in the NFL, then analyzing teams at ESPN. Nobody captures the essence of team-building better than Pat Williams in this awesome book. He goes beyond obvious issues of talent and coaching to uncover the hidden principles for motivating underachievers to become overachievers, and for turning a bunch of individual egos into a cohesive team. Whether you're a business leader, coach, player, or fan, you've gotta read this book!"
—Mike Golic, ESPN commentator and
former NFL defensive lineman

"I always told my Dodgers to play for the name on the front of the uniform, not the one on the back. That's the definition of teamwork. This new book by my friend Pat Williams will really hit home with team-builders everywhere."

—Tom Lasorda, Hall of Fame manager, Los Angeles Dodgers

# EXTREME DREAMS
## *Depend on*
# Teams

Pat Williams
*with* Jim Denney

CENTER
STREET®

New York  Boston  Nashville

Scripture quotations are from the Holy Bible, New International Version®. Copyright © 1973, 1978, 1984 by International Bible Society. Used by permission of Zondervan Publishing House. All rights reserved.

Center Street
Hachette Book Group, Inc.
237 Park Avenue
New York, NY 10017

Visit our Web site at www.centerstreet.com.

Printed in the United States of America

First Edition: July 2009
10 9 8 7 6 5 4 3 2 1

The Center Street name and logo are trademarks of Hachette Book Group, Inc.

Library of Congress Cataloging-in-Publication Data

Williams, Pat
    Extreme dreams depend on teams / Pat Williams with Jim Denney.—1st ed.
      p. cm.
    ISBN 978-0-446-40719-9
    1. Teams in the workplace. 2. Teamwork (Sports) 3. Leadership.
4. Motivation (Psychology) 5. Success. I. Denney, James D. II. Title.
    HD66.W5375 2009
      658.4′022—dc22                                    2008043389

Book design by Charles Sutherland

*To my former teammates at Tower Hill School and Wake Forest University, and the many teammates who have been a part of my life throughout forty-seven years of professional athletics. All the good things that have happened in my career are the result of having great teammates.*

# CONTENTS

# <u>FOREWORD</u>

## *by Patrick Lencioni*
Author, *The Five Dysfunctions of a Team*
and *The Five Temptations of a CEO*

IN A WORLD THAT EMPHASIZES THE INDIVIDUAL, where graduation speeches and Hallmark cards urge us to go out into the world and accomplish anything we set our minds to, something often gets lost: our very human need to enlist the help of others and to give help in the same measure.

As human beings, we were made for teamwork.

This is not to say that individuals should not dream big dreams. There is probably no replacement for individual aspiration and determination when it comes to the initiation of an idea, a plan, an "extreme dream." But when it's time for that dream to take shape and that idea to grow and become a tangible reality, there is no substitute for the power of teamwork. The dream of the individual needs a group of selfless people to come together behind that dream, pool their diverse talents, unify as a team, and make great things happen.

Our society celebrates the individual. The Hall of Fame athlete gazes at us from the cover of *Sports Illustrated*. The corporate CEO looks confidently at us from the cover of *Forbes* or *Business-Week*.

But when the game is over and all the points are on the scoreboard—or when the sales are totaled and the annual report goes to press—what stands out and endures is the accomplishment of the *team*. It's the amazing realization that human beings working together have accomplished far more than the sum of their individual efforts and abilities. Why? Because they committed themselves to something larger than themselves.

They achieved greatness as a team.

Pat Williams knows teamwork inside and out. Drawing from his vast experience as general manager of the world champion Philadelphia 76ers and as the key man in building the Orlando Magic from scratch, as well as from his truly voracious appetite for learning and teaching, he has created the most comprehensive and interesting collection of wisdom on teamwork I have ever read.

From Hank Aaron and John Wooden to Ulysses S. Grant and Peter Drucker, Williams reminds us that teamwork is not merely a concept for corporate off-sites but a principle for accomplishing anything meaningful in the world. With story after story, he illustrates some of the great (and seemingly impossible) achievements that were brought about by teamwork. These stories will captivate you, inspire you, and motivate you to dream some extreme dreams of your own and assemble the teams to make those dreams come true.

So read on, but be forewarned: this isn't a book you'll want to skim lightly for a few quick insights. You'll want to keep it on your nightstand and read it slowly. You'll want to digest the rich lessons of the stories and insights. And you'll want to let the energy in these pages ignite your enthusiasm and your imagination.

You were made to dream. And dreams were made for teamwork.

# FOREWORD

## *by Doc Rivers*

Head Coach, the World Champion Boston Celtics

PAT WILLIAMS HAS DREAMED SOME MIGHTY EX-treme dreams—and his dreams became reality because of the principles in this book. As general manager of the Philadelphia 76ers in the 1980s, he helped build an NBA Championship team. Then he went to Orlando, a city without a big-league sports tradition, and he assembled an organization that transformed the central Florida community into an elite sports venue.

I coached the Orlando Magic for more than four seasons and have made that city my permanent residence ever since. I've spent a lot of time with Pat over the years. I know him well. He's a great friend.

But I'm not writing these words as a favor to a friend. I agreed to write this foreword because Pat has uncovered the essential truths about teamwork and distilled them into this book. He has lived these truths every day for as long as I've known him.

One of the most amazing feats of teamwork this man has achieved involves his incredible family. Using the principles in this book, he teamed up his four birth children with fourteen adopted kids from around the world, plus a daughter by remarriage, and he managed to get them all to live together, fly in formation, and love one another as a team. His kids aren't perfect (whose are?), but they have turned out exceptionally well. That's a remarkable teamwork achievement.

If you're a parent, teacher, coach, or youth worker of any kind, you'll want to soak up the teamwork principles in this book and teach them to the kids under your influence. I was fortunate to have coaches and mentors in my early life who not only taught me the technical skills of basketball, but the life lessons of teamwork: leadership, respect, commitment, discipline, perseverance, unselfishness, and hard work. These are not just teamwork values, they're *life* values—and those values are all over these pages.

It's been fascinating to read Pat's book in the aftermath of the Boston Celtics' championship run—and not just because Pat talks about our championship season in the book. More important, I've been fascinated to see that all the teamwork principles Pat talks about in this book are precisely the ingredients that propelled us to an NBA title in 2008.

Again and again as I read, I thought, *Yes! That's it! He nailed it!* Pat even reveals the secret of *ubuntu*. He gets it. He understands that *ubuntu* is not just a slogan or a gimmick. It's a mind-set, a culture, a way of life. It's the essence of unselfishness and team love.

At the beginning of our championship season, we had a lot of new players, and we had to figure out a way to unite as one. As Pat relates in the book, I encountered this magical Bantu word *ubuntu* by sheer serendipity. It was like a burst of revelation—I knew it was exactly what our team needed.

I studied the writings and speeches of South African archbishop Desmond Tutu. "A person is a person through other persons," he wrote in *No Future Without Forgiveness*. "A person with *ubuntu* is open and available to others, affirming of others, does not feel threatened that others are able and good, for he or she has a proper self-assurance that comes from knowing that he or she belongs in a greater whole."[1] That's the essence of what it means to be a team: I can't be all I can be unless you are all you can be. *Ubuntu* is not just a phrase—it's a way of life.

When I took this concept into the Celtics locker room, the entire team bought into *ubuntu* with a white-hot enthusiasm. They broke out of huddles with a shout of "*Ubuntu!*" They wore *ubuntu* on their wristbands. Most important, they carried *ubuntu* in their hearts and lived it out on the court. The insights of *ubuntu* blended seamlessly with the pride of the storied Celtics franchise and the teamwork traditions of the legendary Red Auerbach.

But *ubuntu* is just one piece of the teamwork puzzle. In this book, Pat puts *all* the jigsaw pieces on the table and shows you how to fit them together. He starts with talent—and he shows that talent is not just about your star players, but also your role-players. During our championship season, the media liked to focus on our "big three," Paul Pierce, Kevin Garnett, and Ray Allen. Within the team, however, we talked about our "big twelve." True teamwork means you play your whole bench. Your opponent may figure out how to contain two or three guys, but no opponent can figure out how to contain twelve guys who function as one, no matter which five are on the court at any one time. Our motto was "strength in numbers."

Pat also talks about such teamwork ingredients as commitment, passion, empowerment, trust and respect, character, and leadership—and by leadership, he doesn't just mean a coach, boss, or CEO. He's talking about building leadership *within* the team, among the players, so that the players lead, motivate, inspire, encourage, and even confront one another for the good of the whole team. As I read about those qualities, I thought, *Yes! That's the Celtics! That's why we are what we are, and how we did what we did!*

It's exciting to see that Pat has not confined the issue of teamwork to the sports world or the business world. Teamwork, he says, is for the *whole* world. Teamwork is the key to healing the planet, giving hope to the human race, putting an end to all the plagues of our society, from crime and poverty to cancer and AIDS.

I know Pat's heart. I've seen him with that wonderful United Nations family of his, and I know that if he could, he'd adopt every homeless kid in the world. And he's gone into the Thirty-third Street jail in Orlando and met with youthful offenders, motivating them to turn their lives around. Pat wants to change the world.

But he's just one guy. And one guy can't do it all by himself. So he's written this book to encourage us all to join him in building teams to change the world. "Dream big dreams!" he says. "Aim high! Higher! Then go assemble the teams to turn those dreams into reality."

Some books can change your life. This one could change your world.

# EXTREME DREAMS
## *Depend on*
# Teams

# INTRODUCTION

## *Going to Extremes*

And if I stand or I fall, it's all or nothing at all;
Darling, I don't know why I go to extremes.

BILLY JOEL, "I Go to Extremes" from
the album *Storm Front* (1989)

CALL ME AN EXTREME DREAMER.

I believe in dreaming big dreams and doing everything on an extreme scale. I could never be a chef, because I couldn't stick to the recipe. I'd figure if a *pinch* of salt improves the soup, imagine what a *cup* of salt would do!

Everything I do, I do to extremes. If I got my way, the book you're reading would be a hundred thousand pages long. Think I'm exaggerating? Just ask my writing partner and my team of editors. Every time we do a book together, they have to gang up on me, put me in a headlock, and *force* me to write "The End" after a mere three hundred pages or so! They shout, "Enough! Enough!" And I shout back, "Let me write! I'm just getting started!"

I'm proud to be an extreme dreamer. The world has been transformed and revolutionized, again and again, by people who dreamed extreme dreams—then assembled dynamic teams to turn those dreams into reality.

Inventor Thomas Alva Edison was an extreme dreamer. Soon

after establishing his workshop in Menlo Park, New Jersey, Edison set a goal of turning out a "minor invention" every ten days and a "big one" every six months. Edison kept faith with his dreams. He was granted 1,093 patents for new inventions—an adult-lifetime average of one new invention every ten to twelve days. James Draper Newton, a friend of Edison's, once asked him how one man could accomplish so much in a lifetime.

"People sometimes talk of me as a lone inventor," Edison replied. "Nonsense! Where would I have been without Charles Batchelor and John Kruesi and all the others? We worked long hours together and nobody ever had a better time. . . . Jimmie, you never saw such a mixed crew as we had at Menlo Park. . . . We all worked as a team."[1]

## "THE LONE EAGLE" WAS NEVER ALONE

And then there was aviator Charles Lindbergh. People called him "the Lone Eagle" because of his 1927 solo nonstop flight across the Atlantic—from New York to Paris in thirty-three and one-half hours. It was an extreme dream—and six famous aviators had already died trying to achieve that dream. Why did Lindbergh succeed where others failed? Because "the Lone Eagle" didn't do it alone. He assembled a first-rate *team* to make his extreme dream possible.

Lindbergh began with two St. Louis businessmen, Harry H. Knight and Harold M. Bixby, who secured the financing for the special plane he needed. Bixby was the head of the St. Louis Chamber of Commerce, and he helped Lindbergh fund his dream in exchange for promoting the city of St. Louis with his airplane (which is why the plane was dubbed *Spirit of St. Louis*).

Once Lindbergh had the money to proceed, he hired aviation engineer Donald A. Hall Sr. to design the lightweight, single-engine monoplane, which was custom-built by the Ryan Aero-nautical Company of San Diego. For two months, Hall put in ninety-hour weeks overseeing a crew of more than fifty people, many of whom worked extra shifts without pay because they believed in Lindbergh's dream. Lindbergh lived, ate, and slept at the Ryan airplane factory (housed in a converted San Diego fish cannery that still smelled of dead fish). He watched the plane-building team assemble every rib and rod, truss and gusset, cable and rivet. The plane went from blueprints to rollout in sixty days.

When Lindbergh took the plane up on its first test flight, he was assisted by two teammates: chief mechanic John van der Linde turned the prop to start the engine, and mechanic's assistant Douglas Corrigan removed the wheel chocks.

So while it's true that Charles Lindbergh, "the Lone Eagle," crossed the Atlantic alone, he couldn't have gotten off the ground without his team.[2]

Dream-builders are team-builders. Extreme dreams really do depend on teams.

## HOW THE BALL BOUNCES

In the late 1970s and early 1980s, I was general manager of the Philadelphia 76ers. A big part of my job was to help recruit a great coaching staff and great players to the team. The Sixers team I helped assemble in 1983 swept the Los Angeles Lakers in the finals, winning the NBA Championship.

I moved to Orlando in 1986 to help launch the Orlando Magic. Once again, I was in the dream-building and team-building business. Soon after we got our NBA expansion team up and running, we got a terrific break. As you may know, the NBA lottery is conducted by whirling Ping-Pong balls in a lottery machine. In back-to-back lotteries (1992 and 1993) those Ping-Pong balls bounced our way, allowing us to acquire two young star players—Shaquille O'Neal and Penny Hardaway.

Suddenly, our little franchise in Orlando was the most up-and-coming young team in sports. We got to the NBA Finals in 1995 and reached the Eastern Conference Finals in 1996. Over my NBA career, twenty-three of my teams have made the NBA Playoffs and five have gone to the NBA Finals.

Now, I don't claim to be able to influence the bounce of a Ping-Pong ball in a lottery machine. Still, there were those in our community, in our industry, and in our Magic organization who began to look at me as some kind of a genius at team-building—a good-luck charm in a three-piece suit. And if people chose to think me a genius, who was I to argue?

I found myself avalanched with requests from corporate America, asking me to speak on the subject of building successful teams in the corporate world. Executives and managers wanted to know: can the principles for building successful sports teams be transferred to the business world? The answer: a resounding *yes*. We were already using the same methods and principles to build not only our high-performing basketball team, but also our high-performing sports entertainment business.

So I decided to organize all I knew about team-building into a system of principles that I could teach to others. I became an absolute fanatic about the art and science (and yes, it's truly both) of putting powerhouse teams together. I was obsessed with taking the lessons of the great sports team builders—Red Auerbach, Don Shula, John Wooden, Mike Krzyzewski, Pat Riley, Tom Osborne, Phil Jackson, Rick Pitino, Vince Lombardi, Joe Torre—and transferring those lessons to the business world, the government, the military, the entertainment world, nonprofit organizations, the religious world. And I've distilled it all into this book.

As I write these words, I am focused on a dream. My extreme dream is to write the best daggone book on teamwork ever written! And to make this dream a reality, I've assembled a fabulous team—my longtime writing partner Jim Denney, publisher Rolf Zettersten at Hachette, editors Cara Highsmith and Holly Halverson, and the rest of the editorial team, plus all of the hundreds of sports and business leaders who have shared their insights with me over the years. They have helped me condense more than four decades of team-building experience, thousands of personal interviews, and countless hours of research into the book you hold in your hands.

Teamwork is one of the least understood, least written-about subjects in the business and management world. I have literally hundreds of leadership books lining the shelves of my personal library—but I can count on both hands all the great teamwork books ever published, with fingers left over. Of the few great teamwork books, some of the most insightful and practical volumes were authored by Patrick Lencioni, founder of the management consulting firm the Table Group. In the opening lines of *The Five Dysfunctions of a Team: A Leadership Fable*, he writes:

> Not finance. Not strategy. Not technology. It is teamwork that remains the ultimate competitive advantage, both because it is so powerful and so rare.
>
> A friend of mine, the founder of a company that grew to a billion dollars in annual revenue, best expressed the power of teamwork when he once told me, "If you could get all the people in an organization rowing in the same direction, you could dominate any industry, in any market, against any competition, at any time."[3]

Patrick followed that book with a sequel, *Overcoming the Five Dysfunctions of a Team*, in which he offered some additional perspective:

I honestly believe that in this day and age of informational ubiquity and nanosecond change, teamwork remains the one sustainable competitive advantage that has been largely untapped. In the course of my career as a consultant to executives and their teams, I can say confidently that teamwork is almost always lacking within organizations that fail, and often present within those that succeed. . . .

[The power of teamwork] cannot be denied. When people come together and set aside their individual needs for the good of the whole, they can accomplish what might have looked impossible on paper. They can do this by eliminating the politics and confusion that plague most organizations. As a result, they get more done in less time and with less cost. I think that's worth a lot of effort.[4]

Once you put teamwork into practice in your organization, these principles will begin transforming *everything*. They will transform how you view the world, including our society and its problems, and the political and environmental issues we face. The principles of teamwork will even impact your belief system. By the time you've finished reading and begin to live the concepts of this book, I believe you'll experience a renewal of optimism and hope regarding the problems we face on a national and global scale—and you'll begin seeing the world through a lens of extreme dreams, extreme possibilities, and the power of teamwork.

The essential principles of teamwork are always the same. They apply whether you're building a professional sports team, a dot-com company, a nonprofit organization, or a military unit. You'll find ideas and inspiration throughout these pages, whether you're reading about Coach Mike Krzyzewski firing up the fans in Krzyzewskiville, or General Patton preaching teamwork to the Third Army before D-Day, or Michelangelo assembling a team of artists to paint the ceiling of the Sistine Chapel. The principles in this book are universal. Regardless of the size of your dream, or the shape of your team, you'll be challenged and inspired in a profound and life-changing way.

I hope you take your time, highlight and underline, scribble notes in the margins, and share these principles with the people around you. If you feel this book has been worth your while, please help spread the word to others. Encourage everyone in your organization, your office, and your family to dream extreme dreams, then put together teams to make those dreams come true.

So turn the page, teammate. *Let's go to extremes . . . !*

# Extreme *Sports* Dreams . . .

## *Depend on Teams*

*Nothing happens unless first a dream.*

Carl Sandburg[1]

In the summer of 1976, the American Basketball Association (ABA) folded. The NBA absorbed four ABA teams and the rest were dissolved. As general manager of the Philadelphia 76ers, I was able to acquire some fine talent from former ABA teams.

Then I caught wind of some *big* news: Julius Erving—the phenomenal "Dr. J"—was unhappy with the New York Nets and wanted out of his contract. I contacted the Nets general manager to find out what it would cost to buy out Erving's contract. Answer: three million dollars for the Nets and three million dollars for Julius Erving himself—a cool six-million-dollar deal in total. No NBA team had ever paid that much for a ballplayer.

I went to Sixers owner Fitz Dixon and told him we had an opportunity to acquire Julius Erving. I expected his eyes to light up. Instead, he looked befuddled. "Tell me, Pat," he said, "who is this Erving fellow?"

Who is this Erving fellow? I needed to make Fitz understand the kind of talent Dr. J represented. I said,

"Julius Erving is the Babe Ruth of basketball." Then I told Fitz what it would cost to acquire him.

Fitz didn't blink when I said, "Six million." He simply asked, "Are you recommending this deal?"

"I believe Julius Erving is worth every penny."

Fitz leaned back, smiled, and said, "Fine and dandy."

With those three words, he made a six-million-dollar decision—and he never regretted it.

During Julius Erving's glory days with the Sixers, he filled our arena with screaming fans and clogged our mailroom with letters from around the world. Of all the athletes I've known and worked with, Doc is the most humble and genuine—no swagger, no inflated ego.

Unfortunately, the same could not be said for the rest of the team. When point guard Lloyd "World B" Free dubbed himself the Prince of Mid-Air, center Darryl Dawkins called himself All-Universe. Steve Mix and Joe Bryant constantly vied for more court time. Everyone wanted twenty shots a night. We made the playoffs, but in the finals against the Portland Trailblazers, the Sixers squandered a 2-0 series lead and were beaten in six games. The sports media called the 76ers a collection of selfish ball hogs who didn't deserve to win—and it was true.

After falling short in the chase for the championship, we launched a marketing strategy that apologized for the previous season while promising better things to come: "We Owe You One." We plastered that slogan all over town. But as the '77–'78 season wore on, we began to regret that slogan. Fans soon jeered, "You owe us *two*!"

### "Mo-ses! Mo-ses!"

We continued tinkering with team chemistry, searching for the right balance of talent and temperament. We sought unselfish players who could play within the system of coach Billy Cunningham. We battled our way into the playoffs, yet we ended the '77–'78 season with frustration. And again in 1979, 1980, 1981, and 1982. We chased our championship dreams—and always came up empty. That slogan, "We Owe You One," haunted us. We wondered if we could ever pay that debt.

NutriSystem founder Harold Katz purchased the Sixers from Fitz Dixon in 1981. He made sure we acquired a dominant center as our spark plug: Moses Malone. It cost Mr. Katz $13.2 million to sign Malone—which worked out to about five hundred dollars per minute of playing time. It was a bargain. Malone's emotional intensity, ferocious rebounding, and effective scoring became the focal point of our team.

Moses was fiercely competitive. The rougher it got, the better he played. His rebounding and shooting percentages actually went *up* as the opposition intensified. He often spoke of himself in the third person: "It's never easy for Moses. Moses got to get out there every night and work hard."

The toughness, selflessness, and work ethic Moses displayed spread throughout the team. Over the years, I've found that key players with outstanding character and a good attitude *always* lift the performance of the whole team.

## "Fo' . . . Fo' . . . Fo'!"

By the end of the 1982–1983 regular season, the Sixers had amassed a phenomenal record of 65-17. Then, just days before the playoffs, the unthinkable happened—

Moses Malone came down with crippling tendonitis in both knees. He couldn't walk, much less play basketball. We literally had to carry him into the hospital for X-rays. Just as Moses was about to lead us into the promised land of an NBA Championship, he was struck down.

The doctors treated Moses with anti-inflammatory medication and wrapped his knees in protective sleeves. He said his knees felt like pincushions. With the playoffs just a day away, Coach Cunningham took Moses aside in the locker room. "Well, Mos'," Billy said, "how are we gonna do?"

Without hesitating, Moses replied, "Fo' . . . Fo' . . . Fo'!" Amazingly, he predicted the Sixers would sweep each round of the playoffs—four games in the quarterfinals, four in the semifinals, and four in the finals.

Billy grinned. "I believe you, Mos'."

The best any team had ever done in the NBA Playoffs was 12-2. Moses was predicting 12-0. He made the same prediction to the fans and the press: "Fo' . . . Fo' . . . Fo'!" That became the Sixers' war cry.

In the first game of the quarterfinals against the Knicks, Moses entered the arena with bags of ice taped to his knees. When it was time to play, the ice came off and he took the court. He gave the team thirty-eight minutes of play, scoring thirty-eight points, seventeen rebounds, and zero limps. And the score? Sixers 112,

Knicks 102. And so it went throughout the quarter-finals. The Knicks fell in four straight.

We faced the Milwaukee Bucks in the semifinals. Off-court, Moses packed his throbbing knees in ice. On-court, he played like a man possessed. After winning three straight games, the Sixers came up short in game four, losing 100–94. Asked if his prediction of "Fo' . . . Fo' . . . Fo'!" had been shattered, Moses shrugged and said, "So it'll be fo'-five-fo'." And it was.

The team we had to beat: the Los Angeles Lakers, the reigning NBA champs, led by Kareem and Magic. It was a punishing, physical series, played out between two evenly matched opponents—but in the end it went exactly as Moses Malone predicted: we swept the Lakers in four.

The Philadelphia 76ers were champions at last! We never imagined it would take so long to deliver on our slogan, "We Owe You One," but we finally got it done.

After the final game, I went to the Sixers locker room to join the party. Champagne spewed everywhere, soaking players in their jerseys and executives in their Italian suits. Moses Malone was still in his sweat-soaked jersey, but he had knotted a silk tie around his neck. He grabbed Coach Billy Cunningham and wrapped him in a bear hug, shouting, "Man, we gonna repeat—and 'peat, and 'peat, and 'peat!"

The taste of victory truly is sweet. But as it turned out, we didn't repeat, nor did we 'peat. We had crested that hill, but we couldn't stay on top.

By 1985, I knew I needed a more extreme dream. I needed—Magic.

## It Takes a Community

I asked myself, *What's the biggest, most extreme dream I could take on?* Answer: building an NBA expansion team. But where? My longtime friend Norm Sonju, who had founded the Dallas Mavericks as an expansion franchise in 1980, suggested Tampa (at the time there was no NBA team in Florida). Norm laid out the challenge I faced. I'd have to raise money, drum up community participation, involve business and civic leaders, assemble an ownership group, get the arena built, and on and on.

The dream was daunting, but it had grabbed my soul and wouldn't let go. I took a speaking engagement in Orlando and an old friend, John Tolson, introduced me to a prominent Orlando businessman, Jimmy Hewitt. When they drove me out to the Orlando airport for my return flight, I asked John and Jimmy if they thought Florida was ready for the NBA. "Absolutely," they chorused.

So I said, "Where would you put the team? Tampa? Miami?" Again they answered in unison: "Orlando!" In those days, Orlando's economy consisted of oranges and Walt Disney World, period. The city didn't even have a skyline! But as the three of us talked on the way to the airport, I became convinced that Orlando was the place to be.

Jimmy Hewitt lobbied the Orlando city government and business community, hired a sports attorney, and began assembling an ownership group. In April 1986, Jimmy Hewitt called me in Philadelphia and said, "Bubba"—(Jimmy calls everybody "Bubba")—"this thing is rolling down the tracks. Time for you to jump on board!"

It would be a leap of faith. I'd have to leave a well-paying job in Philly, uproot my family, and work eighteen-hour days in Orlando without any guarantee we'd get the nod from the league. Orlando had no arena and no history of pro sports. We were competing against proven sports markets like Miami, Toronto, and Minnesota. An extreme dream, to be sure. But this was exactly the challenge I was looking for.

"Jimmy," I said, "I'm in."

We assembled our extreme dream team. Jimmy Hewitt led the effort to involve the city government and promote construction of a new arena. I worked to sell season tickets and sky boxes for a team that had no name and might never exist. Accounting whiz Stewart Crane managed our finances. Jacob Stuart of the Greater Orlando Chamber of Commerce helped us design our political strategy. PR genius Jane Hames plotted our marketing strategy. Doug Minear designed our logo, mascot, and uniforms.

By early 1987, we had our ownership group, led by Bill Du Pont of the Du Pont chemical clan. In April, Bill and his wife, Pam, were golfing at the Winged Foot Golf Club in Westchester County, New York, when Bill got an emergency message from the NBA office: be at the Helmsley Palace Hotel in one hour.

Bill grabbed a quick shower, dashed down the FDR Expressway—and promptly got stuck in New York traffic. He leaped from the car and sprinted down Madison Avenue. Arriving precisely on time, he smoothed out his suit and ambled in. There, the NBA brass gave Bill the news: the Orlando Magic was officially an NBA expansion franchise, slated to play its first game in 1989.

And that's how it began. As I write these words, the Magic has made ten playoff appearances in nineteen years, including a conference title and three division titles—and our most recent season was one of our best yet. Who gets the credit? The *team*!

And when I say *team*, I don't mean just the players. I mean the fans, the business community, the owners, the staff, the coaches, and the players. Walk through the streets, malls, offices, and neighborhoods of central Florida and practically everyone you meet is a member of our team. I often say that it takes five guys on the basketball court to put points on the scoreboard, but it takes an entire community to lift those five guys.

## Teamwork: Key to Perfection

What's the most extreme dream any team could set for itself? How about—*perfection*?

In January 1972, after the Miami Dolphins lost Super Bowl VI to the Cowboys by a humiliating score of 24 to 3, Dolphins head coach Don Shula told his team, "We lost our season today, and there's no way we'll ever get that back."[2] The only way to erase the shame of that loss, he said, was to win it all the following year.

Shula's players got the message. The next season, they envisioned an extreme dream of perfection. They challenged and encouraged one another. If they fell behind, they rallied for a comeback. They shut out two opponents, beating the Baltimore Colts 23–0 in game seven and the Patriots 52–0 in game nine.

In game five, a home game against the Chargers, two San Diego linemen, Deacon Jones and Ron East, broke through the line as quarterback Bob Griese dropped back to pass. Just as Griese got the ball away, East hit him low while the Deacon hit him high. When the dust cleared, Griese was writhing on the ground.

The Miami crowd was strangely silent as medics carted Griese off the field. An ashen-faced Coach Shula sent in backup quarterback Earl Morrall. Griese had a broken fibula (one of the two lower leg bones) and a dislocated ankle.

Morrall led the Dolphins to a 24–10 win over the Chargers. He continued leading the team through the rest of the season and the first game of the playoffs. The Dolphins remained unbeaten game after game. Meanwhile, Bob Griese kept up with the team, attended all the team meetings, and watched game film—just as if he were the starting quarterback.

Shula started Earl Morrall in the first half of the AFC Championship game against the Pittsburgh Steelers. It was a hard-fought game, and the score was 7–7 at the half. In the locker room, Shula took Griese aside and said, "You start the second half." Griese said, "Okay." Then Shula went to give Earl Morrall the news.[3]

Bob Griese later recalled, "It must have been tough for [Shula] to tell Earl that he was putting me in—and it must have been hard for Earl to hear it. But Earl accepted it. . . . Every single player on that team thought in terms of team first, self second."[4]

It was game sixteen of the Dolphins' season—and Bob Griese hadn't played since game five. But he led his team to a 21–17 road victory over the Steelers. Again, the Dolphins were AFC champions. But the big game still lay ahead.

Super Bowl VII, the Miami Dolphins vs. the Washington Redskins, took place on January 14, 1973, at the Los Angeles Memorial Coliseum. The Miami defense dominated, permitting the Redskins to cross midfield just once in the first half and three times in the second. Final score: 14–7. The Dolphins were not only NFL champions but the only team to ever go undefeated and untied through the season and postseason.

Extreme dreams of perfection depend on teams.

## Every Extreme Sports Dream Needs a Team

They called it "the miracle on ice."

The United States Olympic hockey team consisted of young amateurs and college players—all nonprofessionals in the true Olympic tradition. On February 22, 1980, in Lake Placid, New York, they faced a Soviet Union team composed of players whom their government classified as bricklayers, truck drivers, or students, but who were paid to play hockey all year round in world-class training facilities. The Soviet hockey team had not lost an Olympic match since 1968 and had not fallen short of the gold since 1960.

The Americans were seeded seventh in a twelve-team field. Less than two weeks earlier, on February 9, the USA and Soviet teams had played an exhibition match at Madison Square Garden. The Americans lost, 10–3. USA hockey coach Herb Brooks knew he couldn't match the Soviets in talent, strength, or conditioning. To pull off a miracle, he'd have to beat the Soviets with *teamwork*.

Months earlier, when assembling his team, Coach Brooks had sought out players who would put the team ahead of individual glory. He had rejected some of the most talented and accomplished college players because they lacked the unselfishness his team would need. Brooks said he was "looking for players whose name on the front of the sweater is more important than the one on the back."[5]

Coach Brooks put his team through grueling, all-out practices to build stamina and cohesion. He drilled them until they could practically read one another's thoughts. His goal: to transform a collection of individuals into a single organism of many parts all functioning as one. When they failed to play up to their potential, he unleashed his repertoire of stinging rebukes: "You're playing worse and worse every day and right now you're playing like next month." But he also motivated his players with encouragement. Before sending them out on the ice against the Soviets, he told them, "This moment is yours. You're meant to be here at this time."[6]

As the match began, the Soviets scored early, but USA forward Buzz Schneider soon tied the score at one. The Soviets scored again, but forward Mark Johnson answered with a tying goal with a second left in the first period. The Soviets went ahead again—and Johnson hit back, tying the game at three. The normally high-scoring Russians found it nearly impossible to get the puck past goalie Jim Craig, who smothered thirty-six of the Soviets' thirty-nine shots. Finally, with ten minutes remaining, USA's Mike Eruzione teed up a shot that exploded into the net, giving USA a 4–3 lead.

That's when Coach Brooks got *really* nervous. He had seen other teams gain a one-puck lead on the Soviets—and something always went wrong. Brooks shouted, "Play your game! Play your game!"[7]

Team USA played its game. The Americans clung to their razor-thin lead as the crowd counted down the final seconds. ABC sportscaster Al Michaels made the call: "Ten seconds! The countdown is going on right now! Morrow, up to Silk, five seconds left in the game! Do you believe in miracles? *Yes!* Unbelievable!"[8]

In the stands, the crowd cheered, wept, waved American flags, and sang "God Bless America." The 1980 U.S. hockey team had stepped onto the ice as underdogs. They walked off as legends. *Sports Illustrated* named the "miracle on ice" as the greatest sports moment of the twentieth century.[9]

Herb Brooks was killed in a car crash in 2003. Shortly before his death, he told a newspaper interviewer, "We grew up as kids having dreams, but now we're too sophisticated as adults, as a nation. We stopped dreaming. We should always have dreams. I'm a dreamer."[10]

Herb Brooks was an *extreme* dreamer, and he knew how to build a team to make those dreams come true.

So if you have an extreme sports dream, don't do it alone. Dream big dreams, assemble your team, and share the victory with your teammates.

# 1

## *Something Bigger Than Ourselves*

Though one may be overpowered,
two can defend themselves.
A cord of three strands is not quickly broken.

ECCLESIASTES 4:12

TEAMWORK HAS BEEN ONE OF THE GREAT THEMES
of my life for as long as I can remember. As a boy and as a man, as
a team player or a team-builder, I've spent the vast majority of my
years living by the principles of teamwork.

My dad gave me my first baseball glove when I was three and
took me to my first major-league baseball game when I was seven.
Dad, my sister Carol, and I sat in the stands at Philadelphia's historic Shibe Park, scarfing hot dogs and cheering our throats raw
during a Philadelphia Athletics–Cleveland Indians doubleheader.
It was a glorious day, and I was hooked for life on the joyous mys-
tique of teamwork.

When I was twelve, I played on my first baseball team. I loved
the sense of comradeship, the giving and receiving of encouragement, the joy of victory, the shared consolation of defeat, the sense
of belonging, and the pride of realizing, *We're a team!* I've been
involved with team sports nearly every day of my life since then.
That's more than half a century of teamwork experience, from

elementary school to junior high to high school to college to the pros.

I've learned that every important accomplishment in life involves teamwork. The same principles that apply to team sports also apply in the corporate environment, government, the military, the religious world, and in families. As a dad, I helped raise four birth kids and fourteen kids by international adoption, so I was putting teams together every single day to keep our busy household functioning smoothly.

Teamwork is essential to our security and national defense. In *Creating a Culture of Success*, Charles Dygert and Richard Jacobs observe:

> The United States military, in conjunction with its coalition forces throughout the world, emphasizes the importance of teamwork among its various branches. As we watched daily television war briefings by General Brooks on the war in Iraq in 2003, we noticed that he always attributed successes to the "people," not to the technology. He acknowledged that the technology was the best in the world, but emphasized that it was people working together that made the technology effective.[1]

The medical staff of a hospital is also a team. The principles of teamwork are essential to a high-performing, effective lifesaving operation. Business writer William A. Cohen, PhD, offers this insight in *Secrets of Special Ops Leadership*:

> Peter Drucker found an interesting phenomenon in investigating the procedures in a well-run hospital. Doctors, nurses, x-ray technicians, pharmacologists, pathologists, and other health care practitioners all worked together to accomplish a single object. Frequently he saw several work-

ing on the same patient under emergency conditions. Seconds counted. Even a minor slip could prove fatal. Yet, with a minimum amount of conscious command or control by any one individual, these medical teams worked together toward a common end and followed a common plan of action under the overall direction of a doctor.[2]

A business is a team—or should be. This is true whether the business is Microsoft or General Electric or Kelly's Korner Koffeeshop. I have given thousands of speeches to corporate meetings and business conventions, and the number one subject I'm asked to speak on is teamwork. Whenever people come together to achieve a vision, their first priority *must* be to function as a *team*.

## WE WERE MADE FOR TEAMWORK

Why do teams exist? Answer: teams exist to enable people to work together and achieve high goals that would be out of reach for individuals working separately. Teamwork multiplies abilities and strengths. Teamwork enables individuals to complement one another and compensate for one another's lacks and weaknesses. In the first *Rocky* film (1976), boxer Rocky Balboa (Sylvester Stallone) has a conversation with Paulie, the brother of Rocky's girlfriend, Adrian.

"You like her?" asks Paulie.

"Sure, I like her," Rocky says.

"What's the attraction?"

"I dunno. She fills gaps."

"What's 'gaps'?"

Rocky says, "She's got gaps, I got gaps. Together we fill gaps."[3]

That's why we have teams. Teamwork fills gaps.

Phil Jackson, head coach of the Los Angeles Lakers, is known for his mystical approach to basketball. Before leading a team into the playoffs, he gathers his players and reads from Rudyard Kipling's poem "The Law of the Jungle":

> *Now this is the Law of the Jungle—*
> *as old and as true as the sky;*
> *And the Wolf that shall keep it may prosper,*
> *but the Wolf that shall break it must die.*
> *As the creeper that girdles the tree-trunk*
> *the Law runneth forward and back—*
> *For the strength of the Pack is the Wolf,*
> *and the strength of the Wolf is the Pack.*[4]

As a forward for the U.S. women's national soccer team, Mia Hamm scored more international-competition goals than any other player, male or female, in the history of the game. She helped win a Women's World Cup championship in 1999 and was named Women's World Player of the Year in 2001 and 2002 by the Fédération Internationale de Football Association (FIFA). Her teamwork philosophy is simple:

> Soccer is not an individual sport. I don't score all the goals, and the ones I do score are usually the product of a team effort. I don't keep the ball out of the back of the net on the other end of the field. I don't plan our game tactics. I don't wash our training gear (okay, sometimes I do), and I don't make our airline reservations. I am a member of a team, and I rely on the team. I defer to it and sacrifice for it, because the team, not the individual, is the ultimate champion.[5]

Aren't there sports involving *solo* achievements—one person competing for individual glory without a team? What about racing cyclist Lance Armstrong? It's true that Armstrong's seven consecutive Tour de France victories (1999 to 2005) constitute a stunning personal achievement. But few people realize that Armstrong's extreme accomplishment is truly a *team* accomplishment. While Armstrong is the star of the show, he could not achieve victory without his team.

Armstrong was coached by elite cyclist Chris Carmichael, Italian cycling coach Michele Ferrari, and Belgian cycling pro Johan Bruyneel. He has an aerodynamicist who tests his equipment and advises him on the best gear to wear during time trials. A radio headset in his helmet keeps him in contact with his team manager. In every race, he uses three different bikes—for time trials, for racing on the flats, and for mountain racing. His personal mechanic keeps all three precisely tuned to his preferences.

Armstrong's racing team consists of nine cyclists. The other eight cyclists support Lance's strategy and control the tempo of the race. They work much like an offensive line in football, blocking and protecting the quarterback so he can make plays. In *It's Not About the Bike: My Journey Back to Life*, Armstrong observed,

> Cycling is an intricate, highly politicized sport, and it's far more of a team sport than the spectator realizes. . . . On any team, each rider has a job, and is responsible for a specific part of the race. The slower riders are called *domestiques*—servants—because they do the less glamorous work of "pulling" up hills ("pulling" is cycling lingo for blocking the wind for the other riders) and protecting their team leader through the various perils of a stage race. The team leader is the principal cyclist, the rider most capable of sprinting to a finish with 150 miles in his legs.[6]

Armstrong says there is a subtle form of teamwork that takes place even between *opposing* cyclists in the pack (which, in bike-racing terms, is called the *peloton*):

To the spectator [the peloton] seems like a radiant blur, humming as it goes by, but that colorful blur is rife with contact, the clashing of handlebars, elbows, and knees, and it's full of international intrigues and deals. The speed of the peloton varies. Sometimes it moves at 20 miles an hour, the riders pedaling slow and chatting. Other times, the group is spanned out across the road and we're going 40 miles an hour. Within the peloton, there are constant negotiations between competing riders: pull me today, and I'll pull you tomorrow. Give an inch, make a friend. You don't make deals that compromise yourself or your team, of course, but you help other riders if you can, so they might return the favor.[7]

Human beings are designed for teamwork. We have a deep need to achieve extreme dreams through people. Coach Mike Krzyzewski has led his Duke Blue Devils basketball team to three NCAA Championships, ten Final Fours, and ten ACC Championships. "People want to be on a team," Coach K once said. "They want to be part of something bigger than themselves. They want to be in a situation where they feel that they are doing something for the greater good."[8]

As head coach of the Los Angeles Lakers, Pat Riley won back-to-back NBA Championships (1987 and 1988). In 1990, he briefly retired and became a TV sports commentator for NBC. The following year, he took a coaching position with the New York Knicks. In an interview with Dave Anderson of the *New York Times*, Riley explained why he couldn't stay at NBC—and why he couldn't stay away from coaching.

"After the studio show each week," Riley said, "I'd walk out of NBC alone. I'd get in a cab alone. I'd take a flight back to California alone, then the next weekend I'd get on a flight to New York and come back alone. After you've been around a team for thirty years, it's hard being alone like that." Anderson concluded, "Happiness for Pat Riley is coaching an NBA team again."[9] What's true for Pat Riley is true for us all: we were designed to be part of a team, and we are not happy living and working alone.

Even in as highly individual a sport as tennis, people long to be part of a team. Czech-born Martina Navratilova is the former number one women's tennis player in the world. "I like playing on a team," she once said. "That's why I like playing doubles because I like to talk to my teammate, to my partner. I hate being all alone on the court, because when you talk to yourself it's kind of strange. But I love being on a team. It's fun to get that support from your teammates and also to give it, try to figure out what they can and cannot do, and yelling on the sideline."[10]

Debbie Miller-Palmore is an Olympic athlete, a former women's pro basketball player, and the founder of Top of the Key, an organization devoted to developing the athletic, intellectual, and spiritual dimensions of athletes and coaches through basketball camps, clinics, and seminars. "Even when you've played the game of your life," she once said, "it's the feeling of teamwork that you'll remember. You'll forget the plays, the shots, and the scores, but you'll never forget your teammates."[11]

When I was the general manager of the Philadelphia 76ers, I thought that if I could only earn an NBA Championship ring, I'd be riding on a cloud for the rest of my life. When it happened, it was truly as thrilling as I thought it would be—for a while. But the thrill of victory soon wore off. I have a championship ring—but I never wear it. I put that ring in a drawer a long time ago and haven't looked at it in years.

So what do I think about when I remember that championship

season? I remember the *team experiences*, the complex challenge of assembling a team like pieces on a chessboard, the joy of watching everything click, the games, the screaming fans, the camaraderie with the players in the locker room. I remember all of it like it was yesterday. I remember it vividly because I was a team-builder—

And I was a part of a team.

## WHEN IS A TEAM A TEAM?

Extreme dreams come true when the right combination of talent, character, attitude, discipline, and hard work coalesce into a genuine *team*. A great team is an ever-changing puzzle assembled out of moving parts that function together in complex, unpredictable ways. Team-building requires an enormous depth of insight, skill, patience, and a fortunate break or two.

At the heart of teamwork is a concept everybody talks about but few understand. That concept is called *synergy*. The word comes from the Greek *sunergos*, meaning "working together," from *sun* ("together") and *ergon* ("work"). *Synergy* could be defined as the interaction between two or more individuals in such a way that their combined effectiveness exceeds the sum of their individual abilities and strengths. In *The Winner Within*, Pat Riley writes about the synergistic power of teamwork:

> Teamwork is the essence of life.
>
> If there's one thing on which I am an authority, it's how to blend the talents and strengths of individuals into a force that becomes greater than the sum of its parts. My driving belief is this: great teamwork is the only way to reach our ultimate moments, to create breakthroughs that define our careers, to fulfill our lives with a sense of lasting significance. . . .

When our teams excel, we win. Our best efforts, combined with those of our teammates, grow into something far greater and far more satisfying than anything we could have achieved on our own. Teams make us part of something that matters.[12]

Pat Riley is talking about that mystical conjunction called *synergy*.

I've seen situations (and you've seen them too) where a manager or professor or pastor puts people in a room, assigns them a task, and says, "You're a team." Of course, they are *not* a team—not yet. They may be a committee, but they lack the magical synergistic *something* that makes them a true team.

Many organizations claim to believe in teamwork. Few have actually learned what a team is or how to assemble one. You can go to Pep Boys, buy fifty thousand dollars' worth of car parts, take them home, and dump them out in your driveway. But that's not a car. That's just a collection of parts. To be a car, those parts have to be the *right* parts, they have to *complement* one another, and they have to be properly *assembled*.

The same is true of a team.

When you truly have a team and not just a committee, you know it. Why? Because of synergy. When your team is functioning as a team, it will achieve greater things than all your individual team-members could achieve separately. Your team will function cohesively, think creatively, and exceed all expectations.

## THE INVISIBLE HAND

You can start any great enterprise with a team of two. In 1986, the organization we know today as the Orlando Magic consisted of just two people: Jimmy Hewitt and Pat Williams. We had an extreme dream of an NBA franchise in central Florida. We were passionate about that dream, and we quickly recruited others to join our team. Today, the Magic is an enterprise employing hundreds of people, contributing millions of dollars to the central Florida economy. Don't be afraid to start small and dream big. Start with the most basic unit of teamwork: two. Put two people together, apply the lessons and principles of teamwork in this book—and when you need to grow your team, recruit more players.

In 1958, educator Leonard E. Read published an essay entitled "I, Pencil." The essay is written from the first-person perspective of a pencil. The essay begins:

> I am a lead pencil—the ordinary wooden pencil familiar to all boys and girls and adults who can read and write. . . .
>
> I, Pencil, simple though I appear to be, merit your wonder and awe. . . . I have a profound lesson to teach. And I can teach this lesson better than can an automobile or an airplane or a mechanical dishwasher because—well, because I am seemingly so simple.
>
> Simple? Yet, not a single person on the face of this earth knows how to make me.[13]

You might think, *Is that true? No person on earth knows how to make a pencil? Then how are pencils produced by the billions every year?* Answer: the "simple" pencil is constructed of so many different components: wood, graphite, glue, lacquer, metal, and more—that it can be made only by teamwork.

You probably didn't know that the metal ring that holds the eraser is called the *ferrule.* It's made of brass (an alloy of copper and zinc), usually accented with rings of black nickel. How is the brass ferrule formed? How is the black nickel applied? How is the ferrule secured to the end of the pencil? These are all areas of individual expertise.

And what about the eraser? What is it made of? You'd probably say, "Rubber." Well, the rubber in an eraser is merely a binding agent; rubber does not have erasing properties of its own. The actual erasing agent is an ingredient called *factice*, which is made by a process of reacting canola oil with sulfur chloride.

The components of a pencil come from all over the world and require thousands of people with many specialized skills to bring those components together to form a pencil. The straight-grain cedar comes from northern California and Oregon. It is harvested by loggers, cut by mill workers, and shipped by railroad workers. The wood is cut into small pencil-length slats, kiln-dried, and tinted. It is grooved and sandwiched with graphite that was mined in Ceylon and mixed with clay from Mississippi and candelilla wax from Mexico. And the story of the pencil goes on and on in fascinating detail.

No one, not even the president of the pencil company, understands all the processes required to make one simple pencil. Somehow, all of these thousands of people contribute something irreplaceable to the process. The pencil is fashioned by teamwork.

The author of the essay, Leonard Read, adds that there is no "master mind" directing the process. No one forces any of the people in the process to do his or her job. "Instead," he says, "we find the Invisible Hand at work." What is that Invisible Hand? It is the mysterious power of synergy.[14]

Without teamwork, there is no pencil.

And without synergy, there is no teamwork.

## NO DREAM IS TOO EXTREME

In Walt Disney's 1940 motion picture *Pinocchio*, Jiminy Cricket (voiced by Cliff Edwards) sang these words: "If your heart is in your dream / No request is too extreme."[15] No dream of the future is too extreme to reach for, work for, and build for. What about a dream of a world beyond war and racism and hate? An extreme dream—but not *too* extreme. Why not dream it, assemble a team, and make it happen?

What about a dream of a world beyond cancer, AIDS, and other diseases? Or a dream of solving our energy and environmental problems? Or a dream of making the world safe for children—where no child in the world would ever go to bed hungry, or homeless, or physically or sexually abused? Dream it, my friend, then assemble a team and *do* it!

Or what about a dream of colonizing Mars, mining the asteroids, and moving out to the stars? Why shouldn't we? Aim high, dream far! Then make it so!

Teamwork is the ideal environment for solving human problems. Super Bowl champion and college football coach Bill Curry talks about a teamwork phenomenon he calls "the miracle of the huddle," which transcends all differences, erases all distinctions, and bonds people together in a tightly knit brotherhood or sisterhood of teamwork. Curry describes it this way: "The most important thing about sports is the miracle of the huddle. Players of all races, nationalities, religions, backgrounds, and creeds come together as one to accomplish a common goal as a team."[16]

And because teamwork transcends all our petty differences and teaches us to work together for the benefit of all, teamwork is the ideal means of solving all the problems that plague our race and our planet. Individually, we can accomplish next to nothing. But working as a team, there's nothing we can't achieve—

And no dream is too extreme.

# Extreme *Entrepreneurial* Dreams . . .

## *Depend on Teams*

*Entrepreneurs are the foundation of our work-force—it's their ventures that provide jobs. Their entrepreneurial dreams become the backbone of communities. They pay for employees' health insurance, broaden and expand families' life-styles, and set standards for efficiency and pro-ductivity that make American business the best in the world.*

KEP SWEENEY, *The New Restaurant Entrepreneur*[1]

Tech-entrepreneur Charles Katz founded several start-up companies during the dot-com boom; he sold those companies for tens of millions of dollars. Katz learned the value of teamwork at the age of ten.

His first entrepreneurial venture was a snow-shoveling business, which he operated in his subur-ban Washington, D.C., neighborhood. He put together a team of four or five kids, and they went door-to-door, offering their services at three dollars per hour per person. When potential customers said, "No thanks, I'll shovel it myself," he'd point to a clean driveway down the block and say, "We'll make your driveway look just like that!" Often as not, they'd get the job.

"Teamwork was important, of course," Katz recalls. "It was a lot more productive—and a lot more fun—to shovel snow with a bunch of people than it was to do it alone."[2]

Charles Katz learned about teamwork at an early age—and he went on to make millions. What is *your* extreme entrepreneurial dream? Whatever your goals, dream big, aim high, and assemble a team to make it happen.

## An Extreme Global Economy Dream

In 1989, after dropping out of Stanford in his senior year, Joe Liemandt founded Austin-based Trilogy Software, Inc. He was twenty-two years old. When his father learned of his plans, he called Joe a "moron." Today, the Stanford dropout is frequently invited back to Stanford to lecture.

Trilogy is valued at more than $1 billion (of which Liemandt himself owns 55 percent) and remains one of the most successful privately held companies in the world. With overseas offices in Bangalore, India, and Hangzhou, China, Trilogy works exclusively with Global 1000 companies, including British Airways, Ford, Daimler AG, Goodyear, Prudential, and IBM.[3]

Over the years, Trilogy has been profiled by such publications as *Fast Company*, *Forbes*, *Newsweek*, and the *Harvard Business Review*. Trilogy's unusual business model is based on delivering customer satisfaction. The company's revenue and employee incentives are directly tied to the success of the customer. If Trilogy's customers don't make money, neither does

Trilogy. Fortunately, Trilogy's clients *do* make money—tons of it—and that's why Joe Liemandt's company is so successful.

The key to Trilogy's phenomenal success is Liemandt's unique approach to teamwork. That approach is called Trilogy University (TU), an intensive and high-energy orientation program for new hires. Liemandt calls TU "more boot camp than business school." Trilogy's goal is to "recruit 'em young, fire 'em up, and turn 'em loose."[4]

Rather than hiring experienced execs and engineers from other companies, Liemandt prefers to grab smart, enthusiastic young college grads. They go straight from the university campus to Trilogy University, where they undergo a three-month crash course in global economics, software design, and the Trilogy culture. As one TU grad put it, "I wasn't ready for college to end. None of us were. Now it doesn't have to."[5]

The company sends recruiters to university career fairs seeking brash young overachievers brimming with talent, drive, and ambition. Top recruits undergo a grueling interview that typically begins with a handshake and the words, "You'd better impress me." But they are also treated to a kaleidoscope of fun activities, from an afternoon of mountain biking and laser tag to a sampling of uptown Austin nightlife and cuisine. Those who make the cut join the elite and exclusive culture of the "Trilogians."[6]

In a typical year, Trilogy may receive fifteen thousand résumés and applications; fewer than nine hundred prospects will be brought to Austin for interviews; fewer than a third of those will be hired. It's an expensive sifting process, but it yields a significant number of computer wizards who produce millions of dollars' worth of new software packages.[7]

Trilogians love what they do and do what they love. As a result, Joe Liemandt has no clock-watchers on his payroll, and his teams burn a lot of midnight oil. One Trilogian, Joshua Walsky, told *Fast Company*, "People ask me, 'How can you hang out all the time with the same people you work with?' I tell them, 'Well, Trilogy hires people who are smart, talented, interesting, and cool. Those are exactly the sort of people I want to be around.' "[8]

When the people on your team believe in what they do, it's hard to get them to go home. Wouldn't you love to have a team of Trilogians in your office?

## How to Make Extreme Entrepreneurial Dreams Come True

Why is teamwork such a powerful force for making entrepreneurial dreams come true? Let me suggest several reasons:

An atmosphere of teamwork focuses everyone in the organization on a single goal. When the team is aligned in a single direction, the organization moves forward as one.

Teamwork also summons forth every individual's best effort. Each team member thinks, *I have an important part to play. I'm not a spectator; I belong to this team, and I have a stake in whether the team wins or loses.*

As organizations grow, dividing the organization into teams can help maintain an atmosphere of closeness and connectedness. A worker who functions in a fifty-story glass-and-steel edifice honeycombed with cubicles feels like a cog in an impersonal machine. But those who say, "I belong to a team," feel a sense of ownership and belonging.

Teamwork breaks down bureaucratic barriers and rigid thinking, reducing the tendency for people to say, "That's not my job." When people feel ownership of a team and its goals, they pitch in and do what needs to be done, even if a task is not in their job description.

Whatever the extreme dreams of your company, you can assemble teams to turn those dreams into astonishing realities. Here are the essential principles of entrepreneurial teamwork:

## 1. Dream Big, Aim High

Want to open a sandwich shop? Then make sure the sandwiches you build make the world stand up and take notice. Want to start a widget factory? Then manufacture the Rolls-Royce of widgets—the kind of widgets that get you interviewed on every TV show from *Oprah* to *The O'Reilly Factor*. Dream big. Aim high.

During the Vietnam War, Fred Smith was a Marine Corps forward air controller who flew two hundred combat missions in the backseat of an OV-10 Bronco attack plane. He earned the Silver Star, the Bronze Star, and two Purple Hearts.

While in Vietnam, Smith thought often about an extreme dream he'd first set down on paper a few years earlier in an economics class at Yale. In that paper, he had outlined the concept of an overnight air freight system: couriers would pick up packages all over the United States, fly them to a central processing hub, sort and batch them, then fly them out to their destinations—overnight delivery, guaranteed. His Yale professor called Smith's idea unworkable and gave the paper a C+.[9]

After his discharge, Smith put his extreme dream to the test and founded his visionary company, Federal Express, in 1971. His funding came from his $4 million inheritance, plus $91 million in venture capital. Most of the start-up money went to buy a fleet of aircraft. This left very little cash for operating expenses and contingencies. As a result, Smith sometimes asked his employees to hold off cashing their paychecks for a week or two. Some Federal Express pilots even had to purchase jet fuel with their own money to get their planes off the ground. Tom Oliver, former executive vice president of FedEx, recalls, "Our people got the company through those difficult times. Their spirit shaped Federal Express."[10]

Why did FedEx employees go above and beyond the call of duty in those difficult early days? They believed in Fred Smith's extreme dream. They knew that they were part of something that had never been done before—and they believed in the dream.

Big, bold, extreme dreams capture the imagination and fire the enthusiasm. When people believe they are involved in something *big*, they'll sacrifice to make it happen.

## 2. Think "Yin and Yang"

The ancient Chinese taught that the natural world is divided between "yin and yang," between mutually complementary opposites such as light and dark, night and day, summer and winter, male and female. Opposites complement and complete each other, maintaining a dynamic equilibrium. Experience shows that this concept holds true in a teamwork environment—and especially in business partnerships.

The next time you have a scoop of Ben & Jerry's ice cream, remember "yin and yang." High school buddies Ben Cohen and Jerry Greenfield decided to go into business together. They opened their first ice-cream shop after taking a five-dollar correspondence course from Penn State. They divided up the business chores with each partner sticking to his strengths. Ben, the extrovert, went to restaurants and stores, making deals and selling ice cream. Jerry, the introvert, stayed in the shop, testing recipes and manufacturing the product. The key to their success was that each partner had a clearly defined role. "I was doing sales and marketing," Ben Cohen explained, "and Jerry was doing manufacturing. He had complete say over his area of the company, and I had pretty much complete say over mine."[11]

You find the same dynamic in the partnership of Microsoft founders Bill Gates and Paul Allen. Gates was the outside guy—extroverted, always on the road, meeting customers, marketing, and making deals. He was the driven, competitive, financial genius. Allen was the inside guy—introverted, the technical innovator, the manager. Business writer Laura Rich explained: "They were different in every way. . . . It was a good partnership. It was yin-and-yang. . . . Gates wanted more than anything to make money; Allen wanted more than anything to be the first to spot a technological idea. . . . It was a partnership made in heaven—it worked."[12]

The Hewlett-Packard story follows the same pattern. Business writer Charlene O'Hanlon wrote that "Packard and Hewlett were at opposite ends of the personality spectrum." The driven, outgoing David Packard was the perfect complement to the lighthearted, easygoing William Hewlett. Together, they launched their high-tech company in 1939, working out of a one-car garage. Their first big sale was an innovative audio device they sold to the Walt Disney Studio; Disney used it to produce the lifelike stereophonic sound track for the animated feature *Fantasia*.[13]

And speaking of Disney, we find a similar yin-yang dynamic between Walt Disney and his brother Roy. While researching my motivational biography of Walt Disney, *How to Be Like Walt* (Health Communications, 2004), I was fascinated to learn that Walt, the extreme dreamer, owed much of his success to Roy, the accountant and banker.

Longtime Disney employee Pam Dahl told me, "Walt's vision could not have succeeded without Roy. Walt had wonderful, towering dreams, but it was Roy who laid the concrete for those dreams to stand on. Roy has never gotten the credit he deserves for believing in his brother's dreams and getting them built and paid for." And Disney expert Peggy Matthews Rose told me, "Every Walt needs a Roy and every Roy needs a Walt."[14] It's true. Walt never could have created *Snow*

*White* or Disneyland without Roy—and without Walt, Roy never would have become a Hollywood movie mogul.

Finally, there's my friend Rich DeVos, owner of the Orlando Magic. Along with his friend the late Jay Van Andel, Rich cofounded the Amway network marketing company in 1959. Rich is an extrovert, a cheerleader, a motivator, and a salesman. Jay was an introvert, an analyst, a problem-solver. Each admired and respected the strengths of the other. As I wrote in my book *How to Be Like Rich DeVos*, "It was a well-balanced partnership because they complemented each other's leadership strengths while compensating for each other's weaknesses. Decision-making responsibility was shared fifty-fifty."[15]

In forming your teamwork partnerships, think "yin and yang." Find someone who complements you, merge your respective strengths, and achieve great things together.

### 3. Make Sure Your Team Is Well Coached

Coaching teams in the business world requires just the right touch. If you, as the leader or coach, come on too strong and intimidating, you will strike fear in the hearts of your team. Fear squelches communication and suffocates creativity. So you have to maintain a light touch to unleash the talent and imagination of your team.

At the same time, you have to remain vigilant and maintain lines of accountability so that problems don't pile up. When the team needs a decision from the coach, you need to be available to render that decision on the spot so that you don't become a bottleneck, impeding the work of the team.

When you launch a new team, you may have only a few critical days at the beginning of the process where you can provide significant guidance to the players and they will welcome your input. Use that time to project the vision, establish the goals and benchmarks, design the crucial tasks, assign responsibilities, and set a system of incentives and rewards. If you get the team off on the right foot at the very beginning, you will have done your job well. After that, get regular reports on the team's progress. If everything is going well, keep your hands off and let the team do its job.

Once the team is rolling on its own, coach sparingly. Check in at regular intervals, but stay out of the way. Teams develop their own rhythms and chemistry, and if you involve yourself too often, you may upset the smooth functioning of your team.

### 4. Reward Team Attitude and Team Effort

The natural tendency of leaders and coaches is to reward individual achievements. The problem is that when teams succeed, it is often the result of selflessness and sacrifice on the part of people who truly "think *team*" and never get any glory. So the job of the leader or coach is to dig a little deeper, look beyond the flashy accomplishments of the stars on the team, and find ways to acknowledge and reward the hod carriers and role-players. Yes, we should acknowledge individual achievement—but we should also recognize the team as a whole—and especially those self-effacing, self-sacrificing team players who make their contribution without making headlines.

### 5. Decompartmentalize Your Team

A team can't function if the members of the team are isolated from one another. A high-functioning team throws people together and keeps them interacting on a regular basis. Team members should learn from one another—and even learn aspects of one another's roles. If you understand what I do and I understand what you do, we can communicate more effectively, interact more creatively, and even cover for each other from time to time. Mutual cooperation builds camaraderie and discourages turf wars between teammates.

### 6. Make It Fun

Fun fuels great teams. When team players enjoy their work, they don't see it as work. They see it as *fun*.

An experience of fun releases endorphins in the brain, inducing a generalized sense of well-being. When people experience that "endorphin rush," they want to experience it again and again. That's why fun is addictive. When work is fun, *work* is addictive. People want to come in early, stay late, talk about their work after hours, think about their work from sunup to sundown, and solve work-related problems while they're in the shower or brushing their teeth.

As people become comfortable with one another and bond together, they unleash one another's creativity. People feel safe to experiment with extreme possibilities. Soon, brilliant ideas start bouncing off the walls like thousands of Ping-Pong balls. A team environment becomes a hothouse where new ideas are constantly blooming.

And what do you find at the root of all that exciting creativity? *Fun.*

### 7. Think Jazz

Nurture an entrepreneurial spirit in your players. Encourage improvisation, syncopation, and wildly experimental jazz cadenzas. Your team doesn't need you to stand in front of them, waving a baton like a symphony conductor. Let your team find its own rhythms, its own chords.

Learn to tolerate mistakes. The great thing about jazz is that wrong notes don't always sound wrong; they can even sound *cool.* Let people make mistakes, and odds are they will learn wisdom and become more valuable team players as a result.

Avoid rigidity, which leads to bureaucracy. Teams thrive on freedom—the freedom of the entrepreneurial spirit. Freedom builds confidence, and confidence elevates teams. So build teamwork. Think jazz.

## An Entrepreneurial Dream of Changing the World

"Business has to have a conscience," said Rory Stear, founder and chairman of Freeplay Energy PLC.[16] The leader and conscience of Freeplay Energy is a six-foot-seven South African who cares deeply about the needs of the African people. Stear founded his com-

pany in Capetown in 1995 and later moved his headquarters to London.

Freeplay Energy manufactures durable electronic
products that require no batteries and no wall sockets—
hand-powered portable generators, radios, flashlights,
and lanterns. The key to Freeplay's technology, says
*Fast Company*, is

> *a spring made of a two-inch-wide, 20-foot-
> long ribbon of carbonized steel. . . . Turning the
> handle forces [the spring] to wind backward
> onto a bobbin. The force of the spring rewind-
> ing itself drives a set of gears, which in turn feed
> into an electric generator. . . . Winding for thirty
> seconds produces up to an hour of playing time
> on the radio and generates about three minutes
> of light from the flashlight.*[17]

Rory Stear's stated goal is to "empower the global
village" with environmentally friendly products powered by free human muscle or solar energy.[18] For example, Freeplay produces a laptop computer charger
for the One Laptop Per Child program (the program
donates one-hundred-dollar educational laptops to
children in developing nations, where there is often no
electricity). Freeplay also produces radios that enable
villagers to tune in programs that teach the principles
of sanitation, water purification, agriculture, health
care, and AIDS prevention.

While Stear runs the Freeplay company, his
American-born wife, Kristine Pearson, directs the
Freeplay Foundation, an independent charity that
works with other humanitarian agencies to distribute

Freeplay products in the developing world. Kristine Pearson has spent a great deal of time visiting refugee camps and orphanages in such troubled countries as Rwanda, the Congo, and the Sudan. "Renewable energy," she says, "is absolutely central to the growth of the continent. And access to information is key for people to make better choices and improve the quality of their lives."[19]

Freeplay products are attractively styled, rugged, and dependable, so they are best sellers in the retail stores of the developed world, such as Best Buy, Radio Shack, Sports Authority, and Harrods. Profits from sales in the developed world subsidize the distribution of free radios, flashlights, and other devices in Africa, India, and elsewhere. Rory Stear and Kristine Pearson have managed to attract world-class teammates to promote their extreme entrepreneurial dream of changing the world: Tom Hanks, Jimmy Carter, and Nelson Mandela have spoken at Freeplay Foundation events.

Terry Waite—the former Anglican peace envoy in Beirut who was held hostage for 1,763 days—is a foundation trustee. He says,

> *I spent five years in captivity, four of them in solitary confinement. I got no news from the outside world. But near the end of my imprisonment, I did get a small, battery-operated radio. I was terrified that when the batteries died, the guards would not replace them, and I'd be back in total isolation. There are millions of people in this world who are in similar situations—cut off from the flow of information.[20]*

The Freeplay corporation runs on teamwork. *Fast Company* described the teamwork environment at Freeplay, a company without cubicles or private offices:

> *The engineers spend their time in perpetual motion, touching base for thirty seconds here, or two minutes there, swapping information, asking a question, and then returning to their piece of the project. Watching the team work is like seeing professional volleyball players in action—everyone touches the ball, and it never hits the floor. It's easy to understand how this group designed and produced the current version of the Freeplay radio in just fourteen weeks.[21]*

Technology director John Hutchinson underscores the Freeplay team strategy. "For us," he says, "working with these tight product cycles and inventing new technology as we go—it has to be about teamwork. . . . It has to be seamless collaboration."[22]

Hutchinson tells a story that underscores the Freeplay team's commitment to excellence. Years ago, the Red Cross distributed radios to remote villages in Afghanistan, one radio per village. In one village, a boy was given the honor of winding the radio, and everyone would gather around to hear the broadcast. That radio became the hub of village life. One day, the lad turned the handle to wind the radio—and the handle broke. The boy was so upset that he ran away from the village. "If that story doesn't teach us the importance of quality," Hutchinson concluded, "nothing will."[23]

We all want to change the world, but few of us even

know where to begin. Rory Stear and Kristine Pearson refused to be intimidated by the enormity of the world and its problems. They simply dreamed an extreme dream, assembled a team, and started transforming the world, one village—and one radio—at a time.[24]

As you build your extreme entrepreneurial dream, make sure your dream embraces your community and your world. Dream big. Aim high. Make a difference.

## 2

# Principle 1: Top Talent Builds Extreme Dreams

When you build a great team and work with the best, you can't help but improve your own proficiency, the speed and efficiency with which you fast-forward your growth, and the extent to which the work becomes more fulfilling and enjoyable. Working with the best will motivate you to reach new heights.

LORAL LANGEMEIER,
*The Millionaire Maker*[1]

MY FIRST-EVER EXPERIENCE WITH THE NBA DRAFT was a tough lesson.

The year was 1970, and I was general manager of the Chicago Bulls. Jerry Krause was our college scout and he had his eye on Jimmy Collins, a guard from New Mexico State. But our head coach, Dick Motta, came back from an NCAA regional game with a glowing report on a guard from Texas El Paso. "We've got to draft this guy!" Dick said. "He's brilliant! His name is Nate Archibald."

The day of the draft, we contacted Nate Archibald and told him we were interested in him. Our strategy was to take Jimmy Collins on the first round and hope Nate would still be available when our second round pick came up.

Dick Motta was beside himself. He wanted to take Archibald

with our first pick. I said, "Dick, what happens if Nate Archibald isn't there on the second round?"

His grim reply: "Then we'll play against him."

The draft began. We took Collins in the first round, then waited with our hearts in our throats. A few picks into the second round, Cincinnati selected Archibald. Dick Motta put his head in his hands. He was inconsolable.

The outcome: two years after we drafted him, Jimmy Collins didn't pan out in the NBA. Nate Archibald went on to a brilliant fifteen-year career in the NBA and was inducted into the Basketball Hall of Fame.

Without great talent, you cannot rise above mediocrity. Acquiring top talent is the first of the eight keys to making extreme dreams come true—and that can be a lot more difficult than it sounds.

## "TALENT, TALENT, TALENT"

One of the highlights of my life was researching and writing a book called *How to Be Like Coach Wooden* (Health Communications, 2006). John Wooden, the longtime coaching legend at UCLA, allowed me into his life for four and a half years. I interviewed more than eight hundred people who knew him. My goal was to discover what made him so special and why so many people want to be like him. Fact is, if everyone in the world was like Coach Wooden, this world would be almost problem-free.

On a number of occasions, I picked Coach up at his condo in Encino, California. At five o'clock sharp, we headed for the Valley Inn in Sherman Oaks for dinner. That's Coach's favorite dining spot, and if you get there soon enough, you can get the early bird special. Though Coach is in his nineties, his mind is that of a much younger man. His memory is clear, his thinking is sharp, and his sense of humor is subtle and quick. When talking to Coach, you'd better be on top of your game, because he'll pepper you with probing, insightful questions.

One evening, Coach Wooden and I were enjoying his favorite soup course, the Valley Inn's highly acclaimed clam chowder. I asked him, "Coach, what was the one key to your success at UCLA?"

In his quiet, understated way, he replied, "Talent, talent, talent. I never wanted to go into a game unless I had better players than my opponent had."

It's true. Whether you're running an NBA team, a Fortune 500 corporation, or a mom-and-pop widget factory, you've got to have talent in order to compete. Though the talent issue may seem simple on the surface, it's actually amazingly complex. On any team, there are all kinds of jobs to be done, all kinds of positions to be filled, and that means you need all kinds of talent.

I remember how ecstatic our Magic organization was when we drafted Shaquille O'Neal as our center. Yet, as dominant and talented as Shaq was, I wouldn't have wanted five Shaqs on the court—we would have lost every game! In basketball, you've got to have a quick point guard to control the offense and distribute the ball. You've got to have a high-percentage shooting guard who puts points on the board and guards the opponent's perimeter player. You've got to have a small forward who can penetrate to the hole, draw the foul, and get to the line. And you've got to have a big power forward who can score in the low post and rebound aggressively.

Every player has to be custom-fitted to the role. Talented people can be creative, energetic, and inspirational—but they can also be temperamental and difficult to coach. You have to manage all that talent—and the problems that go with it.

To assemble a winning team, choose your players well. You may be stuck with the decision you make for a long time to come, so make sure it's a decision you can live with. Don't let people or circumstances stampede you into a disastrous long-term choice in shaping your team.

When interviewing prospective recruits, ask probing questions that get at the heart of that person's value system and character. Ask anecdotal questions: "What was your most difficult experience at your previous job, and how did you resolve it?" Ask about the candidate's personal goals and dreams: "What do you see yourself doing five and ten years from now?" Look for people whose dreams align with yours. Seek people who think *team*, who want to succeed as part of an organization, not just as individuals.

Notice how a recruit dresses. The way we dress expresses who we are and the attitude we have toward the people around us. Seek out team players who respect themselves, their teammates, coaches, and the organization. Notice too how candidates treat receptionists, clerks, waitresses, drivers, and janitors. People of authentic character treat everyone with respect. Notice whether the candidate respects your valuable time and the time of others.

What if you make a mistake in recruiting a certain person to your team? First, take that person aside and find out what the problem is. Handle the matter quietly, operating on the principle: "Praise in public, correct in private." Odds are, the problem will fall into one of two categories: either the individual lacks the knowledge or skills to carry out his role, or he has a character or attitude defect.

If it's a skill problem, you can correct it by mentoring the individual and helping him acquire the knowledge or skills he needs. But if he has defective character or a bad attitude, the problem may be untreatable. People are amazingly resistant to change—and a bad attitude can spread and infect your team.

Having the *wrong* person in a slot is worse than having *no* person in that slot. The wrong person will throw your team out of balance, make it dysfunctional, and destroy team chemistry. In such cases, the best way to add to your team is by subtraction.

Former Miami Dolphins head coach Don Shula was once asked if luck played a big role in football. He replied, "Sure, luck means a lot in football. Not having a good quarterback is bad luck."[2] Moral: assemble a talented team and you'll improve your "luck"!

## AN ART, NOT SCIENCE

Super Bowls I and II were won by Vince Lombardi's Green Bay Packers. Fittingly, the NFL Championship trophy is known as the Lombardi Trophy. The Green Bay teams he coached were the stuff of legend.

But when Vince Lombardi first arrived in Green Bay as head coach in 1958, the Packers were the worst team in the NFL. The team had not had a winning season in more than a decade. The season before Lombardi's arrival, the Packers had finished with one win, ten losses, and one tie. Green Bay was known as "Siberia." College players feared being drafted by the Packers, and league veterans retired rather than get traded there.

Vince Lombardi took over a Packers team that was undisciplined, disrespectful, and chronically late to practice. Players had so little respect for the coaching staff that they would ignore the coach's play-calling and take themselves in and out of the game whenever they wanted. Upon accepting the job, Lombardi went to church and spent several hours in prayer. Then he went home and spent even more hours with a projector and game film.[3]

Lombardi ran the projector forward and backward multiple times, studying the way each Packer played his role. He took notes, charted plays on yellow legal pads, and wrote meticulously detailed reports on each player—then decided which players to keep and which to cut. He learned that the Packers were strong in a few positions and horribly deficient elsewhere. The defense was a disaster. And the quarterback, he concluded, was a "puzzle." The two standouts were running back Paul Hornung and offensive lineman Forrest Gregg.[4]

As Lombardi rebuilt his coaching team, he chose Norb Hecker as defensive backfield coach—a man without any coaching experience. Several of Hecker's former coaches told Lombardi he knew the game, had good character, and came from a good family. That was enough for Lombardi.

Next, he selected veteran 49ers coach Phil Bengtson as defensive coordinator. He picked John "Red" Cochran to coach the offensive backfield, Tom Fears as receivers coach, and Bill Austin as offensive line coach. Lombardi's coaching staff was an eclectic mix of young and old, untested rookies and experienced veterans. The one common denominator: they all had reputations for intense commitment and good character.

Once Lombardi had his coaching staff in place, he began trading and drafting to assemble his team. He acquired Willie Davis, Henry Jordan, and Bill Quinlan from the Cleveland Browns and teamed them with Packers veteran Dave "Hawg" Hanner, creating one of the most dominant defensive lines in the NFL. He brought in veteran defensive back Emlen Tunnell from the New York Giants, the now-legendary Ray Nitschke as middle linebacker, and Bill Forrester and Dan Currie as outside linebackers. He also brought in a completely new secondary: Willie Wood, Hank Gremminger, Jesse Whittenton, and Herb Adderly.

To rebuild his offense, Lombardi brought in players like running back Lew Carpenter from Cleveland, guard Fred "Fuzzy" Thurston from Baltimore, and quarterback Lamar McHan from the St. Louis Cardinals. He picked backup quarterback Bart Starr, a holdover from the pre-Lombardi Packers, as a potential starter.

Lombardi built the new Packers offense around versatile running back Paul Hornung, who could not only pound the ball but also pass it, receive it, and kick it. Hornung was a hardworking, self-sacrificing, inspirational player, and Lombardi believed he could be the emotional spark plug of the team. Hornung later said that the day Vince Lombardi came aboard as coach "was the start of the eight best years of my life."[5]

Having assembled his team, he began instilling a sense of pride and team spirit, telling them, "You were chosen to be a Green Bay Packer." He instituted a dress code: gray shirt, tie, and green sports coat with the gold Packers logo on the pocket. Donald T. Phillips, in his book *Run to Win*, said, "*Teamwork* was a prominent word in the vocabulary of Vince Lombardi as a head coach. He wanted the Packers to think of themselves as a unit. . . . 'People who work together will win, whether it be against complex football defenses or the complex problems of modern society.'"[6]

He continually experimented with different combinations of players, searching for that elusive goal called *chemistry*. He designed plays in such a way that each player had to execute his assignment perfectly in order for the play to succeed. In a few short years, he took the Packers, once the laughingstock of the NFL, to two straight league championships. Then, once he had taken the Packers as far as they could go, Lombardi resigned, moved to Washington, D.C., and started all over again with the Redskins.

Team chemistry is an art, not a science.

## BETTER TEAMWORK THROUGH CHEMISTRY

As the great Notre Dame head coach Knute Rockne once said, "The secret of winning football games is working more as a team, less as individuals. I play not my eleven best, but my best eleven."[7] Duke basketball coach Mike Krzyzewski agrees: "When you first assemble a group, it's not a team right off the bat. It's only a collection of individuals."[8]

Pat Summitt, coach of the Tennessee Lady Vols basketball team, compares team-building to a jigsaw puzzle:

> You have to ask yourself: What is the whole picture here? . . .
>
> A lot of coaches or managers try to force personnel into a system or framework that doesn't suit them. They have a certain way they think things should be done. What they don't understand, out of stubbornness or ego, is that it may not be the most intelligent use of talent. How many times have you seen a player languish in a lineup, not fulfilling her potential, but as soon as she is traded to another team, she bursts out of her slump? I see that a lot. When you force somebody into a slot, you are inviting disaster.[9]

In 1973, I left the Chicago Bulls and took a position as general manager of the Atlanta Hawks. The roster boasted some outstanding talent, including six-time All-Star "Sweet Lou" Hudson, Walt Bellamy (who had entered the NBA as the number one draft pick overall), and legendary Hall of Famer "Pistol Pete" Maravich. The team was coached by one of the great strategists of the NBA, Cotton Fitzsimmons. With so much talent, I saw an NBA Championship in our future.

Just a few games into the season, I got a rude awakening. This mega-talented team was unraveling before my eyes. During my four years managing the Chicago Bulls, I had never seen our team lose more than three games straight. But the Hawks couldn't even put together back-to-back wins. We lost sixteen of our first seventeen road games after New Year's Day. One of the most talented teams in the NBA ended the season with one of the worst records in the NBA. The reason: *chemistry*. We didn't have any.

Our biggest problem was our biggest star, Pete Maravich. He had incredible moves, plenty of style, and was fun to watch—but he was uncoachable. He wouldn't play within Cotton's system. So we didn't really have a team. We had one thrill-a-minute performer—Pistol Pete—and four other guys who ran around and watched him shoot. That's why we lost.

I left the Hawks after my one and only season in Atlanta. Pete Maravich also left Atlanta, moving to the Jazz for six seasons, and then to the Celtics, where he played alongside Larry Bird for a single season before retiring. In his ten-season NBA career, Pete scored 15,948 points in 658 games for an average of 24.2 points per game. His single-game high was sixty-eight points, and he was named to the All-Star team five times. In spite of his individual achievements, Pete Maravich never won an NBA Championship.

Years after his retirement, Pete had a personal conversion experience that totally changed him. He and I became friends, and he told me that he attributed his lack of a championship ring to immaturity, ego, lack of discipline, and an unwillingness to sacrifice personal glory for the good of the team. If he had made that discovery early in his career, there's no telling what this gifted performer might have achieved.

Longtime Celtics coach Red Auerbach put it this way: "Talent alone is not enough. They said you have to use your five best players, but I've found you win with the five that fit together best."[10] And longtime NBA exec Joe Axelson once told me, "Team chemistry is the most fragile of all chemical mixtures. You never know how you get it, and you never know why you lose it. But when you've got it, you know you've got it—and when you don't, you know that too."

Even though chemistry is an art, not a science, there are specific actions we can take to make great team chemistry more likely to occur. Here are some examples:

## 1. Seek a Balance of Complementary Skills and Personality Types

Make sure you've got some confident yet coachable high-talent leaders, some risk-takers and slam-dunkers, some skilled yet humble role-players, some motivators and cheerleaders, and some tough-minded spark plugs. Assemble a well-rounded, well-balanced mix of skills and temperaments.

## 2. Manage Conflict; Don't Fear It

Poor interpersonal chemistry can destroy a team. Great chemistry can enable a team to soar. Conflict on a team is not always a symptom of unhealthy chemistry. It often means that strong, committed personalities are contending for their vision of success. Creative solutions often arise out of such ferment.

In *The Five Dysfunctions of a Team: A Leadership Fable*, Patrick Lencioni tells us that it is often the *fear of conflict*, not conflict itself, that causes team performance to break down. He relates a fictional conversation between Kathryn Petersen, CEO of a company called DecisionTech, and subordinates Nick and Carlos, on the subject of conflict in a corporate team environment. Kathryn speaks first:

> "If we don't trust one another, then we aren't going to engage in open, constructive, ideological conflict. And we'll just continue to preserve a sense of artificial harmony."
>
> Nick challenged, "But we seem to have plenty of conflict. And not a lot of harmony, I might add."
>
> Kathryn shook her head. "No. You have tension. But there is almost no constructive conflict. Passive, sarcastic comments are not the kind of conflict I'm talking about."
>
> Carlos weighed in. "But why is harmony a problem?"
>
> "It's the lack of conflict that's a problem. Harmony it-

self is good, I suppose, if it comes as a result of working through issues constantly and cycling through conflict. But if it comes only as result of people holding back their opinions and honest concerns, then it's a bad thing. I'd trade that false kind of harmony any day for a team's willingness to argue effectively about an issue and then walk away with no collateral damage."[11]

An honest, respectful clash of viewpoints can be one of the healthiest and most constructive processes a team can experience. As a team leader, use conflict as a creative force to unleash new ideas and new approaches. Never fear conflict; instead, manage conflict well. Make sure your team players know how to trade opposing viewpoints without trading insults or trading blows.

If you find that disagreements habitually deteriorate into bickering over personality issues and petty turf battles, then you probably have a rivalry of egos on your hands, resulting from mutual incompatibility. That's bad chemistry—and bad chemistry wastes time and energy. Don't allow bitterness to poison your team.

### 3. Remove Bad Apples

Sometimes the problem is one individual who refuses to play by the rules. He doesn't respect his teammates. He interrupts. He ridicules ideas. Sometimes, this problem can be cured by reminding the individual to abide by team rules. If one or two warnings don't get his attention, then he's off the team.

Your goal is to assemble a cohesive group of people who represent a diversity of skills, personality types, temperaments, and points of view—but who share an absolute *unity of purpose*. Once you achieve that, you've got *chemistry*. You've got a platoon of people who are ready to go to war for one another.

Most important, you've got a *team*.

## EVERY PLAYER NEEDS TO KNOW HIS ROLE

It's been called "the most shocking moment in NFL history." On November 18, 1985, the New York Giants played the Washington Redskins at RFK Stadium.

In the second quarter, Redskins coach Joe Gibbs called for a flea-flicker pass. Quarterback Joe Theismann took the snap and handed off to running back John Riggins, who took a few steps—then turned and tossed the ball back to Theismann. Looking downfield, Theismann searched in vain for his receivers. Turned slightly to the right, his blind left side was exposed.

Theismann knew that one of the most dangerous defensive backs in the NFL, Lawrence Taylor, was coming from the left side. But he was confident that Redskins left tackle Joe Jacoby could handle Taylor. Problem: Theismann didn't know Jacoby was on the sidelines, replaced by shorter, slower Russ Grimm.

Lawrence Taylor tore through Grimm like he was made of tissue paper. Theismann never saw Taylor coming. He was still holding the ball, looking for an open receiver, when Taylor steamrolled him. Theismann heard a pair of loud pops as he fell, like both barrels of a shotgun. One pop was his shinbone breaking. The other was his calf bone.

The next thing Theismann knew, he was under a pile of bodies with his lower right leg bent at a forty-five-degree angle, the bone jutting through flesh. Since that night, neither Theismann nor Lawrence Taylor has been able to watch the video of that play—

The play that ended Joe Theismann's career.

Nobody did anything wrong that night. Theismann played the game the way it's supposed to be played. So did Lawrence Taylor. Offensive linemen like Jacoby get tired and have to take plays off. Russ Grimm did the best he could, but he was no match for future Hall of Famer Lawrence Taylor. In football, and in life, bad things happen. In this case, a bad thing happened to Joe Theismann because a dependable role-player was on the sidelines instead of in the trenches.[12]

What is a role-player? He or she is a player on the team who fills a crucial slot but rarely gets the glory. Role-players are the backbone of every team. They practice, train, work, and condition themselves as hard as any star player. A great role-player has good character traits—especially humility. While sitting on the bench, the role-player is totally absorbed in what happens on the field, analyzing the opposition, watching for weaknesses, and searching for windows of opportunity. When the role-player's name is called, he jumps off the bench, hits the ground running, and plays aggressively.

Often, when a coach sends a role-player into the game, you can literally see a wave of enthusiasm and energy ripple through the team. Sometimes that is the mystical moment when the game's momentum shifts.

Everyone wants to be a starter. It takes a special kind of person to be a role-player. As NBA coach Pat Riley observes, "Teamwork multiplies the potential of everyone on [the team]. The key to teamwork is to learn a role, accept that role, and strive to become excellent playing it."[13]

In his book *Wooden on Leadership*, Coach John Wooden honored one of the great role-players on his UCLA Bruins basketball team:

> Swen Nater understood that his greatness came in practice rather than in games. He served his team as a backup center behind the significant skills of Bill Walton. This positioning allowed Bill to sharpen his abilities in practice against a center, Swen, who was also tall and talented. (Swen could have been a starter on almost any other team in the country.)

Before Swen joined us, I clearly explained to him what specific role he would play on the team and how valuable it would be to the team. He took on the task, eagerly accepted his role, and helped UCLA win two national championships.

Was Bill Walton greater than Swen Nater? It's a question that has little relevance to me in the context of leadership and team productivity. Both young men attained greatness in performing their specific and important roles as it best serves their team. . . . Each role offers the opportunity to achieve personal greatness.[14]

Coach Wooden had a favorite analogy he used with his UCLA teams. A team, he said, is like a powerful car. The stars like Bill Walton or Kareem Abdul-Jabbar are the engine, providing the power. But a car needs more than a powerful engine in order to go places. If a tire is flat, the car is stuck—and the engine is no help. Even parts as small as the lug nuts are necessary—because if "the lug nuts are missing, the wheels come off." The lug nuts, of course, are the role-players. Coach Wooden explains:

A lug nut may seem like a little thing, but it's not. There is a role that each and every one of us must play. We may aspire to what we consider to be a larger role, or a more important role, but we cannot achieve that until we show that we are able to fulfill the role we are assigned. It's these little things that make the big things happen. The big engine is not going to work unless the little things are being done properly.

Remember that Michael Jordan was with the Chicago Bulls for several years before he ever played in a championship game. Was he talented? Of course he was, but that powerful engine called Air Jordan was in a car with some parts that were not functioning properly.

Of course, when I told the players about their roles and the car with the powerful engine, new tires, and tight lug nuts, I also reminded them the car needed a driver behind the wheel or it would just go around in circles or smash into a tree.

I told them the driver was me.[15]

It's tough being a role-player instead of a starter. Everyone wants the applause and recognition of stardom. No one goes into any team endeavor thinking, *My goal is to become anonymous!* So it's important to help your role-players understand their importance to the team—and to the dream.

Rick Pitino coached the University of Kentucky basketball team to an NCAA Championship in 1996 and is currently head basketball coach at the University of Louisville. He was once asked how he handles bruised egos when he shuffles the starting lineup. Pitino replied:

> I don't ever get them to think it's benching or a demotion. I explain it to them this way: I had one of the greatest college teams of all time at Kentucky in 1996. On that team there were seven guys [who went on to play] in the NBA. I started the five best players, and we lost the second game of the season because it wasn't a group that was cohesive.
>
> And then I took a walk-on point guard, gave him a scholarship and made him a starter. He was totally willing to sacrifice for the good of the team and worked to make other players better. He didn't care about scoring; he didn't mind doing the dirty work. He just wanted to make the other people better. The other person who became a

[substitute] still played the same amount of minutes and I made him understand, this is just about making the team better—it has nothing to do with your significance to the team.

We didn't lose another game until the end of the season, and we won a championship, all because that young man accepted his role.[16]

Whitey Herzog has been a major-league baseball outfielder, scout, manager, general manager, coach, and farm system director— so he's been involved in team-building throughout his career. In *You're Missin' a Great Game*, he talked about the need to take good care of your role-players: "A lot of the time, I spent more time with my twenty-fourth guy than I did with my stars. They *needed* your attention; the star already got plenty. Maybe I appreciated them because they were the kind of players I used to be. My lesser guys won me a lot of ball games, and some of them are still my best friends."[17]

Another great baseball manager, four-time World Series champion Joe Torre, agrees: when role-players believe they are making a contribution, teamwork happens. In *Joe Torre's Ground Rules for Winners*, he explains:

Here's my motto: *Every employee must feel useful.* In order to build teamwork, you must acknowledge each individual's worth, letting him know that his role, no matter how seemingly minor, is a vital cog in the team's efforts. When you grant your stars, your role players, and everyone in between the same level of attention, you lay the groundwork for an unselfish team spirit. . . .

Making time for team players is no panacea for their problems, but it's a fundamental rule of sound managing. It creates the space in which you can get to know them;

let them know you; solidify trust; and resolve unspoken issues. Your one-on-one dialogues with team players are motivational building blocks—the basis for the creation of teamwork.[18]

Drew Bledsoe was drafted first overall by the New England Patriots in 1993, and he quarterbacked the team from 1993 to 2001. He made only one Super Bowl appearance, a 35–21 loss to the Green Bay Packers in Super Bowl XXXI. In March 2001, the Patriots signed him to a ten-year contract for more than $100 million—but he played only one more season with the Patriots. In game two of the 2001 season, he sustained a chest injury when he was hit by a Jets linebacker while scrambling for the sidelines.

Bledsoe's injury allowed backup quarterback Tom Brady to show what he could do. Brady proceeded to take the Patriots to the Super Bowl. Bledsoe got to play in only one more game—the AFC Championship game against the Steelers—after Brady suffered an ankle injury in the second quarter. Though Bledsoe had a great game, completing 10 of 21 for 102 yards, one TD, and no interceptions, Coach Bill Belichick gave the starting nod to Tom Brady for Super Bowl XXXVI.

The hardest thing for Bledsoe was getting his adrenaline pumped up in one game only to be sidelined for the biggest game of all. Even so, he accepted his benching with good grace. "There's a right way to do things and a wrong way," he explained. "The right thing is to step back and accept a different role than I'm accustomed to and do whatever I can in that role to not only help Tom, but help the team prepare. Every quarterback, if you play long enough, goes through some very difficult times."[19]

On February 3, 2002, Drew Bledsoe was at the Superdome in New Orleans for Super Bowl XXXVI. He stood on the sidelines, ready to play if he was needed. He never got the chance. Though the St. Louis Rams were heavily favored to win the Super Bowl that year, Tom Brady led the Patriots to the team's first NFL Championship.

Bledsoe was a role-player that day. His role was to wait and be ready.

Extreme dreams depend on every player knowing his role, accepting his role, and carrying out his role like a professional. To build your winning team, *acquire top talent*—including talented role-players.

## ALL SIZES, SHAPES, AND COLORS

When you acquire top talent, you break down artificial barriers that divide people, including race, gender, and economic class. You treat people as *people*, and you take advantage of all the strengths that diversity can bring to your team.

One of my longtime friends in baseball was the late Danny Murtaugh, who spent twenty-nine years with the Pittsburgh Pirates as either a player or a manager. On September 1, 1971, Danny sat in his office at Three Rivers Stadium and wrote down his starting lineup for the game that evening against the Philadelphia Phillies: Rennie Stennett, second base. Gene Clines, center field. Roberto Clemente, right field. Willie Stargell, left field. Manny Sanguillen, catcher. Dave Cash, third base. Al Oliver, first base. Jackie Hernandez, shortstop. Dock Ellis, pitcher.

Danny didn't notice anything unusual about the lineup. He was simply putting together the best available mix of talent to go up against the Phillies and their left-handed pitcher, Woodie Fryman. When the game began, no one in the stands or the press box noticed anything unusual. But Danny Murtaugh had unintentionally made baseball history. Though Jackie Robinson had broken the color barrier almost a quarter-century earlier, this was the first time a major-league ball club had fielded a team consisting entirely of nonwhite players, both African-Americans and Latin Americans.

Bruce Markusen, manager of program presentations at the Baseball Hall of Fame in Cooperstown, New York, reflected on Danny's decision:

> In 1971, the Pirates represented baseball's most heavily integrated team, with black and Latino players accounting for nearly fifty percent of the club's roster. The Pirates also featured one of baseball's most harmonious teams, with friendships and gatherings often crossing racial lines. White players often socialized with black and Latino players, either at bars and restaurants after games, or at barbecues and parties organized by one of the team's leaders, Willie Stargell. Considering the unity of the team, the players' reaction to the all-black lineup was not surprising. "We had a loose group, [so] we were all laughing and hollering about it and teasing each other," says [pitcher Steve] Blass. "I thought that was a great reaction."[20]

Pirates first baseman Bob Robertson, who did not play that night, recalled Danny Murtaugh's Pirates as a ball club in which race was simply not an issue. "That was the type of ball club that we had," Robertson said. "It didn't make a difference if you were black, yellow, green, purple, whatever. We enjoyed each other's company. We got along fine. We had a lot of respect for one another."[21]

Was Danny *trying* to make a social statement with that lineup card? Al Oliver, who played first base that night, didn't think so. "I think Danny was just putting the best team on the field," he said. "What it came down to was that the Pirates were not afraid to draft black and Latino players because they were interested in one thing . . . winning."[22]

After the game, a reporter asked Danny if he was aware that he had just fielded the first all-minority team since the end of Negro League baseball. "Is that a fact?" said Danny. "To tell you the truth, I never thought about it. . . . All I knew is that I had nine Pirates out there on the field."[23]

As you build your team, start with talent. Acquire top talent, regardless of what size, shape, or color it comes in. That's the first step in achieving your extreme dreams.

# Extreme *American* Dreams . . .

## *Depend on Teams*

*There are those who will say that the liberation of humanity, the freedom of man and mind is nothing but a dream. They are right. It is the American Dream.*

ARCHIBALD MACLEISH, poet and
librarian of Congress[1]

The year 1776 was the year of the Great Experiment. Nothing like it had ever been attempted before. Down through history, the human race had been ruled by tyrants, dictators, and plutocrats—but people had never before tried to govern themselves.

A few American patriots had a dream: "We hold these truths to be self-evident, that all men are created equal, that they are endowed by their Creator with certain unalienable Rights, that among these are Life, Liberty and the pursuit of Happiness." The notion that human beings are created equal and ought to be free was an extreme dream in 1776. In much of the world, it is still an extreme dream today.

That original American Dream Team included Thomas Jefferson, Benjamin Franklin, John Adams, George Washington, Alexander Hamilton, James Madison, and Thomas Paine. Each team member had a distinct role to play—and if any one of them dropped the ball at a crucial moment, the dream would have failed.

Washington was the strategist of the Revolution. Franklin was its conscience and philosopher. Adams was the motivator and driving force behind the Revolution. Hamilton was its financial wizard. Paine was the pamphleteer and marketing genius of the Revolution. Madison was the architect of the Constitution. And Jefferson was the spokesman and poet laureate of the American Dream. Every member of the team left his own distinct fingerprints on the Dream that became America.

## Jefferson: Architect of an Extreme Dream

In June 1776, the Second Continental Congress chose thirty-three-year-old Thomas Jefferson to draft the Declaration of Independence. Jefferson was a lawyer, architect, farmer, philosopher, and scholar. Proficient in five languages, he had studied the Greek and Roman classics and the Old and New Testaments in their original languages. Jefferson was inspired by the Israelite Moses, who set up the world's first representative form of government, organizing a million Israelites into subgroups and sub-subgroups. To Jefferson, this seemed like a brilliant blueprint for self-government—and it became the foundation of our representative democracy.

Historians say Jefferson wrote a complete draft of the Declaration in seventeen days—and probably wrote most of it in one day. The section accusing England's King George III of tyranny was largely adapted from the Constitution of Virginia, which he cowrote with George Mason and James Madison.

The other sixteen days were probably spent on the first three paragraphs, which included the line: "We hold these truths to be self-evident. . . ." It's not surprising that this section would absorb so much of Jefferson's time and energy. Those paragraphs set forth the extreme and enduring dream of America and defined who we are and why we exist as a free and equal people.

## An Early American Dream Team

After Jefferson completed a suitable draft of the Declaration, he gave it to Benjamin Franklin and John Adams for their critique. Franklin made nearly fifty corrections, including a change to the preamble. Instead of Jefferson's "Life, Liberty and Property," Franklin suggested "Life, Liberty and the pursuit of Happiness." Later, the document was revised by a full session of the Continental Congress—much to Jefferson's dismay. Many historians, however, feel the document was stronger after being edited by the entire team of founding fathers.

The official signing of the Declaration took place on August 2, 1776. First to sign was John Hancock, who wrote his name with a grand calligraphic flourish. Then he turned to the other founding fathers and encouraged them to act as a team. "There must be no pulling different ways," he said. "We must all hang together."

"Yes," Franklin agreed, "or most assuredly we shall all hang separately."[2]

When the signing was complete, fifty-six names were affixed to the document—and every signer knew Franklin was serious about hanging separately. The penalties for treason against the British Crown included not only hanging, but disembowelment, beheading, and being drawn and quartered.

The signers were leaders of their communities and had much to lose. They included lawyers, judges, merchants, traders, and plantation owners. Before the Revolutionary War ended, five of the signers were tortured to death by the British. A dozen had their homes burned to the ground. Nine were killed in the war. Others lost sons and other family members.[3]

The American Dream was forged in war and baptized in blood. The founding fathers could have chosen quiet, secure lives as British colonial subjects. But they valued liberty more than safety. They put their lives and livelihood on the line, hung together as a team, and hammered the extreme American Dream into reality.

## E Pluribus Unum

The founding fathers were not perfect men. They had their blind spots, which prevented them from seeing that the phrase "all men are created equal" should refer to all Americans, including African-Americans, Native Americans, and women. Yet the grand ideas of the Declaration of Independence laid the groundwork for the recognition of the equality and rights of *all* people, regardless of color or gender.

It's significant that the first martyr of the American Revolution was Crispus Attucks, a man of both African and Native American ancestry. He and four other men were killed by British troops in the Boston Massacre of 1770. Their sacrificial deaths had a direct role in sparking the American Revolution. Whenever I go to Boston, I stop at the Granary Burying Ground and pay my respects at the place where Crispus Attucks is buried, along with Paul Revere, John Hancock, Samuel Adams, and other heroes of the Revolution. I always remember that a courageous person of color gave his life for the extreme American Dream.[4]

The beauty of the American Dream is that it comes in all colors. The source of our American strength is the same thing that makes any team strong: diversity expressed through unity.

Great teams thrive on diversity, with each team member having a unique set of skills, filling a unique role. Yet great teams are also unified behind a single purpose. All of those diverse talents and personalities *must* unite around a single goal. A divided team is destined to fail. As Americans, we should see ourselves as a diverse assemblage of personalities, backgrounds, viewpoints, and abilities, united by an extreme dream—the American Dream of equality and freedom for all.

Not all the patriots of the American Revolution were transplanted Englishmen. Some Revolutionary heroes had names like Friedrich Wilhelm von Steuben, the Marquis de Lafayette, Casimir Pulaski, and Thaddeus Kosciusko.[5] Some had Native American or African ancestry like Crispus Attucks. Every one of those names is as American as apple pie. People came from across the sea, joined our team, and fought for the extreme American Dream. "No other nation," former British prime minister Margaret Thatcher once said, "has so successfully combined people of different races and nations within a single culture."[6] It's the dream of freedom and equality that binds us together.

That's why the motto on the Great Seal of the United States of America is the Latin phrase *E pluribus unum*—"Out of many, one."

## A Witness to History

For two seasons in the early 1960s, I played minor-league baseball, catching for the Philadelphia Phillies farm club in Miami. In the summer of '63, I said good-bye to my brief pro-baseball career and packed up my belongings for the long drive north to Bloomington, Indiana. I was going to Indiana University to complete my master's in physical education. I called my mom and told her I'd visit her in Delaware before going on to Indiana.

"I've got a better idea," Mom said. "Meet me in Washington, D.C. I'm going to the March on Washington to hear Dr. Martin Luther King Jr. He's giving a speech at the Lincoln Memorial on August 28."

Mom had been involved in social causes for as long as I could remember, and she was a fan of Dr. Martin Luther King Jr. His fame had been established eight years earlier during the bus boycott in Montgomery, Alabama.

I drove up from Florida and met Mom and my sister in Washington. I will always be grateful that Mom arranged for me to be standing in that vast crowd on the National Mall in front of the Lincoln Memorial. The weather was hot, humid, and miserable—but once Dr. King stood up to speak, no one noticed the weather. Thanks to my mother, I was a witness to history and among the first people on the planet to hear Dr. King's historic "I Have a Dream" speech.

In that speech, he talked about the extreme dream of freedom and equality in America—a dream unfulfilled. "Even though we face the difficulties of today and tomorrow," he said, "I still have a dream. It is a dream deeply rooted in the American Dream. I have a dream that one day this nation will rise up and live out the true meaning of its creed: 'We hold these truths to be self-evident, that all men are created equal.'"

It was years before I began to fully appreciate the importance of that moment. Every so often, something happens to drive home the meaning of Dr. King's dream in a new and powerful way. I had one such experience while this book was being written.

In July 2008, I went to Alabama as a guest of my friend John Merrill. John introduced me to Ed Bridges, the executive director of the State Archives of Alabama, and we went on a tour of the historic sites of the great civil rights struggle of the 1950s and 1960s. We went to the Cleveland Avenue bus stop where Rosa Parks boarded a municipal bus on Thursday, December 1, 1955. Then we went a block farther, to the place where she was forced off the bus for refusing to give her seat to a white passenger.

John and Ed took me to the beautiful white-trimmed, redbrick Dexter Avenue Baptist church that, in 1955, was led by a twenty-six-year-old pastor named Martin

Luther King Jr. I went down into the basement where, the night of December 2, a few dozen community leaders planned the historic boycott of the Montgomery bus system—a boycott that would bring racial segregation to its knees. There I met a church deacon, a man in his mid-eighties. He had actually been present at the meeting when the boycott was planned. I felt I had encountered a living figure from history.

The meeting in that basement was a team strategy session. Dr. King articulated the extreme dream of moving the nation beyond the hurt and injustice of segregation and Jim Crow laws. Those in attendance represented a mix of skills, viewpoints, and backgrounds. Some were highly educated intellectuals, others were working-class people—but they were all united behind one dream. Together they planned how the boycott would be carried out—the funding that would be needed, the car pools that would provide alternative transportation, and so forth. Teamwork was the key to keeping the boycott in force for the long haul.

And it *was* a long haul. The boycott ultimately lasted 381 days. It ended on December 20, 1956, after the U.S. Supreme Court ordered the Montgomery buses desegregated. When the court ruling came down, Dr. King sent a message to the African-American community around Montgomery, which I quote in part:

> *Remember that this is not a victory for Negroes alone, but for all Montgomery and the South. Do not boast! Do not brag!*
>
> *Be quiet but friendly; proud, but not arrogant; joyous, but not boisterous.*
>
> *Be loving enough to absorb evil and un-*

*derstanding enough to turn an enemy into a friend.*[7]

That, of course, is what great teams do. They are gracious in victory, and courteous to opponents—even unjust opponents. Rosa Parks and Dr. King and their team of committed activists showed us the power of moral suasion and civil disobedience—

And the power of an extreme dream and a committed team.

The future of America depends on all of us joining the team, letting go of the things that divide us, and holding on to our unity. That's the American Dream.

And that's American teamwork.

# 3

# Principle 2: Great Leaders Build Extreme Dreams (Part 1)

My sports were team sports, ice hockey and baseball. The whole team dynamic is similar in business. Leadership is earned.

JAMES McNERNEY JR.,
CEO, Boeing Company[1]

THE THINGS YOU HAVE TO DO TO RUN AN NBA TEAM!

It was the fall of 1982, and I was general manager of the Philadelphia 76ers. We were at the beginning of what would turn out to be our championship season. We had brought in the mighty Moses Malone from the Houston Rockets, but we had to cut a couple of players to make room on our roster. All the remaining players arrived for the first day of training camp except starting point guard Maurice "Mo" Cheeks. He hadn't informed anyone he'd be late for camp, so his no-show was a mystery.

I made a few worried calls and finally located him in Chicago. Turned out he was concerned about his contract, which still had four years remaining. Mo had seen the Sixers deal a couple of players away, and for some reason, he thought he was next. I called him and said, "Mo, just get on a plane and get to Philly right away."

"I want to stay with the Sixers. I don't want to be traded."

"Mo," I said, "we don't want to trade you. You're part of this team."

"I need to hear it from Mr. Katz," Mo said, referring to owner Harold Katz.

"I'll set up a meeting with Mr. Katz. You can see him tonight. As soon as you get into town, come straight to the Bellevue Stratford Hotel."

"Okay."

"Whatever you do, don't talk to any reporters."

"Okay."

I hung up knowing I needed to handle the situation with kid gloves. If the media got wind of Mo's dissatisfaction, it would mean bad publicity for the Sixers.

Harold Katz was being honored that evening at a black-tie dinner at the Bellevue Stratford. While the dinner took place, I paced the lobby, waiting for Mo to arrive. As soon as he climbed out of his taxi, I grabbed him by the sleeve and rushed him across the lobby. I kept my head on a swivel, watching for reporters. As near as I could tell, no one had seen Mo enter the hotel—and I intended to keep it that way.

But Mo was a famous face in Philadelphia. Where could I stash him until Mr. Katz could get away from the dinner? Then I had an inspiration.

"Where are you taking me?" he asked, frowning.

"Trust me," I said, hustling him into the elevator.

We got off the elevator on an upper floor. At the end of the hallway was a little balcony. Well, it was actually more of a window ledge with a railing and some potted palms. You had to open some glass doors to get to the ledge, which was just big enough for one person.

"Mo," I said, "I want you to stand on that ledge—and it would help if you'd crouch down behind the potted palms so no one can see you from the hallway."

"You want me to wait out there? Do you know how high we are?"

"Mo," I said, "you're not afraid of heights, are you?"

"Well, no, but—how long do I have to wait?"

"A few minutes."

Mo grudgingly agreed to hide on the ledge. I went downstairs and checked on the banquet. It dragged on, one dull testimonial after another. I groaned and went upstairs to check on Mo.

When I looked at the glass doors, I couldn't see Mo—just the fronds of the potted palms. Had he gotten tired of waiting? Was he holding a press conference?

I opened the glass doors a crack. "Mo?"

His face appeared. Not a happy face. "Williams! What's taking so long?"

"Mr. Katz should be out any minute. You doing okay?"

"I think I'm catching a cold."

"Just a few more minutes, Mo."

"Williams, this is the dumbest—"

I shut the door.

After fifteen minutes or so, the banquet ended and Mr. Katz emerged. I took him aside, explained the situation, and asked him to wait in an empty conference room. Then I went upstairs and got Mo off the ledge. The three of us sat down and Mo explained why he hadn't shown up at training camp.

Mr. Katz sat back with an astonished look on his face. "Is that all you want?" he said. "A guarantee you'll play out your contract? You've got it! In fact, I'd be happy to extend your contract a few more years."

Maurice Cheeks reported for training camp the next morning and proceeded to give us one of the best seasons of his NBA career. Today, Mo is still with the Philadelphia 76ers—as head coach.

When you're a leader of a team, you never know what new problems will land on your plate each day. All you know is that you'd better be ready to solve them. It helps to have a potted palm or two handy in case of emergencies.

## THE SEVEN SIDES OF LEADERSHIP

There are no great teams without great leaders. Over the years, I've made an intensive study of leadership through observation, reading, and interviewing literally thousands of great leaders. I have talked to coaches at every level, from high school to the big leagues. I have spoken with military leaders, such as General Colin Powell and General Tommy Franks. I have spoken with great religious and humanitarian leaders such as Billy Graham, Charles Colson, and Marian Wright Edelman. I have cabinets filled with notes on every aspect of leadership. I have a leadership library in my home with (at last count) 510 books by such authorities as Alan Axelrod, Warren Bennis, Peter Drucker, John Maxwell, Jay Strack, and more—and I have read, highlighted, and annotated every volume.

In my career as a player and a sports executive, I received the best leadership training anyone could ask for. My mentors included the great baseball owner-promoter Bill Veeck, Philadelphia Phillies owner Bob Carpenter, Miami farm club general manager Bill Durney, minor-league manager Andy Seminick, minor-league owner R. E. Littlejohn (the Spartanburg, South Carolina, Phillies), college baseball coach Jack Stallings, and my high school coaches Bob DeGroat and Peanuts Riley. From a half century of team experience and leadership training, I've concluded that the essence of leadership can be distilled to seven qualities I call the Seven Sides of Leadership. They are:

1. *Vision.* A great leader must have a vision, an extreme dream toward which he or she is leading the team.
2. *Communication Skills.* Communication is essential to teamwork. Great leaders exemplify and teach healthy communication skills to their teams.
3. *People Skills.* Leaders must know how to motivate and empower people to work together. People skills can be learned and improved with practice.
4. *Character.* People choose whether or not to follow a leader based largely on that leader's character.
5. *Competence.* The word *competence* begins with *compete.* The players on a team want to know that their leader can make them competitive and lead them to victory.
6. *Boldness.* Leaders of extreme-dream teams must be decisive and daring. Bold leaders build high-achieving teams.
7. *Servanthood.* Genuine leadership is not about being a boss. It's about being a servant. Extreme dreams don't happen unless a leader stoops to serve.

Some people are born with a few of these qualities. No one is born with them all. So in order to become leaders, we have to build these traits into our lives.

We can acquire and improve each of these Seven Sides of Leadership. We can practice our visionary skills, improve our communication and people skills, commit ourselves to character growth, gain confidence and boldness through experience, and choose an attitude of servanthood. The more complete we become in the Seven Sides of Leadership, the more effective we are as leaders.

Leadership is the ability to achieve goals through people. Coaches achieve wins and championships through their players. Business leaders achieve market share, ROI, and increased stock value through managers and employees. A government leader achieves political and social betterment through the people in his or her administration. Military leaders achieve battlefield objectives and ultimate victory through their soldiers.

Every leader is in the people business. If you want to gauge the effectiveness of a leader, all you have to do is look at his team and see what his players have accomplished. Great leaders achieve great results.

Leadership is not handed out automatically along with the title. Leadership is *earned*. If you've got what it takes, your team will follow you anywhere. If not, you're going nowhere. To be a leader who inspires a devoted followership, you need the Seven Sides of Leadership.

## THE FIRST SIDE: VISION

A vision defines what your extreme dream will look like when it is achieved. You, as the leader, impart your vision to the team, giving your players a goal to compete for. Players who are committed to an extreme vision will pay any price and persevere through adversity to make that vision a reality.

Vision generates energy and passion. It transmits excitement and intensity from your soul to the soul of your team. Your vision should be so simple and memorable that you could state it on a T-shirt. Come to think of it, handing out "vision shirts" to the team is not a bad idea!

As leadership guru John Maxwell observes, "Vision is everything for a leader. It is utterly indispensable. Why? Because vision leads the leader. It paints the target. It sparks and fuels the fire within, and draws him forward. It is also the fire lighter for others who follow that leader."[2] A common, shared vision enables teams to achieve unity in the midst of their diversity.

President Ronald Reagan came into office with an extreme dream of liberating people from communist oppression. To achieve that dream, President Reagan drew upon the power of vision—a vision he announced to the entire world on June 12, 1987. On that day, he gave a powerful speech before the Brandenburg Gate in Berlin. "General Secretary Gorbachev," he said, "if you seek peace, if you seek prosperity for the Soviet Union and Eastern Europe, if you seek liberalization: Come here to this gate! Mr. Gorbachev, open this gate! Mr. Gorbachev, tear down this wall!"[3]

At the time, skeptics said that President Reagan had announced a dream so extreme it could never be realized in our lifetime. But President Reagan was more than a visionary. He was a team-builder. Not only did he assemble a White House team to pursue that goal through a combination of diplomacy and military might, but he also drew upon a team of key international players to take a united stand against the "evil empire" of the Soviet Union: Polish-born Pope John Paul II joined President Reagan in speaking out strongly against Soviet oppression. Reagan supported the efforts of Czech dissident Vaclav Havel and Polish Solidarity leader Lech Walesa in their demands for political reform behind the Iron Curtain. And Reagan joined forces with America's staunchest European ally, Prime Minister Margaret Thatcher of Great Britain; from both sides of the Atlantic, they spoke against communism with one voice.

In November 1989, two years after President Reagan delivered his Brandenburg Gate speech, the people of Berlin began tearing down the Berlin Wall, and the West German government couldn't stop them. Two years after that, the Soviet Union collapsed.

Media mogul Ted Turner had a vision for a global 24-7 cable news channel. Amazingly, no one at the three big networks had ever thought of it before. CBS, NBC, and ABC all had globe-spanning news divisions, and it would have been comparatively simple for them to feed news to a twenty-four-hour cable news desk. But the networks lacked vision, so they devoted all their resources—millions of dollars' worth of equipment, infrastructure, and personnel—to producing one half hour of news per night.

Ted Turner didn't have network news-gathering resources, but he did have a vision. In 1980, shortly before launching his Cable News Network, he said that CNN "won't be signing off until the world ends. We'll be on, and we will cover the end of the world, live. . . . When the end of the world comes, we'll play 'Nearer My God to Thee' before we sign off."[4] Ted Turner's vision put twenty-four-hour cable news on the map.

A vision should be extreme, bold, and even intimidating. The team members need to know they are not being asked to climb a little hill. They are being challenged to scale Mount Everest. The rewards: fabulous. The stakes: unbelievably high. The odds: nearly impossible. Extreme dreams should be as difficult as ending the Cold War or reinventing the news business. If it was easy, you wouldn't need teams.

When your team catches the vision you have cast, you'll see your vision multiplied a dozen or a hundred or a thousand times over. As your vision is implanted in the minds of your players, it will be magnified into an unstoppable, synergistic force for transformation. Your life, and the life of every member of your team, will be forever changed by the dynamic power of that vision.

## THE SECOND SIDE: COMMUNICATION

Great leaders are great communicators. They convey optimism and hope. They inspire and motivate. They teach and encourage. Above all, they communicate the vision.

Remind your players often of your vision. Make sure they can recite it in their sleep. Any team member who cannot articulate the vision will be out of sync, so hammer the vision home in speeches and one-on-one conversations. Billboard it on banners and posters, in newsletters and e-mails. Remind your players that each one has an individual stake in the vision. Everything they do must be focused on turning the vision into reality.

Here are some suggestions for improving communication on your team:

### 1. Be Aware of Body Language

Communication is more than just words. Our eyes communicate. Our facial expressions communicate. Our gestures and body language communicate. The tone of your voice actually communicates more information than your words. If you say to someone, "I'm so glad you're here," in a voice full of enthusiasm, with your eyes alight and a smile on your face, your message will come through loud and clear. But say those same words in a sarcastic tone while rolling your eyes and folding your arms in front of your body, and you will totally invert the meaning of your words. When you communicate, remember that people listen with their ears—and their eyes.

### 2. Commit Yourself to Continuous Improvement as a Communicator

If you are not a confident speaker, do something about it. Join a local chapter of Toastmasters International, the nonprofit organization that helps people improve their public speaking and leadership skills. Take a speech course from your local community college or university. Or take private training from an executive coaching company.

In the early 1960s, when I was in Miami learning how to run a minor-league baseball team, one of my duties was promotion.

We used radio extensively and one of our best friends in radio was a popular young talk-show host. He broadcast from a houseboat called *Surfside 6*, tied up near the oceanfront Fontainebleau Hotel in Miami Beach. (The boat was featured in the early '60s TV series *Surfside 6*.)

I would accompany one of our team's players or coaches to the boat, and I'd sit and watch while the radio host would interview our guy for an hour. I took note of everything the host did—the way he asked questions, the way he hunched forward and listened to the answers, the way he responded with insightful follow-up questions. I still apply the lessons I learned to the local radio shows I host today in Orlando.

You've undoubtedly heard of that talk-show host. He's still in broadcasting—only now he does his show from the CNN studios in Los Angeles instead of a houseboat. His name: Larry King. Over the years, Larry has been a good friend. He's endorsed my books, interviewed me on his radio show, and appeared on my local radio show in Orlando. Larry offers this advice on effective communicating:

> Whether you are talking to one person or several thousand, there are keys to communicating effectively. One thing I've learned is that there's nobody you can't talk to if you understand the basics: honesty, the right attitude, interest in the other person, and openness about yourself.
>
> No matter how much we know about communication, we can continue to improve the way we talk and achieve the success and confidence that comes with that improvement. After all, every successful person is in the communication business.[5]

### 3. Be a Good Listener

Look people in the eye, give them your full attention, and offer verbal feedback: "Really? . . . I agree. . . . Exactly!" Use "reflective listening," and repeat back that person's key points in your own words to make sure you've heard correctly: "In other words, I'm hearing you say . . ." People can tell when you're listening with half an ear—so it's important to listen with both ears, both eyes, and both hemispheres of your brain. Larry King explains why listening is such an important component of communicating: "I remind myself every morning: Nothing I say this day will teach me anything. So if I'm going to learn, I must do it by listening."[6]

### 4. Keep It Loose

Encourage a relaxed atmosphere where people are invited to speak freely. Most face-to-face communication goes better over coffee or tea or some other beverage. Good news sounds even better with a warm, steaming cup in your hands—and bad news seems not quite so bad.

T. Boone Pickens Jr. chairs the BP Capital Management fund; his current net worth is estimated at around three billion dollars. His advice: "Keep things informal. Talking is the natural way to do business. Writing is great for keeping records and putting down details, but talk generates ideas. Great things come from our luncheon meetings, which consist of a sandwich, a cup of soup, and a good idea or two. No martinis."[7]

### 5. Face-to-Face Communication Is Best

If you want to communicate only data (such as the time and place for a team meeting), e-mail is fine. But most of the communication that takes place on teams is too important to entrust to e-mail. When you need to offer encouragement or deal with a problem, say it face-to-face. Make sure your players receive not only your words, but your eye communication, your body language and gestures, and your tone of voice. Make your point with impact. Make it in person.

### 6. Communicate with Energy

When you are animated and expressive, your message has impact and makes a deeper impression on your listeners. When speaking to an audience, get out from behind the lectern and *move*. Walk from one side of the stage to the other—or even go out into the audience. Use big arm gestures to make your point. Make eye contact with specific people in the audience. As Alan Fox, director of StoryFocus Communications, puts it, "All the good communicators have lights in their eyes; there's a sparkle in there. How do you turn your headlights on?"[8] Your "headlights" are your personal energy. When you speak, make sure your personal high beams shine brightly.

### 7. Be Accessible

If you're the coach, let the team know you're available anytime. Walk the corridors, take your meals in the lunchroom, mingle with people, and greet them by name. You're not just improving communication—you're building team relationships.

### 8. Fix Problems, Not Blame

If you punish mistakes, people will keep you in the dark. Masao Nemoto, former senior managing director of Toyota Motor Corporation, once wrote down his "Ten Principles of Management Effectiveness" to remind his associates of Toyota's values. The first rule: *Never punish for mistakes.* Why? Because punishment squelches communication.[9]

### 9. Continually Teach Good Communication Skills

Team leaders need to teach and exemplify good communication skills. In addition to teaching basketball, Mike Krzyzewski teaches his Duke players to communicate:

> Effective teamwork begins and ends with communication. . . . However, communication does not always occur naturally, even among a tight-knit group of individuals. Communication must be *taught* and *practiced* in order to bring everyone together as one. . . .
>
> On the basketball court, there is very little time to get your message across. In the heat of the game, a basketball team speaks a different language; it is not a language based on long sentences, but it is a language nonetheless. To acclimate our team to speaking this language, we do not merely drill defensive stances and positioning in our practices, we drill talking. When you talk, your body reacts, your hands get ready, and your mind becomes prepared to respond, even under pressure.[10]

### 10. Keep It Simple

The most effective communication is always the simplest. My friend Doc Rivers, former Orlando Magic head coach, won his first NBA Championship as head coach of the Boston Celtics in 2008. During that season, a reporter asked Doc what the Celtics would do to facilitate ball movement. Doc's reply: "Pass." Now, that's keeping it simple![11]

Another leader who understands the importance of simplicity

is Pastor Andy Stanley, founder of North Point Ministries, one of the fastest-growing religious ministries in the United States. He says, "Every time I stand to communicate, I want to take one simple truth and lodge it in the heart of the listener. I want them to know that one thing and know what to do with it."[12]

### 11. Be an Encourager

Your job as a leader is to help your players see themselves as winners. Basketball coach Rick Pitino has led teams from three different schools (Providence, Kentucky, and Louisville) to the NCAA Final Four. In *Success Is a Choice*, he tells a story about the importance of communicating encouragement. It's the story of Anthony Epps, a starting point guard at Kentucky—an "unsung hero," in Coach Pitino's words. He played a key role in Kentucky's national championship, freely dishing the assists while rarely turning the ball over. Even so, the media gave him little attention so Anthony felt he had no future in pro basketball.

Coach Pitino wanted Anthony to believe in himself and commit himself to improvement through the summer. So Coach Pitino called the young man into his office and said, "Everyone's talking about all the other guys having a chance to play in the NBA. No one ever mentions you. How do you feel about that, Anthony?" Anthony replied that his skills probably weren't up to that level. Pitino answered, "Let's take a look at your skills. You had a three-to-one ratio of assists to turnovers, which is excellent. You guarded the other team's best point guard. You thought 'pass before shot.' You have the humility to sacrifice yourself for the good of the team. We could not have won the national title without you."[13]

Coach Pitino went down a list of Anthony Epps's strengths, then pointed out two areas where Anthony could improve: his foot speed and his first step. "If I were you," Pitino said, "I wouldn't let a lack of foot speed or a lack of a quick burst on my first step prevent me from being a pro. The first thing I would do tomorrow would be to go out and begin working to improve my foot speed and my first step. And I would see this as a golden opportunity. Because you have as much right to make it to the NBA as anyone else on this team, and you can't let that opportunity pass."[14]

After that talk, Pitino concluded, Epps "became a motivated player. Why? Because he wanted to give himself every opportunity to open doors in his future. What I did was enable him to dream. . . . That's what motivators do."[15]

### 12. Keep It Focused

Communication should always have a clear purpose. Give people specific action steps you want them to take. Whenever you finish talking to your team, they should know exactly what you expect of them.

## THE THIRD SIDE: PEOPLE SKILLS

The set of skills we call "people skills" can be summed up as the ability to work with people in order to inspire them to achieve a goal. If you can't achieve results through people, you can't lead your team. As financier-philanthropist John D. Rockefeller once said, "The ability to deal with people is as purchasable a commodity as sugar or coffee. And I will pay more for that ability than for any other under the sun."[16]

There are many individual skills under the heading of "people skills." Leaders need to be good delegators. They have to be able to evaluate the talent, character, and attitude of players. They need a sense of fun, a sense of humor. They need to be emotionally warm and vulnerable, not cold and unapproachable.

Sometimes leaders hide behind closed doors and isolate themselves from the team. They do this to protect themselves against interruptions and intrusions—but a leader's *job* is to deal with people and problems, which come in the form of interruptions and intrusions. If you retreat from your players, you are not leading your team.

One of my leadership mentors was Bill Veeck, who owned and operated such ball clubs as the Cleveland Indians, the St. Louis Browns, and the Chicago White Sox. He was always out among his players, talking to them, joking with them, and asking about their lives and their families. He had his office door removed from its hinges so his door would never be closed to anyone. Bill always answered his own phone and his own mail. He was available whenever I had a question, and he made a huge impact on my life.

As CEO of General Electric from 1981 to 2001, Jack Welch acquired a reputation for uncanny business insight and people skills. He is married to Suzy Wetlaufer Welch, a former editor of *Harvard Business Review*. In a column posted at The Welch Way: The Official Website of Jack and Suzy Welch, they observe that a big change takes place in a person's values and priorities upon becoming a leader:

> Being a leader changes everything. Before you are a leader, success is all about you. It's about your performance. Your contributions. It's about raising your hand, getting called on, and delivering the right answer.
>
> When you become a leader, success is all about growing others. It's about making the people who work for you smarter, bigger, and bolder. Nothing you do anymore as an individual matters except how you nurture and support your team and help its members increase their self-confidence. Yes, you will get your share of attention from up above—but

only inasmuch as your team wins. Put another way: Your success as a leader will come not from what you do but from the reflected glory of your team.[17]

Danny Litwhiler is a former major-league outfielder who played from 1940 to 1951 with the Cincinnati Reds and other teams. Now in his nineties, Danny recently published a book, *Living the Baseball Dream,* in which he recalls his experiences in the game. He describes manager Luke Sewell of the Reds as a man with great baseball skills but few people skills. "He was expressionless with the players," Litwhiler said. "If you did something good, Luke would say nothing, as if to say, *That's what you're getting paid for.* If you did something wrong, he would say nothing. . . . Players often wondered what Luke thought."[18]

On one occasion, when the Reds were playing the Phillies at Shibe Park, Danny went to the plate and faced Phillies pitcher Ken Heintzelman. Ken hung a curveball—and the instant the ball left his hand, Heintzelman shouted, "Oh, no!" He knew he'd blown it. Danny knocked that ball way out over the roof of the double-deck bleachers—home run.

Luke Sewell watched from his position as third-base coach. After Danny crossed the plate, Luke came over, clapped Danny on the back, and said, "That was the funniest thing I ever heard or saw in baseball. When Heintzelman pitched the ball, he yelled, 'Oh, no!' It was almost like he was trying to get the ball back!" Danny concluded, "That was the only complimentary thing I ever heard Luke say in regard to my play or any other player's performance."[19]

That's a fond memory for Danny Litwhiler, but it's also sad. Players are hungry for feedback and affirmation. They need leaders with strong people skills.

Contrast Danny's experience with that of NFL tight end Chad Lewis, who has played for the St. Louis Rams and the Philadelphia Eagles. Though he played only half a season with the Rams, he has high regard for Dick Vermeil, then head coach of the Rams.

"I developed great respect for Coach Vermeil that season," Lewis recalls. "He cares so much about his players. He has every player to his house for dinner in the offseason and he cooks for them—eight to ten players at a time with their wives or girlfriends. That's just how he is. . . . Players love Dick Vermeil."[20]

The acid test of Coach Vermeil's people skills came when he called Chad Lewis into his office during week nine of the season. It was bad news: Vermeil had to cut Lewis from the roster—and he was actually in tears as he gave Lewis the news. "I didn't want to do this," Vermeil said. "I love having you around. I know we're going to win the Super Bowl and I wanted to put you on the injured reserve for that, but the more I thought about that it wasn't fair to you. I know you're going to do great things. I want you to have that opportunity. I'm going to do what I can to get you a job."[21]

The next day, Coach Vermeil called Chad's wife, told her how sorry he was, and asked if there was anything he could do to help the family. "Chad's going to be fine," he reassured her. "No one does that!" Lewis concluded. "And it wasn't just me. [Coach Vermeil] was like that with all his players. I've talked to him several times since. It's always a handshake and a hug."[22]

The key to people skills is a genuine love for people. You can't fake that, at least not for long. We define ourselves by the way we treat other people. The things we say and do for others will determine how we are remembered after we're gone.

The greatest people skill of all is compassion.

# 4

## Principle 2: Great Leaders Build Extreme Dreams (Part 2)

There are different ways to lead, but I've always felt that it's better if other people follow me because they want to follow, not because I've been put up there as the leader and they have to follow.

TONY DUNGY, head coach,
Indianapolis Colts[1]

WE'VE JUST LOOKED AT THE FIRST THREE SIDES of leadership: vision, communication skills, and people skills. Now let's continue on to the final four sides of leadership: character, competence, boldness, and servanthood.

### THE FOURTH SIDE: CHARACTER

General H. Norman Schwarzkopf commanded the victorious Coalition Forces during the Gulf War of 1991. Earlier in his career, Schwarzkopf was the number two man in charge of Army personnel. His boss was a three-star general. One morning, Schwarzkopf came into the office and saw his boss walking out, leaving Schwarzkopf in charge. It was Schwarzkopf's first time filling in for the boss, so he peppered the general with questions: What if such-and-such happens? Should I call you if there's a problem?

The general turned to Schwarzkopf and said, "Whatever comes up, simply follow rule number fourteen."

"What's rule number fourteen?"

"When placed in command, take charge."

Still unsure of himself, Schwarzkopf asked a few more questions.

The general replied, "Follow rule number fifteen."

"What's rule number fifteen?"

"When in command, do the right thing."[2]

Schwarzkopf never forgot rules fourteen and fifteen—nor did he forget the lesson the general had taught him: leadership is rooted in character. To be a leader, you have to take charge and do the right thing. That's what people of character do.

There are many components that constitute good character, including honesty, integrity, courage, responsibility, dependability, a strong work ethic, perseverance, humility, and a commitment to being a good influence on others. Character makes leadership possible. Teams must be able to trust their leaders, and trust is based on character. If a team can't rely on a leader's honesty and integrity, the players won't respect him and follow him.

Many people think talent and charisma are adequate substitutes for character. Not true. Ability and charisma are the outward trappings of a leader. Character is the inner reality.

A leader without character is just a boss—and potentially a tyrant. Character is all that keeps leaders from abusing their position and inflicting harm on the people around them. Theodore Roosevelt, the twenty-sixth president of the United States, knew the danger posed by people with leadership skills and personal magnetism, but without an inner core of character. He said, "To educate a man in the mind and not in morals is to educate a menace to society."[3]

When I think of a leader of great character, I think of George Washington. After the passage of so many years, you might think Washington is more of a myth than a real man. But those who knew him testify that he was a genuine human being, with human flaws, but also with a deep core of character. One man who knew Washington well was Thomas Jefferson. He wrote:

> I think I knew General Washington intimately and thoroughly; and were I called on to delineate his character, it should be in terms like these. . . . His integrity was most pure. . . . He was, indeed, in every sense of the words, a wise, a good, and a great man. . . . On the whole, his character was, in its mass, perfect, in nothing bad, in few points indifferent; and it may truly be said that never did nature and fortune combine more perfectly to make a man great and to place him in the same constellation with whatever worthies have merited from man an everlasting remembrance.[4]

Historian David McCullough, Pulitzer-winning author of *1776* and *John Adams*, remarks on the fact that the Revolutionary War was a young man's cause, and that Washington, one of the oldest of the founding fathers, was only forty-three years old when he took command of the Continental Army. Neither Washington nor any of the other revolutionaries had any experience in starting a new country. "They were winging it," McCullough said. "They were improvising."[5]

Why did the Continental Congress choose Washington to lead the Army? Though he had served in the French and Indian War, Washington had never before led an army into battle. He had no track record as a military leader. "He was chosen," McCullough explained, "because they knew him; they knew the kind of man he was; they knew his character, his integrity. . . . He was a man people would follow. And as events would prove, he was a man whom some—a few—would follow through hell."[6]

Another insightful historian, Stephen E. Ambrose, also assesses George Washington as a leader of consummate character:

> Washington's character was rock solid. He was constant. At the center of events for twenty-four years, he never lied, fudged, or cheated. He shared his army's privations. . . . They respected him, even loved him. Washington came to stand for the new nation and its republican virtues, which was why he became our first President by unanimous choice. . . . In his ability to persuade, in his sure grip on what the new nation needed (above all else, not a king), and in his optimism no matter how bad the American cause looked, he rose above all others. He established the thought, "We can do it," as an integral part of the American spirit. . . .
>
> He resisted efforts to make him into a king and established the precedent that no one should serve more than two terms as President. He voluntarily yielded power. His enemy, George III, remarked in 1796, as Washington's second term was coming to an end, "If George Washington goes back to his farm he will be the greatest character of his age." Napoleon, then in exile, was as stunned as the rest of the world by Washington's leaving office. He complained that his enemies "wanted me to be another Washington."[7]

You may ask, "Didn't Washington own slaves?" He did. "Well, doesn't being a slave-master disqualify Washington as a leader of character?" Stephen Ambrose neither rationalizes nor defends slavery, but he does point out, "Of the nine Presidents who owned slaves, only Washington freed his." Many people today suggest that those who founded our nation are unworthy of honor because of that issue. Ambrose replies:

> [The founding fathers] established a system of government that, after much struggle, and the terrible violence of the Civil War, and the civil rights movement led by black Americans, did lead to legal freedom for all Americans and movement toward equality. . . . Of all the contradictions in America's history, none surpasses its toleration first of slavery and then of segregation. . . .
>
> Slavery and discrimination darken our hearts and cloud our minds in the most extraordinary ways, including a blanket judgment today against Americans who were slave owners in the eighteenth and nineteenth centuries. That the masters should be judged as lacking in the scope of their minds and hearts is fair, indeed must be insisted upon, but that doesn't mean we should judge the whole of them only by this part.[8]

One of the most revealing tests of human character is that which takes place at the end of life. Historian Peter R. Henriques of George Mason University describes how George Washington faced this final character test. In 1799, Washington wrote down his thoughts about death in a letter, saying, "When the summons comes I shall endeavour to obey it with good grace." Henriques notes that Washington "hoped that in facing death he would do nothing to sully the reputation he had spent a lifetime building."[9]

In mid-December of that year, after inspecting his farm on horseback in freezing rain, Washington fell ill with an infection that turned into pneumonia. He had probably contracted acute epiglottitis due to a bacterial infection. Henriques writes:

The pain associated with acute epiglottitis is intense, but the truly frightening aspect of the disease is the obstruction of the larynx that makes both breathing and swallowing extremely difficult. The first thing an infant learns to do is breathe and the second is to swallow. To have these two absolutely basic functions dramatically impaired is very frightening to anyone, no matter how brave and courageous he or she might be. Like any mortal, George Washington had to face the terror of air hunger, of smothering and gasping for each breath.

While the General received excellent medical treatment consistent with medical knowledge of the time, virtually every single action in fact compounded his suffering and hastened his demise. . . . Washington was bled four different times, losing approximately five pints or over eighty ounces of blood! Purgatives, emetics, and blistering greatly added to his discomfort without benefiting his condition. Washington's words, "I die hard," were certainly accurate. . . . He died as he lived, and his final words and actions reveal a great deal about the man and his character.[10]

History records that Washington, in his final hours, showed extraordinary compassion to everyone around him. Washington reassured the nervous doctor who bled him, "Don't be afraid." And when his personal secretary Tobias Lear strained to move Washington so he could breathe, the dying man apologized to Lear for burdening him. He urged his African-American servant, Christopher Sheels, to sit down and rest. Though he could scarcely speak, he took time to dictate some final changes to his will. In the end, he thanked his physicians for their efforts. Not once during his final ordeal did he complain about his suffering. His last words, recorded in the journal of Tobias Lear, were, " 'Tis well."[11] Those are the words of a man whose life was shaped by character.

Columnist Thomas Sowell laments the fact that we Americans sometimes elect leaders without regard to their character. Citing the scandal-ridden presidencies of Richard Nixon and Bill Clinton, Sowell observes, "Presidents of the United States lacking character and integrity have inflicted lasting damage on the office they held and on the nation."[12]

Character is vastly more important than intelligence. Just ask Charles Colson. The founder of Prison Fellowship and the Wilberforce Forum, Colson achieved the rank of captain in the United States Marine Corps. In a commencement address at Geneva College in Pennsylvania, he said:

> I was a Marine officer. When you're going into combat, the most important thing is that you can depend on the fellow in the next foxhole to be there if the shooting begins. I cared a whole lot more about his character than I did his IQ, because my life depended on his character. And as you go through life, whether it's in the military, or whether it's in your businesses, or whether it's in your churches, or whatever walk of life, and certainly in your family, someone is going to depend more on your character than your IQ.
>
> Build and develop your character.[13]

I once heard former congressman J. C. Watts speak on character at a convention in Scottsdale, Arizona. He asked, "How many of you husbands think the character of your wife is important? And how many of you wives think the character of your husband important? Yes, I thought you would. Now, don't tell me that the character of our leaders doesn't matter. You can no more have leadership without character than you can have water without the wet."

People are counting on us—and we'd better have a steel core of character that can withstand temptation, pressure, and adversity. If our players can't have faith in our character, what right have we to ask them to follow us?

## THE FIFTH SIDE: COMPETENCE

A leader is a problem-solver, salesman, teacher, organizer, change agent, crisis manager, and more. How do you become competent in all these areas? Only one way: experience. A team will follow a leader with a strong track record, because competence inspires confidence. Teams want to be led by proven winners.

New York Yankees owner George Steinbrenner once said: "If you can't sit in the saddle, you can't lead the charge."[14] More than three decades ago, Steinbrenner formulated "George Steinbrenner's Seven Commandments for Leaders." These seven principles are not actually commandments but questions—and the answers to these questions determine one's competence as a leader:

1. Does he win?
2. Does he work hard enough?
3. Is he emotionally equipped to lead the men under him?
4. Is he organized?
5. Is he prepared?
6. Does he understand human nature?
7. Is he honorable?[15]

Answer yes to all seven questions, and you have a leader who is *competent* to lead.

Former General Electric CEO Jack Welch offers "Six Rules for Successful Leadership." Here are his rules (along with my commentary in parentheses):

1. Face reality as it is, not as it was or as you wish it were.
   *(Be honest with yourself!)*
2. Be candid with everyone.
   *(Tell the truth to everyone, especially your players.)*
3. Don't manage, lead.
   *(Be a leader, not a bureaucrat. Envision an extreme dream, then lead your team to the promised land.)*
4. Change before you have to.
   *(Don't respond to change—initiate it!)*
5. If you don't have a competitive advantage, don't compete.
   *(Conserve your strategic resources by choosing your battles wisely.)*
6. Control your destiny, or someone else will.
   *(Pursue your own extreme dreams, assemble a great team to get there, and don't let circumstances or people keep you from your goal.)*[16]

Those are teamwork words to live by from a leader who exemplified all six rules. During his two decades as CEO of GE, Jack Welch faced reality, told the truth, led his company to the brink of the next millennium, initiated profound structural change, transformed the company, closed down or sold factories and divisions that couldn't compete, and carefully controlled GE's destiny. He became known for his blunt candor and his high expectations for GE executives. Welch rewarded top-performing executives with stock and cash incentives. He did away with layers of management hierarchy, making GE less rigidly bureaucratic and more responsive to change.

The company expanded enormously under Jack Welch's leadership. During his tenure, GE revenues rose from roughly $26.8 billion to nearly $130 billion, and the market value soared from $14 billion to more than $410 billion. Welch literally turned GE into the biggest and most valuable corporation in the world. No wonder *Fortune* magazine named him "Manager of the Century" in 1991.[17]

Competency in the sports world is measured by wins and championships. Competency in the church world is measured by church growth. Competency in the military world is measured by success on the battlefield. And competency in the business world is measured by financial statements and stock value.

## THE SIXTH SIDE: BOLDNESS

Leaders must be bold. You can't be a leader if you do not possess boldness, because there is no such thing as a "timid leader." Every great achievement in history is a monument to the boldness of some great leader.

Boldness is a multifaceted quality. Let me suggest seven specific ingredients, which, taken together, make up a bold leader:

### 1. Decisiveness

Leadership is decision-making. The best decisions are made cleanly, without waffling or second-guessing. American journalist Gordon Graham once said, "Decision is a sharp knife that cuts clean and straight; indecision, a dull one that hacks and tears and leaves ragged edges behind it."[18] Or, as someone else has said, "Once you make a decision and the die is cast, murder the alternatives."

Be bold! Decide—and don't worry if you made the right decision. Instead, motivate your team to *make* it the right decision. Indecision is contagious. Hesitant leaders produce hesitant teams.

### 2. Courage

Bold leaders are courageous. Genuine courage is not the absence of fear, but the willingness to do the thing that scares you. Someone once said, "Courage is fear that has said its prayers." Courage is not a feeling. It's a *decision*—the decision to do the right thing in spite of our fears.

### 3. Confidence

Leaders must have bold confidence in themselves and in their teams. Confidence is infectious, empowering players to believe in themselves. Genuine confidence isn't arrogance; it's simply the "can-do" attitude of a leader who has done it before and can do it again.

### 4. Initiative

Bold leaders don't wait for events and circumstances to turn in their favor. They take the initiative and control the future. They continually look ahead, see what's on the horizon, and seize the moment before it arrives.

### 5. Perseverance

Bold leaders don't give up. They don't complain about adversity. They deal with it and stick with it until they succeed.

## 6. Ruggedness

A bold leader cares little about his or her own comfort. He or she knows that nothing great has ever been achieved within a comfort zone. Bold leaders are willing to leave the safety of the shore and head out to sea for a life of adventure.

## 7. Inner Security

Bold leaders are secure within themselves. They don't worry unduly about what others think of them. When attacked or criticized, they hardly notice because their souls are protected by rhinoceros-tough armor. They are willing to stand alone against peer pressure, temptation, conflict, and controversy. As Margaret Thatcher once observed, "Being prime minister is a lonely job. In a sense, it ought to be: You cannot lead from the crowd."[19]

Yes, leadership is a lonely business. Theodore Roosevelt described that kind of bold but lonely leadership in a speech at the Sorbonne in Paris in 1910:

> It is not the critic who counts: not the man who points out how the strong man stumbles or where the doer of deeds could have done better. The credit belongs to the man who is actually in the arena, whose face is marred by dust and sweat and blood, who strives valiantly, who errs and comes up short again and again, because there is no effort without error or shortcoming, but who knows the great enthusiasms, the great devotions, who spends himself for a worthy cause; who, at the best, knows, in the end, the triumph of high achievement, and who, at the worst, if he fails, at least he fails while daring greatly, so that his place shall never be with those cold and timid souls who knew neither victory nor defeat.[20]

During the Civil War, President Abraham Lincoln placed General George McClellan in charge of organizing the Army of the Potomac. McClellan, a competent and meticulous planner, did an excellent job of training the troops—but he lacked boldness. He analyzed problems to death. He preferred caution over courage.

In the Peninsula campaign of 1862, McClellan faced an undermanned, ill-equipped enemy. Confederate Major General John B. Magruder brilliantly played upon McClellan's indecisive nature. He marched a small squad of troops in circles past the same position, so that the squad looked like a battalion. He moved snipers around and had them take potshots at McClellan's forces from different locations. As a result, McClellan thought he faced a massive Confederate army when his forces could have overwhelmed the modest Rebel forces at any time.

When McClellan asked the War Department for more soldiers, President Lincoln personally replied, "You now have over one hundred thousand troops. . . . You had better break the enemies' line from Yorktown to Warwick River at once. . . . I have never written you, or spoken to you, in greater kindness of feeling than now, nor with a fuller purpose to sustain you—*but you must act*."[21] Lincoln underlined those last four words.

Amazingly, McClellan ignored the president's orders. In fact, a few days later, a reconnaissance force under Brigadier General William F. Smith broke through the thinly defended Confederate line. Smith wanted to press the attack—but McClellan ordered Smith to retreat.

President Lincoln's patience finally came to an end. He left the White House and rode to McClellan's headquarters in Virginia for a face-to-face talk. The general was nowhere to be found (perhaps deliberately so). Exasperated, Lincoln returned to the White House, summoned his advisers, and said, "If General McClellan does not want to use the army, I would like to *borrow* it for a time." Soon afterward, Lincoln relieved General McClellan of command.[22]

McClellan's lack of boldness undoubtedly prolonged the war, perhaps by two years or more, at a cost of thousands of lives on both sides. After the war, journalist John Russell Young asked General Ulysses S. Grant to evaluate the man. Grant replied, "McClellan is to me one of the mysteries of the war."[23]

Bold leaders must make decisions and seize opportunities. The failure to decide is itself a decision—and a poor one.

Boldness is a crucial trait for business leaders. Prime example: Intel Corporation. Founded in 1968 as Integrated Electronics Corporation, Intel is now the world's largest maker of semiconductors. The personal computer revolution is based on Intel's x86 series of microprocessors, found in most PCs. The company was founded by Robert Noyce and Gordon Moore and came to dominate the computer industry under the bold leadership of Andrew Grove. During Grove's tenure as CEO (1987 to 1998), he oversaw the growth of Intel's market capital from $18 billion to $197 billion.

Dr. Noel M. Tichy teaches organizational behavior at the University of Michigan. In *The Leadership Engine*, he attributes Intel's phenomenal success to Andy Grove's bold leadership:

> Every two years, Andy Grove plunks down about $2.5 billion to build a plant to produce a new type of microchip. This is essentially a bet on the future of Intel's new technology. So far, the bets have paid off big for Intel. Is Grove lucky, or a great gambler? Hardly. Grove is a great leader who looks for opportunities to change his company before the market changes ahead of it, and then makes it very clear to people what mountain they are about to climb.[24]

Tichy adds that Andy Grove has "a leadership quality that I have come to call 'edge': the ability to make tough decisions and the willingness to sacrifice the security of today for the sake of a better future. . . . The people who succeed, the winners, are the ones who have edge."[25]

What Tichy calls "edge," I call boldness. Tichy learned the term "edge" from "the ultimate Mr. Edge," former General Electric CEO Jack Welch. Tichy once went to Welch's office to interview him about leadership. Welch told him, "A leader's got to have edge. . . . A lot of people have good ideas, and good values, and they can even energize others. But for some reason they are not able to make the tough calls. That is what separates, for me, whether or not someone can lead a business."[26]

Tichy quotes Andy Grove on the importance of boldness (or edge) in business:

> I can't help but wonder why leaders are so often hesitant to lead. I guess it takes a lot of conviction and trusting your gut to get ahead of your peers, your staff and your employees while they are still squabbling about which path to take, and set an unhesitating, unequivocal course whose rightness or wrongness will not be known for years. Such a decision really tests the mettle of the leaders. By contrast, it doesn't take much self-confidence to downsize a company—after all, how can you go wrong by shuttering factories and laying people off if the benefits of such actions are going to show up in tomorrow's bottom line and will be applauded by the financial community?[27]

Talleyrand, the first prime minister of France, once said, "I am more afraid of an army of a hundred sheep led by a lion than an army of a hundred lions led by a sheep."[28] So be a lion and be bold! Decide firmly, act courageously, display confidence, seize the initiative, persevere to the end, live adventurously, and stand strong.

Set an example of boldness and you will summon the confidence of your team.

## THE SEVENTH SIDE: SERVANTHOOD

Whether in business, sports, government, the military, or the religious world, a leader *must* be a servant. If you're not willing to serve, you're not qualified to lead.

Michael Bergdahl worked alongside Wal-Mart founder Sam Walton at the company's Bentonville, Arkansas, headquarters. In his book *What I Learned from Sam Walton*, Bergdahl writes, "Wal-Mart leaders embrace a philosophy called 'servant-leadership,' which simply means that if you are a leader you need to put the needs of your people first. . . . When you boil it all down, the secret to Sam Walton's leadership philosophies is servant-leadership."[29]

Sam Walton practiced this philosophy whenever he visited Wal-Mart stores. His employees (called "associates" within the Wal-Mart culture) loved him and flocked to him—and Walton was never happier than when "rubbing elbows with the troops."[30]

In March 1992, President George H. W. Bush presented Sam Walton with the Presidential Medal of Freedom. Sam was dying of cancer at the time. Michael Bergdahl recalls that, in the final weeks of his life, Walton had a hospital bed moved into his office so that he could stay on the job. He used an "anti-gravity pen" to scribble notes on his clipboard while lying flat on his back. Bergdahl concludes:

> Sam modeled these servant-leadership behaviors to the very end of his life. I can still remember in his final

days, seeing Sam Walton in his office laying flat on his back in a hospital-type bed taking chemotherapy treatments while he continued to work. I can assure you he didn't do it to make people feel sorry for him; he did it because he intended to keep working until the very end of his life. . . . The sight of him lying there in his office in the final days of his life, continuing to work from a hospital bed, is an inspirational image burned forever into my memory.[31]

Bosses give orders. Servant-leaders offer guidance. Bosses intimidate. Servant-leaders motivate. Bosses wield power. Servant-leaders empower others. Bosses throw their weight around. Servant-leaders delegate authority. Bosses say, "You work for me." Servant-leaders say, "We work together." Bosses demand sacrifice. Servant-leaders exemplify sacrifice. A leader who is not a servant is just a boss.

NFL coach Tony Dungy is a consummate leader—and a servant. He has collected two Super Bowl rings, one as a defensive back with the Pittsburgh Steelers in Super Bowl XIII, the other as head coach of the Indianapolis Colts in Super Bowl XLI. He once talked about his leadership role:

> There are different ways to lead, but I've always felt that it's better if other people follow me because they want to follow, not because I've been put up there as the leader and they have to follow. To do that, you have to earn people's trust and their respect; and the way to do that is to show them you are there to help them. . . .
>
> I really try to, number one, be a role model and serve my team spiritually. I want to teach them as much as I can about football and how to be better players; but I also want to help them be good people.[32]

Tom Osborne was the head coach of the University of Nebraska football team from 1973 to 1997. He served six years in the House of Representatives from Nebraska's Third Congressional District. His Cornhuskers finished in the top fifteen of the final AP poll twenty-four out of twenty-five seasons, won national championships in 1994 and 1995, and shared a championship in 1997. When he retired from coaching, his record was an astounding 255-49-3. Tom Osborne stresses the importance of being a servant as well as a leader:

> We are called to serve rather than be served. . . . The coach is truly a servant of his players. He may be a disciplinarian and stern at times; however, his primary motivation from a spiritual perspective is to serve and to care for those with whom he has been entrusted. . . . As a coach, there is a temptation to consider oneself preeminent and look at players as pieces of the puzzle who enable the coach to achieve his goals. When I viewed myself as a servant of the other coaches and players, things went better on our team and for me personally. This does not mean that I was any less demanding or did not expect great effort and solid preparation. It did mean, however, that I was there to do whatever I could to help them accomplish team objectives and mature into better people.[33]

General David Petraeus is commanding general of the Multi-National Force in Iraq. He is a remarkable man: West Point graduate, class of 1974, top 5 percent of his class; master's in public administration (1985); PhD in international relations (1987), Woodrow Wilson School of Public and International Affairs at Princeton. One of the world's leading experts on counterterrorism, he is the chief architect of the "Surge" strategy that is bringing peace, stability, and political reconciliation to war-torn Iraq.

In a 2008 *Wall Street Journal* column, Peggy Noonan revealed a little-known story about General Petraeus that sheds light on him as a leader—and as a servant. In September 1991, General Petraeus commanded the Third Battalion of the 101st Airborne at Fort Campbell, Kentucky. During a "live-fire" training exercise, a soldier tripped and his rifle discharged, hitting General Petraeus in the chest. A helicopter airlifted Petraeus to Vanderbilt University Medical Center in Nashville.

A civilian surgeon was called to Vanderbilt in time to see the helicopter land. General Petraeus was brought out on a gurney, pale from loss of blood, but conscious. The surgeon told him, "I have to make a decision whether to take you straight into surgery or give you blood and get you stabilized first."

"Do the surgery," the general said. "Let's get on with it."[34]

The doctor took General Petraeus into surgery, removed the bullet and a piece of lung, and stopped the internal bleeding. The operation went well, and the next day, General Petraeus asked to be transferred to the base hospital so he could be closer to his men. He was concerned that his soldiers would worry about him if he didn't return to the base right away. The general got his wish.

The general's surgeon, Dr. Bill Frist, was eventually elected to the United States Senate and served as Majority Leader. After Frist moved to Washington, he and General Petraeus became good friends. They ran together in the Army ten-miler in Washington, and Senator Frist visited General Petraeus in Iraq to personally gauge the progress of the war. The doctor-turned-senator feels privileged to see firsthand how a servant-leader responds when his life is on the line: the general's only thought was for his troops. That is leadership, that is servanthood, and that is true greatness.

## ONE LEADER, SEVEN SIDES

So these are the Seven Sides of Leadership. To be a great leader of an extreme-dream team, you must have vision, communication skills, people skills, character, competence, boldness, and servanthood. Remove any one of these qualities from the equation, and leadership falters.

Every one of the Seven Sides of Leadership is a learnable skill or a character quality you can *choose* to build into your life. So choose it, learn it, and live it. Teamwork begins with the person in charge—

And that person is *you*.

# Extreme *Exploratory* Dreams . . .

## *Depend on Teams*

*But I put forth on the high open sea*
*With one sole ship, and that small company*
*By which I never had deserted been.*

DANTE ALIGHIERI, *The Divine Comedy*,
"Inferno," Canto XXVI[1]

Sir Ernest Henry Shackleton (1874–1922) dreamed of reaching the most extreme location on earth: the South Pole. He made five Antarctic expeditions, the most famous being the third, the Imperial Trans-Antarctic Expedition aboard *Endurance*, 1914–1916.

To assemble his team for that expedition, Shackleton wrote a letter to the *Times* of London, announcing his intention to go to the South Pole and inviting people to apply for a place on the team. He warned that conditions would be harsh, the risk would be great, and the pay would be low—more a token honorarium than a salary. He received five thousand applications, including three from young women.

Shackleton chose his team with care. He didn't look merely for talent, physical strength, and proven skills. He also looked for intangible qualities of attitude, character, and team spirit—qualities that would transform a collection of separate individuals into that synergistic union of souls called a *team*. In *Leading at the Edge*, Dennis N. T. Perkins wrote about Shackleton's unusual approach to recruiting his team:

> *Reginald W. James, selected as* Endurance *physicist, described his peculiar interview: "Shackleton asked me if my teeth were good, if I suffered from varicose veins, if my circulation was good, if I had a good temper, and if I could sing. At this question I probably looked a bit taken aback, for I remember he said, 'Oh, I don't mean any Caruso stuff; but I suppose you can shout a bit with the boys?'"*
>
> *The question about singing had become one of Shackleton's stock queries, and his touchstone for a man's team spirit.*[2]

Shackleton's ship, the *Endurance*, left London on August 1, 1914, the same day Germany declared war on Russia—the beginning of World War I. Shackleton paused for a week in Plymouth to offer his ship to Great Britain for the war effort, but the British Admiralty telegrammed a one-word reply: "Proceed."

*Endurance* crossed the Antarctic Circle on December 30 and sailed on toward the Weddell Sea. The plan was for six men to be set ashore on the Antarctic coast. Those men were supposed to traverse the continent by dogsled, reach the South Pole, then move on to the opposite coast on the Ross Sea, where they would be picked up for the voyage home. On January 10, 1915, lookouts caught their first glimpse of the Antarctic continent. On the eighteenth, the ship became trapped by pack ice and could not be freed. The *Endurance* was stranded a thousand miles from the nearest inhabited land.

Weeks passed, then months. The men lived aboard the icebound ship, surviving on meager rations. Shackleton knew he had to keep up the morale of his crew if they were to survive the brutal Antarctic winter. His lighthearted manner gave everyone the confidence to believe everything would turn out all right. Shackleton treated his men as equals and pitched in with the "grunt work," such as serving meals and scrubbing decks. He organized entertainment nights with music and skits and encouraged the men to stay fit by playing soccer or racing dogsleds on the ice.

On May 1, the sun went below the horizon—and wouldn't reappear until early September. For four months, it was nighttime at noontime. Day after day, the men could hear the ice floes pressing against the hull of *Endurance*, cracking and warping her timbers. The sounds of snapping planks were as loud as gunshots.

By October 24, a massive shelf of ice broke through the hull, and water poured in. Shackleton ordered the men to remove all lifeboats, provisions, and equipment from the ship. For weeks, *Endurance* slowly settled into the water. Finally, on November 21 the ship abruptly went down by the bow, disappearing within minutes.

The crew knew the world did not expect their return until February, so their chances of being rescued were nil. Just before Christmas, the men set off in an attempt to cross the ice shelf, hoping to reach Paulet Island,

250 miles away. They took as much food and survival gear as they could carry, plus three lifeboats for the sea crossing. But the buckling sea ice prevented them from traveling more than a mile and a half a day. Shackleton, realizing it would take nearly a year to reach land, called a halt.

They established a base they called "Patience Camp." By late March 1915, with provisions running low, the crew began to kill and eat the sled dogs.

On April 8, the ice floe where they camped split in two, leaving them on a small, unstable triangle of ice. If it broke up, Shackleton and his men would have no hope of survival. The following day, they launched out in the lifeboats. They threaded their way slowly around dangerous ice floes in temperatures as low as –20 degrees F, with their food and strength dwindling. On April 14, they reached the southeast coast of Elephant Island, but its perpendicular ice cliffs afforded no place to come ashore.

They rounded the island and found a narrow strand of beach. Elephant Island, they knew, was uninhabited. The nearest help was eight hundred miles across the Southern Ocean, at South Georgia Island. Shackleton selected five other men, and they outfitted one boat to make the journey. They launched on April 24, leaving twenty-two men on Elephant Island, trusting Shackleton's promise to return.

The journey in the twenty-two-foot boat was harrowing. Shackleton and his companions braved gale-force winds and fifty-foot waves. Cloud cover was so heavy the navigator could only take star readings four times during the journey. Several times, the boat was swamped by waves of icy water. The men bailed for their lives, and several times they thought their cause was lost.

After seventeen days at sea, the lifeboat arrived on the west coast of South Georgia. The men removed the heavy screws that held the lifeboat together and inserted them into the soles of their boots as makeshift ice cleats. They trekked thirty-six hours without sleep, crossing the mountainous spine of the island and arriving at the Stromness whaling station on the east coast on May 20.

Shackleton and his men were picked up by the whaler the *Southern Sky*, which took them to Elephant Island to attempt a rescue of the remaining men. An ice shelf prevented the *Southern Sky* from reaching the island; the attempt was abandoned.

The Uruguayan government lent Shackleton a trawler, *Instituto de Pesca No. 1*, but this attempt at rescue was also thwarted by ice. A third attempt aboard the British schooner *Emma* also failed. The Chilean government then lent Shackleton a steamer, the *Yelcho*, for a fourth attempt—

And on August 30, 1916, the *Yelcho* reached the coast of Elephant Island. Shackleton saw a crowd of thin, malnourished men waving and cheering on the shore. He had left them there four months earlier. With tears blurring his eyes, he counted the men—twenty-two! They were all alive!

From the time he left England until the day he rescued his men from Elephant Island, nearly twenty-five months had passed. Shackleton failed to reach the South Pole—but he succeeded in his most important mission: he kept his team alive.

When Shackleton returned to England in the fall of 1916, the public showed little interest in his story. World War I was in full fury (two men from his expedition later died in that war), and Shackleton hadn't even reached the Pole.

But with the passage of time, the story of the *Endurance* expedition became revered as one of the most inspiring tales of courageous leadership and teamwork ever told. Sir Ernest Henry Shackleton had an extreme explorer's dream—a dream of reaching the bottommost point on the planet and trekking across the frozen continent—and he refused to let go of that dream.

In 1921, he set off on another expedition, intending to circumnavigate the continent of Antarctica aboard a ship called the *Quest*. A number of men who had accompanied him aboard the *Endurance* went with him on the *Quest*. On January 5, 1922, as the ship neared South Georgia Island, Sir Ernest Shackleton suffered a massive heart attack and died. He was forty-seven years old.

Sir Ernest Shackleton never achieved his extreme dream of going to the South Pole—yet his legacy of leadership lives on. His story is a testimony to the strength of the human spirit—and the power of teamwork. Even when the dream fails, a committed team can rise up, overcome adversity, and carve out a place in history. Extreme dreams of human exploration depend on great leaders and great teams.[3]

## 5

# Principle 3: Commitment Builds Extreme Dreams

*If you aren't going all the way, why go at all?*

> JOE NAMATH, retired NFL
> quarterback, New York Jets[1]

IN THE SUMMER OF 1999, WHEN DOC RIVERS CAME aboard as head coach of the Orlando Magic, he wanted to send a message to his leading scorer, point guard Darrell Armstrong—so he sent it by FedEx.

When Darrell answered his door, the delivery man put a FedEx envelope in his hands. Ripping the envelope open, Darrell was surprised to find a sheet of paper with three words typed in the center: "Are You Committed?"

Darrell later told *Sports Illustrated*, "It wasn't just the words on the paper that impressed me. It was that Doc only lives about fifteen minutes from my house, and still he sent those letters overnight!"[2]

Great teams are committed teams. Players must be committed to one another, to the coach, and to the extreme dream. They must be committed to excellence, perseverance, competition, and winning. Commitment must be total, unconditional, and absolute.

The simplest and most succinct expression of commitment

I've ever heard is that two-word statement, "I'm in." NBA coach Pat Riley has said that there are only two options when it comes to commitment: "You're either IN or you're OUT. There's no such thing as life in-between."[3]

If you're a leader, you must demand total commitment from your team. Not just obedience—commitment. Team members who merely obey orders will stand where you tell them to stand, do what you tell them to do, and put forth the minimum amount of effort. But players who are *totally committed* will give you a degree of intensity and persistence that far exceeds anything you would ask of them.

## THE POWER OF COMMITMENT

To the average Joe, a "team" is simply a group of people all wearing the same uniform. But if you've ever been on a *real* team, a *committed* team, you know that's not true. Teamwork is all about commitment. Without commitment, you have no team.

Challenge your team to total commitment: "If you put on the uniform but you're not committed to our common dream, then you're an impostor. If you're not 1,000 percent committed to your team, then please do everyone a favor and walk away. You shouldn't be in this game—you're holding everyone else back."

Pat Riley put it this way: "When a player totally commits to me, I commit to him. I know which guys I'd want to jump into a foxhole with."[4] Why is commitment so important? Because commitment leads to winning. For the team that is totally committed, *all things* are possible. Here's how it works.

Commitment seals off escape. It burns all your bridges behind you. When you're truly committed, you look only forward, never back. Decisions are easier to make, because you have already crossed "retreat" and "surrender" off your list.

This intense degree of mental focus, born of total commitment, enables you to function at the peak of your abilities. Commitment is your best defense against hesitation and indecision. When there is only one direction to go, *you go*. The moment you fully commit to your extreme dream and cut off all avenues of retreat, people and circumstances align and help you reach your goal.

Winning demands hard work and an unselfish attitude. Commitment energizes players to put in the preparation needed to build a team of winners. When Pat Riley was head coach of the Lakers, he said:

> Few people realize that beneath the surface glitter, the players bring a fanatical depth of preparation in every game. Their apparently spontaneous creativity and effortless innovation is actually the product of hundreds of hours of hard practice sessions. With that devotion to hard work, the Lakers have made a covenant with each other to put aside selfishness so that the team can achieve its goals, saying, "Whatever it takes for the team to win, I'll do it."[5]

Commitment powers perseverance. If you are totally committed, you refuse to give up. If an opponent knocks you down, you *will* get up. Staying on the canvas is not an option. You have to keep fighting.

Recently, while driving on the highway near Orlando, I saw a recruiting billboard for the United States Marine Corps. The headline read, "We don't take applications, only commitments." That's a powerful statement. The Marines understand commitment better than anyone else in the world. That's why you can hand the Marines any "impossible" assignment—and they will get it done. In his book *Corps Business: The 30 Management Principles of the U.S. Marines*, David H. Freedman observes:

The Marine motto is, of course, the Latin phrase *semper fidelis*, or "always faithful." This motto, which might be uttered, heard, or read a hundred times or more in a Marine's typical day (usually condensed to *semper fi*), is as noteworthy for what it does not attempt to convey as for what it does. It does not explicitly exhort Marines to do a great job, protect the country, be brave, or exalt the organization. It simply demands that every Marine remain committed to the Corps and to other Marines, unconditionally and forever.

Clearly the Marine Corps is asking a bit more of its members than do other organizations. In companies where it's every person for himself or herself and the only sure way to obtain commitment is through stock options, it would simply seem ludicrous to ask for unqualified lifetime loyalty. That's too bad, insists [Major General Emil "Buck" Bedard]. "The best way to measure an organization is by the loyalty it inspires, bottom line," he says.[6]

What about your organization, your team? Does it inspire loyalty and commitment? Are your players totally committed to your extreme dream? Is there a spirit of *semper fidelis* in your organization? Make sure your players know: "You're either *in* or you're *out*."

### "CHOOSE ONE CHAIR"

Someone once said that the hardest part of running a marathon is lacing up your running shoes. As a marathon runner myself, I can tell you it's true. The hardest part about marathoning is making that first commitment. Once you are fully committed to being a marathon runner, the rest is just hard work and perseverance.

Commitment *must* be focused on a single goal, a single purpose, a single destination. You cannot "commit" yourself to a dozen different things at once. That's not commitment—that's multitasking. A committed person is obsessed with one extreme dream. To be "committed" to a dozen goals is to be committed to none. An extreme dream is all-consuming. It demands *total* commitment.

Italian tenor Luciano Pavarotti (1935–2007) was one of the truly great vocal performers of our time. His reputation extended from the world of opera to the world of popular music. Born in Modena, Italy, the son of a baker, Pavarotti dreamed as a boy of becoming a professional soccer player—but it soon became clear that his talents didn't match that dream.

At the same time, he was taking voice lessons, and his teacher encouraged him to consider a career in music. So Pavarotti studied music in college, but upon his graduation he couldn't decide if he should go into teaching or pursue a career as a professional singer. Teaching would provide a steady, secure living, while the life of a professional singer was notoriously insecure—some singers starved while only a few achieved soaring success. Pavarotti asked his father for his advice. "Luciano," his father replied, "if you try to sit in two chairs, you will fall between them. You must choose one chair."[7]

Pavarotti chose professional singing. It was more difficult and frustrating than he even imagined it would be. Beginning in 1961, he took roles in opera houses across Italy and from Spain to Turkey. Finally, in 1966, he received his big break, appearing at Milan's La Scala; two years later, he debuted to enormous acclaim at the Metropolitan Opera in New York City. His father had given him brilliant advice: choose one chair.

Luciano Pavarotti made his choice—and conquered the music world.

Fred Smith Sr. (not to be confused with Fred Smith, the

founder of FedEx), was a business consultant, public speaker, author, and mentor to many executives and leaders, including John Maxwell, Ken Blanchard, Zig Ziglar, and myself. Fred was a great proponent of total commitment. He once said, "Commitment is essential for victory in an individual's life. Committed lives have meaning, accomplishment, purpose, and excitement. . . . Tentative lives are never victorious. Have you ever read a biography [of] someone who lived tentatively and became a hero?"[8]

A commitment to an extreme dream is like a marriage commitment. You wouldn't think of going into marriage with the thought, *I hope this marriage thing doesn't cut into my dating.* No, a marriage commitment is absolute and all-consuming. You say, "I am committed to this person, totally and forever." If you enter into marriage thinking, *If it doesn't work out, I can always quit,* then you already have one foot out the door. The first time your marriage relationship faces a big test, your halfhearted "commitment" will collapse—and so will the marriage.

The same is true of a commitment to an extreme dream. The leader must be totally, irrevocably sold out to the dream. The team members must be absolutely committed to the leader, to the team, and to the dream. Halfhearted "commitment" will kill your dream faster than any obstacle or opposition.

Don't allow semicommitted players onto your team. If anyone shows signs of mental reservation, of an "I-can-bail-out-anytime" attitude, either set that player straight or remove him in a hurry. That kind of thinking can infect the team.

Wise people know: commitment powers winning. Businesswoman and author Mary Crowley commented: "One person with a commitment is worth more than a hundred people who only have an interest."[9] Anthropologist Margaret Mead said, "Never doubt that a small group of committed people can change the world. It is the only thing that ever has."[10] And leadership guru

John Maxwell said, "Ordinary people with commitment can make an extraordinary impact on their world."[11]

## COMMITMENT: THE KEY TO TURNAROUND

Dennis Green was named head coach of the Minnesota Vikings in January 1992, a team coming off two lackluster seasons in a row. Green swiftly turned things around. During his first six years as head coach, Denny Green's Vikings reignited a once-dispirited fan base and qualified for the playoffs every year but one. The high point of Green's Minnesota coaching career was the 1998 season, when the Vikings lost only one regular-season game, set a record for most points scored in a season (later broken by the Patriots), and failed to reach the Super Bowl only by losing the NFC Championship game to the Falcons in overtime.

Ray Didinger interviewed Denny Green for the book *Game Plans for Success*, and Green recalled his arrival in Minnesota. Some five thousand Vikings ticket-holders had canceled their season tickets in disgust over the previous season. So Green criss-crossed the Twin Cities and spoke at every Rotary and Lions Club meeting, trying to rebuild goodwill. He recalled:

> One man said something that really stuck with me. He said he had been a season-ticket holder since the Vikings were founded in 1961 and had supported the team through the four Super Bowl losses, but he was ready to give up after the 1991 season.
>
> He said, "I could accept losing, but it broke my heart when they didn't even try."
>
> I promised him that attitude would change. I said as long as I was coach of the Vikings, the team would play hard every week. We might not win every week, but there

would never be a question about our effort. I meant that and I've done my best to instill that commitment in our team.

Winning stems from commitment, and commitment begins with attitude. That has been true since the beginning of time. If you take over an operation where the attitude stinks, you have to address that situation first before you can begin solving the other problems.[12]

Vince Lombardi took the same approach when he became head coach of the Green Bay Packers in 1958—then the worst team in the NFL. The last season before Lombardi arrived, the Packers finished with a dismal 1-10-1 record. The players were undisciplined, out of shape, and disrespectful toward the coaches. Lombardi dealt with that in a hurry, cutting bad-attitude players off the roster while demanding absolute commitment from the players he retained.

During a practice session, Lombardi saw linebacker Ray Nitschke loafing through a scrimmage. "Mr. Nitschke," Lombardi called out, "I have read that you are the best linebacker in the NFL. But after watching you just then I find it hard to believe. Now, do it again!"[13]

On the next snap, Ray Nitschke exploded forward, picked up a rookie lineman by his shoulder pads, tossed him into center Jimmy Ringo, and kept going. As halfback Paul Hornung recalled, "It took them two minutes to get the rookie to come to."[14]

As leadership expert Donald T. Phillips reflects in his book *Run to Win*, "When Lombardi confronted a member of his team, he was forcing the individual to *think* about his *personal* commitment to the organization and to his own performance."[15]

Vince Lombardi constantly talked about commitment. "Individual commitment to a group effort," he once said, "is what makes a team work, a company work, a society work, a civilization work."[16] And Lombardi didn't demand anything from his players that he hadn't already demanded of himself. "I don't know how else to live," he once said. "Unless a man believes in himself, and makes a total commitment to his career, and puts everything he has into it—his mind, his body, and his heart—what's life worth to him?"[17]

After completing his amazing turnaround of the Green Bay Packers and coaching them to five NFL Championships (with a record of 141-39-4 during his tenure), Vince Lombardi accepted the head coaching position with another team that sorely needed a turnaround, the Washington Redskins. At a February 7, 1969, press conference announcing his hiring by the Redskins, Lombardi issued this promise: "I will demand a commitment to excellence and to victory. That is what life is all about."[18]

## COMMITMENT: THE KEY TO COMPLETENESS

A wish can become an extreme dream when you back it up with commitment. We can achieve things we never thought possible when we add the power of commitment. Sharon Wood, the first North American woman to climb Mount Everest, put it succinctly: "Level of commitment equals level of performance."[19]

Commitment holds teams together through times of adversity and discouragement. When players are committed to one another, they make one another better. They hold one another accountable, spur one another on, and lift one another up. As Pat Riley observed, "Teamwork requires that everyone's efforts flow in a single direction. Feelings of significance happen when a team's energy takes on a life of its own."[20]

Talk of commitment is cheap; the real thing is costly. Commit yourself and your team to the dream, then see it through to completion. Odds are, you *will* succeed, because the very nature of commitment is that there's no giving up until victory has been achieved. And what if you fail? You'll still have succeeded in one very important challenge: you'll have conquered the fear that holds most people back—the fear of trying.

My friend Bobby Bowden is the head college football coach of the Florida State Seminoles, a position he's held since 1976. His teams have won twelve conference titles and two national championships. Bobby was inducted into the College Football Hall of Fame in 2006.

I well remember the shock and sadness I felt on hearing that Bobby's fifteen-year-old grandson, Bowden Madden, and Bowden's dad, John, had been killed in a three-vehicle accident in late 2004. John, who played football for Bobby at Florida State from 1978 to 1981, was married to Bobby's youngest daughter, Ginger, until their divorce earlier that year. The accident happened on a Sunday night on Interstate 10. The funeral took place on Thursday—the day before Florida State's season opener against the Hurricanes of Miami at the Orange Bowl. Many wondered if Bobby would skip the game because of his loss.

Game day arrived and Bobby Bowden was where he always was, striding the sideline, emotionless on the outside, heartbroken within. He had made a commitment to his team and he would keep it, no matter how much he hurt inside. Bobby's son Jeff, who was the Seminoles' offensive coordinator, had told reporters earlier in the week, "Dad doesn't show his emotions to a heavy degree, but it has been difficult for both of us to concentrate at times."[21]

Seminoles linebacker Buster Davis spoke of the way Bobby Bowden kept his commitment to the team despite his loss. "We know what [Coach Bowden] must have been going through," Davis said, "but he never showed his emotions. . . . We really got the sense that he didn't want us thinking about what he was going through."[22]

At the ACC press conference two days before the game, Bobby spoke publicly about his loss. "This is life," he said. "I experience it with my players a lot. I have a player who loses a mother or a player who loses a father or a player who loses a brother. Of course, after it happens to you, you realize that somebody can't tell you how it feels. . . . I believe I can sympathize a little bit more."[23]

Those were the emotions Bobby took into the Orange Bowl that night. It was a grueling, low-scoring, defense-dominated game. Bobby Bowden's Seminoles played with a lot of heart, no doubt wanting to win the game for their coach. After all, the Seminoles had lost to the Hurricanes in their last five meetings, and no one at Florida State wanted to extend that streak by one more game.

Late in the fourth quarter, the Seminoles led 10 to 3. With 3:58 to play, Florida State attempted a thirty-four-yard field goal that would have put the game out of reach for the Hurricanes— but Miami blocked it and got the ball back. The Hurricanes drove eighty yards in five plays—then scored, tying the game at 10. Another Miami touchdown in overtime, and it was over. Bobby Bowden's Seminoles had lost six straight to Miami.

As Bobby walked toward the tunnel, some rowdy Miami fans shouted taunts at him. Did they know he had just buried his grandson? Were they ignorant? Stupid? Drunk? It didn't matter. Bobby was so lost in his thoughts that he scarcely heard them.

He went to the press room to answer questions about the game. He explained the loss in simple terms: "We had our chance to put them away and we didn't. They had a chance to put us away and they did." All the reporters' questions were about football— though one reporter asked if it was hard coaching that night. "It wasn't hard to be here coaching this game," Bobby replied. "But it was hard for my mind not to be somewhere else."[24]

Eventually, the reporters left—all but *Tampa Trib* columnist Joe Henderson. He noticed Bowden getting up from the table, shaking his head, and saying to no one in particular, "It's awful. Just awful." Henderson knew Bobby wasn't talking about football. Joe Henderson went outside and hung around with the Seminole players as they waited to board the bus, collecting quotes for his column. He was about to leave when he heard, "Hey, Joe!" The columnist turned and saw Bobby Bowden walking to the bus. Bobby tossed something to Henderson, and the columnist caught it—the Florida State cap Bobby had worn during the game. In a soft voice, Bobby added, "Give that to your grandson." Then he climbed aboard the bus.[25]

The next day, Joe Henderson told that story in his newspaper column and concluded, "One day I'll tell a grandchild about a remarkable guy who happened to be a football coach. That guy has strength, values, and he sees the good in people."[26]

Bobby Bowden is committed to his players, to the game of football, and to the extreme dream of winning the national championship. He has achieved his football dream twice in his career, but it didn't happen in 2004. That was a tough year for Bobby as a coach. It was an even tougher year for him as a family man. Football losses hurt. But family losses have a way of putting football losses in perspective.

Commitment is the key to teamwork. And it's the key to winning.

But more than that, commitment is the key to being a complete human being like Bobby Bowden.

# Extreme *Creative* Dreams . . .

## *Depend on Teams*

*There must be bands of enthusiasts for everything on earth—fanatics who share a vocabulary, a batch of technical skills and equipment, and, perhaps, a vision of some single slice of the beauty and mystery of things, of their complexity, fascination, and unexpectedness.*

ANNIE DILLARD, *An American Childhood*[1]

*Question:* Who painted the ceiling of the Sistine Chapel in the Vatican?

*The Standard Answer:* A lone genius named Michelangelo.

*The Truth:* A team of artists, technicians, and assistants, led by Michelangelo.

When Michelangelo Buonarroti was commissioned in 1508 by Pope Julius II to paint the ceiling of the Sistine Chapel, he knew the challenge was too great for his skills alone. The ceiling consisted of fifty-eight hundred square feet of plastered surface. He had to create key scenes from the book of Genesis, transfer the drawings to the ceiling, then apply paint to the wet plaster before it hardened. He'd have to perform his artistry while standing on a scaffold with his neck craned back—not lying on his back, as many people assume.

Michelangelo was mentored in the Florentine studio of Domenico Ghirlandaio, who was not only a master artist but a master delegator. While assisting Ghirlandaio, Michelangelo learned the principles of creative teamwork. He also became acquainted with many fellow artists who studied under Ghirlandaio. Michelangelo brought a number of these artists from Florence to assist him in the Sistine project.

While Michelangelo created the principal drawings and painted the key figures himself, he assigned his assistants to mix plaster and paint, make brushes, and transfer Michelangelo's original paper drawings to the plaster ceiling, using a grid system to enlarge the images. He also assigned his assistants to paint lesser scenes and figures. His team included biblical scholars Tommaso Inghirami and Schmuel Sarfati, who gave him insight into Old Testament symbolism.

Michelangelo personally designed a new scaffold after rejecting a flimsy platform constructed by the pope's carpenter. He made painter Francesco Rosselli foreman over a team of carpenters who constructed the new scaffold, based on Michelangelo's blueprints. Rosselli also helped prepare the ceiling for painting.

When some early paintings were ruined by a fast-growing mold, Michelangelo's Florentine friend, fresco painter Jacopo l'Indaco, invented a new mold-resistant plaster formula. Other artists who assisted Michelangelo included Giovanni Montorsoli, Francesco Granacci, Giuliano Bugiardini, Raffaello da Montelupo, and Silvio Cosini.

Michelangelo sought out the best artists and

craftsmen he could find, paid them well (sending the bill to the pope), gave them time off when they were sick, praised excellent work—and held them accountable for mistakes. Intensely passionate about his art, he demanded that everything be done his way—yet he encouraged his assistants to add their own artistic flourishes to his creation.

Some sections of the ceiling are clearly the work of Michelangelo's hand. Others, such as the three panels of the life of Noah, are believed to be almost entirely the work of assistants, with only minimal contribution by the master himself.[2]

As Warren Bennis said on the *NewsHour with Jim Lehrer* (PBS, March 26, 1997), "When you ask people who painted the Sistine Chapel, what comes to most people's minds, the correct answer is Michelangelo. But it was Michelangelo plus thirteen terrific artists and a crew of two-hundred that did the Sistine Chapel. So all throughout history it's been a group, a creative group."[3]

If you want a painting to hang on the wall, all you need is one talented artist and a two-by-three-foot canvas. But if you have an extreme artistic dream of transforming a chapel ceiling into fifty-eight hundred square feet of art that endures for the ages, you need one inspired leader plus one talented team.

Extreme *creative* dreams depend on teams.


## The Utopian Dreamer


When I moved to central Florida to help build the Orlando Magic, I noticed that everywhere I looked, I saw the impact of one man: Walt Disney. Walt never lived in Orlando, yet the culture of central Florida has been shaped by his vision.

While helping to build the Magic organization, I received invaluable assistance from Disney executives, including some who had known Walt personally. They told me story after story about this extreme dreamer—and I was captivated. I became obsessed with the life and mind of Walt Disney. I read every Disney biography ever written. I interviewed almost every person alive who knew him, including his daughter, Diane Disney Miller, and his nephew, Roy E. Disney. Then I wrote a Disney biography called *How to Be Like Walt* (Health Communications, 2004).

Though I never met Walt, I feel I've come to know him well. In my own way, I've devoted my life to doing what he did—dreaming extreme dreams, then assembling the teams to make those dreams come true.

There was an almost perverse stubbornness to Walt's extreme dreams. He once said, "If [the Disney Studio] management likes my projects, I seriously question proceeding. If they disdain them totally, I proceed immediately."[4] Once Walt knew the dream was extreme enough, he'd assemble just the right mixture of talents, temperaments, and personalities to turn that dream into a reality.

In the 1950s, Walt ignored the advice of the experts and pushed ahead with plans for an amusement park called Disneyland. His brother and business partner, Roy O. Disney, was appalled. "Walt," he said, "we're in the motion picture business, not the roller coaster business." But Walt was committed to his dream. He sold his home in Palm Springs, borrowed against his life insurance, and sent Roy out to make a TV deal to fund his dream. Then Walt assembled a team of artists, architects, engineers, and other experts to hammer his dream into a reality.[5]

A true utopian, Walt had extreme dreams of transforming the world. He envisioned a science-fictional concept called EPCOT—an Experimental Prototype Community of Tomorrow. The center of his city of tomorrow would be enclosed beneath a transparent, air-conditioned dome. Around this hub he would place futuristic homes, green parks, sports and entertainment complexes, and hotels. His monorail mass-transit system would eliminate cars, smog, stoplights, and traffic jams. As journalist Howard Means of the *Orlando Sentinel* observed, "If anyone in this century could have pulled off a successful utopia, it would have been Walt Disney."[6]

If cigarette smoking hadn't taken him from us in the prime of his creative life, Walt surely would have built his utopian dream. I interviewed Walt's longtime artist and associate John Hench, who joined the Disney team in 1939 and remained with the company for sixty-five years. He said,

*Walt's brother Roy told me about his last visit to Walt in the hospital, when Walt was talking very excitedly about the Florida Project [EPCOT]. It was as if Walt could see this map on the ceiling, and he was describing it to Roy, explaining why we'd have to build an east-west road running through, and so on. Walt could see the whole thing in full detail. He died the next morning—but he died the way he had always lived: focused on his dreams. Walt was ob-sessed, and that's why he achieved the things he did.*[7]

After Walt's death in 1966, the Disney Company scaled back Walt's dreams. The company built a Florida theme park called Epcot—but it's a pale shadow of Walt's city of tomorrow. If Walt had lived another ten years, the world would certainly be a much different—and much better—place.

## The Ultimate Dreamsmith—and Teamsmith

Songwriter Richard M. Sherman, who with his brother Robert wrote the songs for such films as *Mary Poppins* and *The Jungle Book*, told me that Walt "would give you a challenge and say, 'I know you can do this.' He made you believe anything was possible. He made you proud to be on his team. And it really was a team effort—Walt would roll up his sleeves and go to work alongside the rest of us."[8]

Walt was the ultimate dreamsmith—and the ultimate teamsmith. He was constantly tinkering with the chemistry of his team. Layout artist Frank Armitage, who worked on *Sleeping Beauty* and *The Jungle Book*, told me, "The way Walt could combine people was amazing. He mixed people the way we mix paint. He knew how to put the right group of people together to produce the best results. In the early days, Walt would have writers, artists, and story artists all together. . . . They built on each other's ideas and produced amazing results."[9]

Walt believed that the best teams involved a balance of contrasting and complementary personalities. He would always put quiet, reflective people together with talkative, energetic people. He put cautious types together with bold risk-takers. His experiments always paid off. Robert W. Butler, coauthor of *Walt Disney's Missouri*, summed up Walt's creative approach: "It was all about teamwork with Walt Disney."[10]

What is your extreme creative dream? Don't try to do it alone. Build a team, find the right balance of talent and personality, then paint your own Sistine Chapel or build your own Disneyland.

Dream big dreams, build a great team—then go forth and astonish the world.

# 6

# Principle 4: Passion Builds Extreme Dreams

Winning is the ultimate prize, and it takes hard work to achieve it. But it's hard to win without having a passion for the game. You need that passion to make you play harder in the fourth quarter, when you're dead tired. You need the passion on fourth-and-one from the goal line. You need that passion to work out in the offseason when you'd rather be playing with your kids.

EMMITT SMITH, retired NFL
running back, Dallas Cowboys[1]

THERE HAS NEVER BEEN AN NBA GAME LIKE IT—NOT before, not since. On December 13, 1983, in the rarefied air of Denver's mile-high McNichols Sports Arena, two teams left Planet Earth and entered an alternate zone of reality.

In a triple-overtime game that lasted three hours and eleven minutes, the Denver Nuggets and Detroit Pistons combined to take 251 shots, make 93 assists, and collect 113 rebounds. An NBA-record four players scored more than 40 points each; a dozen players—six on each team—scored in double figures. To this day, it remains the highest-scoring game in NBA history, with a final score of 186–184—a combined total of 370 points.

Those who were on the hardwood that night say it was more than just a basketball game. It was a *spiritual* experience. Denver's Alex English (who scored forty-seven points that night) recalled, "Everybody was just flowing. It seemed like nobody could miss a shot." His teammate Kiki Vandeweghe (fifty-one points) said, "You hear people talk about a 'zone' for individual players. That night . . . we were in it."[2]

Detroit's players felt it too—a sense of transcendence, of being part of an experience that was more than just a game. Kelly Tripucka (thirty-five points) recalled, "Somewhere along the way you get a sense of it. You feel it coming on."[3]

Isiah Thomas, who collected a career-high forty-seven points that night, recalled, "Everybody was playing great. It was just one of those games where everything goes in."[4]

## THE "ZONE" EXPERIENCE

My friend Chuck Daly (who later coached the Magic) was the Pistons head coach. Going into the game, he knew that the Nuggets, coached by Doug Moe, counted on running and scoring, not defense, to win. So, before the game, Daly joked with Moe, "Why don't we just say that the first team to score 140 points is the winner?" Chuck later said, "Little did I know how prophetic I would be."[5]

Chuck turned his Pistons loose to run and gun with the Nuggets. Doug Moe also coached with a loose, hands-off style, letting his players find their own rhythm. The result was a strangely magical game that ebbed and flowed at a frenetic yet fluid pace. "It was basketball at its purest," said Alex English. "Free-flowing, with the pressure off the players. . . . No one was limited or afraid to try things."[6]

In the first overtime, the Nuggets moved out to a five-point lead. Then the Pistons surged back, powered by a three-pointer by Isiah Thomas—amazingly, the first trey of the game. With the score tied at 159, Isiah attacked with an apparent game-winning layup—but the officials ruled that it came after the buzzer.

Tripucka was the Pistons' scoring leader in the second OT—but it also ended with a tie, 171–171. The Nuggets pulled out to a 179–177 lead in the third OT—but with 1:41 remaining, the Pistons battled back to a 186–181 lead. With twenty-eight seconds remaining, the Nuggets' Richard Anderson hit a three-pointer—Denver's only trey of the night—to bring his team within two—

And that was the score, Detroit 186, Denver 184, when the buzzer ended the strangest, highest-scoring game in NBA history.

What happened to those two teams on a December night in 1983? What was the mysterious force that seemed to elevate all the players on both teams? And remember, it wasn't just one team but *both* teams that experienced this mile-high miracle. The players can't explain it, but they have a name for it: they were "in the zone."

During his thirteen-year career with the Boston Celtics, six-foot-ten center Bill Russell powered his team to eleven NBA Championships. In his memoir *Second Wind*, Russell wrote about his own experiences "in the zone":

> Every so often a Celtic game would heat up so that it became more than a physical or even mental game, and would be magical. . . . When it happened I could feel my play rise to a new level. It came rarely, and would last anywhere from five minutes to a whole quarter or more. . . . It would surround not only me and the other Celtics but also the players on the other team, and even the referees. . . .
>
> We'd all levitate. And then the game would just take off, and there'd be a natural ebb and flow that reminded

you of how rhythmic and musical basketball is supposed
to be. I'd find myself thinking, "This is it. I want this to
keep going," and I'd actually be rooting for the other team.
When their players made spectacular moves, I wanted
their shots to go in the bucket. That's how pumped up
I'd be.[7]

The intense competition and high level of performance by
players on both sides seem to trigger the magic of "the zone."
It's almost as if the entire game is being played from a musical
score, as if each move has been choreographed, each shot pre-
destined. This is basketball raised to a spiritual plane. Russell
goes on to describe the beautiful and fleeting nature of "the
zone" experience:

> I'd be putting out the maximum effort, straining,
> coughing up parts of my lungs as we ran, and yet I never
> felt the pain. The game would move so quickly that every
> fake, cut, and pass would be surprising, and yet nothing
> could surprise me. . . .
> But these spells were fragile. . . . Once a referee broke a
> run by making a bad call in my favor, which so irritated me
> that I protested it as I stood at the foul line to take my free
> throws. "You know it was a bad call, ref," I said wearily. He
> looked at me as if I was crazy, and then got so angry that I
> never again protested a call unless it went against me. Still,
> I always suffered a letdown when one of those spells died,
> because I never knew how to bring them back; all I could
> do was keep playing my best and hope.[8]

Mysterious and magical, "the zone" confers superhuman performance and superhuman endurance. It even alters the flow of
time. . . .

## TIME DILATION

Detroit forward Kelly Tripucka said of the 1983 Pistons-Nuggets game: "We were running as fast as we could. But the way the points were coming, and the way people were shooting . . . I swear it felt slow out there."[9]

That eerie sense of time dilation has been described by players in other sports as well. For example, Atlanta Falcons linebacker Will Overstreet once said, "When you make a great play, everything slows down. You can see it all happen. I see everything happening in slow motion, and then once the play is over everything speeds up and is back to normal. . . . It's the best feeling in the world. You know it's about to happen, and it happens."[10]

John Brodie, quarterback of the San Francisco 49ers from 1957 to 1973, spoke of experiencing moments when "time seems to slow way down in an uncanny way, as if everyone were moving in slow motion. It seems as if I had all the time in the world to watch the receivers run their patterns, and yet I know the defensive line is coming at me just as fast as ever."[11]

Baseball players speak of that same eerie sensation, where time seems to dilate and everything goes miraculously right. Shortstop Michael Young of the Texas Rangers, a former American League batting champion, said, "You're seeing the ball well and the game is really slowed down. You're not thinking about anything; you're just using your instincts."[12]

And Don Mattingly (nicknamed "Donnie Baseball"), Yankees first baseman from 1982 to 1995, said, "When you're seeing the ball well, your confidence is just sky-high. You're not worried about getting behind in the count, you're laying off bad pitches, you're not swinging over strikes. When you're in that situation, everything seems like it slows down for you a little bit."[13]

"The zone" is as big a factor on the mound as it is at the plate. Former catcher Tim McCarver cites his St. Louis Cardinals teammate, pitcher Bob Gibson, who had a phenomenal season in 1968. That year, Gibson set a record ERA of 1.12, the lowest single-season earned run average of any pitcher in the modern era. During that season, he pitched 47 scoreless innings and 13 shutouts.

Interviewed by Lawrence Shainberg in the *New York Times*, McCarver recalled, "Gibson was on a mission. You could see it in his eyes. He had tremendous energy and animation, a confidence that he could do anything . . . [and] put the ball anywhere he wanted. I'd just put my mitt out, and he'd put the ball in it."[14]

Shainberg concludes,

> Even statisticians acknowledge that such performances as Gibson's—or Joe DiMaggio's 56-game hitting streak in 1941, or Orel Hershiser's string [in 1988] of 59 scoreless innings—rise so far above the norm that there is no room for them on probability curves. So much do they exceed common levels of mastery that they seem, like a mutation in evolution, to define a new order of existence.[15]

Such seemingly superhuman performances can be found in every arena of athletic competition. Shainberg writes,

> Basketball players say that when they play in the zone the basket seems bigger, and they feel an almost mystical connection to it. Ted Williams, the legendary hitter for the Boston Red Sox, has said that sometimes at bat he could see the seams on a pitched ball. And the former collegiate gymnast Carol Johnson remembers that on good days the balance beam was actually wider for her, so that "any worry of falling off disappeared."[16]

## THE STITCHES ON A FASTBALL

We can't talk about "zone" experiences without a nod to Michael Jordan. He seems to play the game in a totally different time continuum than mere mortals. He has said that he often experiences the game at a different pace than the fast-break pace the spectators see. "Basketball," he once said, "is like meditation to me."[17] His midair hand-switch layups and his floating jump shots not only defied Newton's law of gravitation but appeared to stop time in its tracks as well. How he did it, not even Michael himself seemed to know.

Jordan's "in the zone" performance was never more stunningly on display than in game one of the 1992 NBA Finals against the Portland Trail Blazers. NBC sportscaster Marv Albert recalls that he and fellow broadcasters Mike Fratello and Magic Johnson talked to Michael before the game. The subject of their conversation: three-point shots. Albert said, "Michael's one of these guys who would say, 'Today I'm going to be an assist guy,' 'Today I'm going to do this'—you know, control the game. . . . And [that day] he said he felt he had to shoot threes."[18]

So the game got under way—and Michael Jordan came out firing threes! In fact, he drained six three-point field goals and scored thirty-five points in the first half, setting two NBA Finals records. After hitting his sixth trey, Jordan jogged past the announcers' table, grinned at Albert, Fratello, and Johnson, put his hands up, and shrugged.

"He comes out and hits six," Marv Albert concludes, "and he gave that expression when he looked over to the table—he shrugged, like, 'I can't believe I'm doing this.' That was a major moment." A major moment indeed. To this day, that game is referred to as "The Shrug Game."[19]

Dr. Stuart Hameroff of the Center for Consciousness Studies, University of Arizona, offers this theory to explain Jordan's outstanding ability:

> Athletes like the basketball player Michael Jordan are able to excel because the other teams' players seem to be reacting in relative slow motion. Physical speed aside, this may occur by an increase in the frequency of conscious events. For example if Jordan is having 60 conscious events per second, and the players defending him are only having 40 conscious events per second, Jordan has 50 percent more perceptions, decisions and reactions over any given time interval than his opponents, who will appear to him to be in slow motion.[20]

In "the zone," people experience a magnification of their abilities, awareness, and endurance. They think more clearly and react more quickly than their talents and abilities should allow. "The zone" is an altered state of consciousness and creativity. Writer-philosopher Andrew Cooper observes,

> The zone. All athletes know it, strive for it, prize its attainment. It is that realm of play in which everything—skill, training and mental discipline—comes together, and players feel themselves lifted to a level of peak performance in which limits seem to fall away. . . . In the zone, the extraordinary capacities that lie within each individual are made manifest. To grasp this hidden dimension is to transform the very meaning of athletic play.[21]

Almost everyone who has experienced "the zone" reports a sensation of the slowing of time. How do we account for this time dilation effect in "the zone"? Psychologist Robert E. Ornstein of Stanford University explains that as the brain attempts to "increase the amount of information processing in a given interval, the experience of that interval lengthens." In other words, under certain circumstances, the brain—or at least certain centers in the brain—process information so rapidly that time actually seems to pass more slowly.[22]

So when Ted Williams was "in the zone," he could actually see a 95-mile-an-hour pitch approaching as if it were moving at half that speed; he literally could see the stitches on the ball—and that special ability enabled him to clobber pitches that other batters would whiff. It also means that as Michael Jordan went up for a jump shot, his brain was processing information so quickly that he seemed to have extra time to target the basket, then make all the tiny muscular adjustments to produce a perfect shot—swish![23]

## "IN THE ZONE" OVER FALLUJAH

Kirsten A. Holmstedt, in her book *Band of Sisters: American Women at War in Iraq,* tells the story of two Army pilots, Captain Robin Brown and Chief Warrant Officer Jeff Sumner. While flying their Kiowa Warrior helicopter at a very low altitude—a mere one hundred feet—near Fallujah, Iraq, the aircraft was rocked by an explosion. The Kiowa instantly lost engine power and hydraulics. Brown and Sumner had to take flawless, lightning-quick action or die. Holmstedt writes:

> As the aircraft dropped to the ground, Brown focused on the positive. This might work out. She considered all the steps as they were happening. It felt like the action was occurring in slow motion and very deliberately. While she thought through each step, she felt calm and detached. She didn't have time to think about anything else. Only, *What's my next step?*[24]

Working as a team, Brown and Sumner kept the rotors in auto-rotation to slow the descent. They managed to bring the helicopter down in a semicontrolled crash. The wounded craft landed heavily but safely on its skids. Brown and Sumner were alive.

Holmstedt relates what Captain Robin Brown experienced during the near-catastrophic descent: "It felt to Brown as if fifteen seconds had passed from the time they were struck to when they hit the ground. It was more like half that time. In combat, senses come alive and perception of time slows down. Like a car accident, everything seemed to happen in slow motion."[25]

Eugene G. D'Aquili and Andrew B. Newberg, in their book *The Mystical Mind*, suggest that when the brain's limbic system is triggered by intense emotional experiences, people suddenly acquire an amazing ability "not only to remain calm in life-threatening situations but to think clearly, rationally, and often in 'slow motion.' Thus, human beings would be able to rely upon their most valuable asset in times of extreme crisis—they would be able to use their brains efficiently, indeed, hyper-efficiently."[26]

Clearly, the same processes within the brain that slow down time in life-threatening emergencies are also available to athletes in moments of extreme high performance—that is, when they are "in the zone." What is the *one* common denominator between these two experiences, the life-threatening emergency and the "zone" experience? I'm convinced that it's a thing called *passion*.

What is passion? As I define it, passion is an emotional obsession so intense that it grips you, motivates you, fires your imagination, and defines you. An athlete with a passion for basketball is driven by the game. He eats, sleeps, and breathes basketball. Love of the game possesses him, and there is no substitute for it. Losing a basketball game is unacceptable. Just the sight of a basketball makes a player's hands twitch. He wants to hold the ball, dribble, shoot, and score. Whenever he's away from the game, he goes into withdrawal. That's *passion*.

What does that kind of passion have to do with life-or-death emergencies, like being shot out of the sky over Fallujah? Simply this: we all have a passion for living. We have an instinct for survival—and one of the sites in our brains that process threats to our survival is also the site that processes our emotions—the limbic system.

I believe our passion for living, our passion for performing, our passion for athletic competition, our passion for winning—all the passions that we care so intensely about—may well be mediated through the limbic system of our brains. It may be that it is there, in the emotion-processing structures beneath the rational cerebral cortex, that the miracle of "the zone" takes place.

Now, I don't claim to be an expert on the human brain. Bottom line, it really doesn't matter whether the precise location of the "in the zone" site is the limbic system or the second joint of your left big toe. All that really matters is that "the zone" experience seems to be triggered primarily by intense emotion—by *passion*. And if I'm right, if it is truly our passion that tips us into "the zone," then that is a radical insight. It means *we can actually create the conditions* that transport us to "the zone" of transcendent performance—

We can *choose* to go to the zone and *remain* there.

When Captain Brown and Chief Warrant Officer Sumner were falling out of the sky, they instantly entered "the zone." They were only one hundred feet above the ground, little more than treetop level. They had practiced emergency landings before— but from an altitude of one thousand feet, not one hundred. In their practice sessions, there had been plenty of time to think and respond—but in the real emergency, there was no room for error.

Something happened to Brown and Sumner as their helicopter fell. They went into "the zone." Time slowed down. Concentration intensified. Awareness was magnified. They reacted more rapidly and accurately than they would have thought humanly possible—and they landed safely. Why? *Because they had a passion to live.* The strong, passionate emotions of their survival instinct kicked in, activating the centers of their brains, which enabled the two pilots to function hyper-efficiently.

A well-trained, well-conditioned warrior who is passionate about living will enter "the zone"—and so will a well-trained, well-conditioned athlete who is passionate about the game. That's where extreme dreams come in. Modest dreams and minor goals do not inspire passion. But an extreme dream fires the imagination and captivates the soul of every member of your team. An extreme dream ignites the passion that lifts players into that magical, mystical "zone" where dreams come true.

## "THE ZONE" IS FOR EVERYONE

I've had that "in the zone" experience four times during my playing career. The first time was in a high school basketball game. On that particular night, I reached a level where every shot I put up from the outside went in. I could see the ball leave my hands, I knew it would go in—and it did. I saw everything happening in slow motion. I had never heard of such experiences before, and I had no name for what happened to me that night—but I knew I had experienced something rare and wonderful.

I attended Tower Hill School, a prep school in Wilmington, Delaware. One time, our baseball team played at Philadelphia's Germantown Academy. In that game, everything again seemed to happen in slow motion. I'd stand at the plate, and it was as if I could take my time watching each pitch, deciding whether it was a ball or a strike. I could literally see the stitches on the ball—I saw everything with absolute clarity as if time were standing still. I hit two home runs that day and a line-drive single. (The next day we played against my uncle's Haverford School team. Knowing how well I had played against Germantown, he intentionally walked me four straight times.)

It happened one time during my college career at Wake Forest University. We were playing a game at Georgia Southern University in Statesboro. As Yogi Berra would say, it was "déjà vu all over again"—an unexpected recurrence of an almost mystical sense of being "in the zone." That day, I went four for five, including a home run on a fake bunt and swing.

Finally, in my first year in pro ball (1962 in Miami), we were playing in Tampa against the Reds' farm club in the Florida State League. I got four hits that night, and again it was as if everything around me slowed down and the ball practically stood still over the plate—it was like hitting off a batting tee.

So there you have it—I was "in the zone" four times in my rather mediocre playing career. And that just goes to show that being "in the zone" is an experience that's available to anyone. If I had only known how to reach that "zone" on a more consistent basis, who knows what kind of playing career I might have had?

Lawrence Shainberg observes, "One mystery of the zone is that entry to it is not restricted to the elite."[27] In other words, "the zone" is not just for the professional athletes. Amateur athletes can get into "the zone" as well. In fact, "the zone" is accessible even to nonathletes. Basketball, baseball, and football players know what it feels like to be "in the zone." But so do many actors, dancers, musicians, artists, writers, public speakers, business executives, salespeople, and on and on.

Television writer Michael Cassutt described an "in the zone" experience he once had as part of the writing team for a CBS television drama in the late 1980s:

> We were scrambling late at night to add a holiday element to an episode that had to start filming in the morning.

In the middle of the scramble, I sat down with the script and a pencil (of all things) and—with no prior thought or discussion, sitting on the couch in an office filled with producers, assistants and actors, just closing my eyes and picturing a conversation, I wrote a scene about a homeless teen recalling the best Christmas he'd ever experienced. It took all of fifteen minutes. I handed in the pages to be typed into the script. Half an hour later the typist returned, tears streaming down her face, demanding to know how I'd done that.

I didn't know. I had just been In the Zone.[28]

"The zone" is for everybody. And passion is the key.

### "UPLIFT YOUR TEAM!"

Duke basketball coach Mike Krzyzewski knows that passion must come not only from the five players on the court, but from the all-important "sixth man," the fans. In his book *Five-Point Play*, Coach K talks about how he involved the "sixth man," fired up their passion, and made them an integral part of the Blue Devils' 2001 NCAA Championship season.

One of the biggest events on the Duke University calendar is the home game against the University of North Carolina. It's a huge celebration for the Blue Devils' student supporters, who call themselves "the Cameron Crazies" after Duke's Cameron Indoor Stadium. They paint their faces white and blue, wear "Sixth Man" T-shirts, and they jump and scream whenever the opponent has the ball. Because of the "sixth man," Cameron is a tough house for visiting teams.

The Crazies are so passionate about their team that they camp out and party for weeks in a tent city called Krzyzewskiville to secure their place in line for tickets to the big game. The night before the game, Coach K comes out and talks to the two thousand or more Crazies who are gathered there. "It's really not a pep rally," Krzyzewski explains. "It's a team meeting. And these kids know it."[29]

Every year, Coach K's talk has a different theme. Before this particular game, Krzyzewski chose to talk about what he called "the Fist." He made a fist and said:

> When we take the court, we have to be together—like a fist. . . . When you're having a bad day, you must allow the others to step up for you, or to pat you on the back and say, "C'mon, get with it!" or to get in your face and try to snap you out of it. And you, in turn, will not say, "Leave me alone, I want to be miserable today." That is unacceptable on our team. . . . We do not have a bad day because we observe the five points of THE FIST.[30]

He went on to talk about the passion of the Duke players— how they huddle before the game, put their fists together, and shout, "One, two, three—WIN!" Five players with a single passion for winning. But five isn't enough. There needs to be a sixth man in that huddle. So, Krzyzewski said, "When we get into that huddle, I want you all to reach out from the stands and put your fists in, too. If you do that, I believe we're going to win. I believe in us and I want you to believe in us, too. . . . Uplift your team. Uplift us."[31]

Then Coach K removed his Duke jacket to reveal the T-shirt he wore underneath. It was the same T-shirt that was the informal "uniform" of the Cameron Crazies, with the words "Sixth Man" emblazoned across the front. All around Krzyzewskiville, a deafening cheer went up, and it went on and on. Finally, when the Crazies began to quiet down, Coach K concluded, "I'll be wearing this under my shirt during the game to keep you guys close to my heart."[32]

Whatever arena you play in, make sure you stir the passion of your players—and your "sixth man." You don't want an arena full of spectators, but an arena filled with passionate team players who are lifting up your team and energizing their efforts. The passion of the crowd magnifies the passion of the players.

## PASSION SHOWS

One of the great privileges of my life was becoming personally acquainted with one of my boyhood heroes, Boston Red Sox legend Ted Williams. There are many stories from Ted's playing days that illustrate his passion for baseball. Let me share two.

In 1941, two years after his major-league baseball debut, Ted Williams was having a phenomenal year. That was the year he batted .406 with 37 home runs, 120 runs batted in, and 135 runs scored. It was also the rookie season of Yankees shortstop Phil Rizzuto. When the Red Sox played the Yankees, Ted Williams routinely got to second base. While at second, edging toward third, Ted would talk to Rizzuto and even struck up a friendship with Rizzuto that was part rivalry, part mutual respect.

On one of his visits to second base, Williams complimented Rizzuto: "You play hard." Then he added, "I love this game, and you better love it too."[33]

That was vintage Ted Williams—pure baseball passion.

One of Ted's biggest fans was the famed "beat generation" poet and novelist Jack Kerouac of Lowell, Massachusetts. Before writing such explosive novels as *On the Road* and *The Dharma Bums*, Kerouac was a sports reporter for the *Lowell Sun*. Beginning in 1939, he often hitchhiked to Boston's Fenway Park just to watch Ted Williams play. He later said, "The thing I loved about Williams was his glee. He had great glee."[34]

How about you? Do you have great glee? Do you have an intense, consuming passion for the work you do?

Marques Johnson, an NBA guard-forward who played for the Milwaukee Bucks, L.A. Clippers, and Golden State Warriors, had a career in pro basketball from 1977 to 1990. He once said,

> It's the sport that I love, not the business. The business end messes everything up. I almost wish there was no money in it, then we could all go out and enjoy playing like we did when we were kids. I'd still play if there was no money, because it's the best game there is, and you can play all the time if you want. . . . When I'm playing ball, it's like I'm not even part of the earth—like I belong to a different universe.[35]

That's passion talking.

Shawn Finney is an assistant basketball coach at Marshall University in Huntington, West Virginia. He once told Mike Kilduff of the *Sporting News*,

> When I was a junior in high school, I was out mowing the grass and the lawnmower blade broke off and hit my leg. I went running over to my house, and my father comes out and my mom's in a little bit of a panic. They scoop me up, and I'm in the car flying to the hospital and all I'm saying is, "I'm not going to get to play basketball. I'm not going to get to play basketball." My mom says, "You'll get to play basketball. You'll get to play basketball." And I tell her, "Yeah, but not tonight."[36]

To a player with passion, the game is more important than the pain.

Outside linebacker Andy Russell was an early mainstay of Pittsburgh's legendary "Steel Curtain" defense. He played for the Steelers in 1963 and from 1966 to 1976. During his rookie year, Russell was in a huddle when he saw defensive lineman Ernie Stautner approach with his thumb broken. It was so bad that the flesh at the base of the thumb was torn and the bone was protruding.

Andy Russell described what Stautner did as he entered the huddle: "He takes his thumb in his hand and he wrenches it down into his fist. Doesn't show it to anybody. Doesn't say anything. Looks up and says, 'What's the defense?'"[37]

So they ran a few more plays and forced the other side to punt. As the Steeler defense came off the field, Russell watched Stautner. He figured the lineman would ask for the team doctor and leave the game for the hospital. Wrong.

"Give me some tape," Stautner said. Russell saw the lineman sit down at the end of the bench, "like a great warrior licking his wounds alone."[38] Stautner wound several rolls of tape around his hand until his fist was a huge mass of tape. Then he went back into the game. He played every down, using his bandaged paw like a club.

Andy Russell was astounded. "After the game," he recalled, "I watched as the doctor cut off the tape. Blood trickled from the wound and I felt nauseous. I thought, What kind of man could ignore a compound fracture? Doesn't he feel pain like the rest of us? Maybe, I worried, I don't belong in the NFL."[39]

How did Andy Russell explain Stautner's ability to play through pain? One word: passion. "I'm thinking, this is just unbelievable," Russell said. "That is passion for what you do. That guy was making no money. He just loved to play. What a commitment."[40]

## PASSION LIVES ON

Johnny Unitas was a skinny, awkward kid with a passion for football. When he was in junior high, his teacher asked the students what they planned to do when they grew up. Johnny replied, "I'm going to play pro football." When he got to high school, his teacher, Sister Theresa Marie, thought that his surname was an omen of future greatness. "Unite us?" she said. "You must be the leader!"[41]

Passed over by several universities, Unitas was accepted by the football program at the University of Louisville, Kentucky. The day of his first weigh-in, the six-foot-one string bean of a quarterback tipped the scales at 145 pounds. Because of budget cuts in the Louisville athletic program, the football program played one-platoon football—players had to play both offense and defense. So Johnny Unitas quarterbacked on offense, then switched to linebacker or safety on defense and kick returner on special teams.

Married and with one child, Unitas was employed as a steelworker and played semipro football for six dollars a game with the Bloomfield Rams from Pittsburgh's east end. In 1956, Unitas borrowed gasoline money from friends so he could attend an open tryout with the Baltimore Colts. The Colts signed him as a backup quarterback. When starting QB George Shaw went out with a broken leg in a game against the Chicago Bears, Unitas took the field. Though the Colts lost that game, Unitas led his team to victory over the Green Bay Packers and the Cleveland Browns. The following season, he led the Colts to a 7-5 record, the team's first winning season.

During a seventeen-year career in the NFL, Johnny Unitas racked up a record 2,830 completions for 40,239 yards and 290 touchdowns. He was the first QB to throw for more than 40,000 yards—and he did so in 12- and 14-game seasons as opposed to the 16-game seasons played today. Between 1956 and 1960, he threw touchdown passes in 47 straight games—a streak that has never been equaled. After surviving numerous injuries, including a punctured lung and a mangled right arm, Johnny Unitas acquired a reputation as the toughest guy in football.

While playing for the Baltimore Colts, Unitas kept his job with Bethlehem Steel in Pittsburgh. In those days, pro football didn't pay very well, and most players in the game had "regular jobs." In 1958, Johnny Unitas led the Colts to an NFL Championship, beating the New York Giants, 23–17, in the first overtime game in NFL history. That nationally televised game has been called "the greatest game ever played" and it produced a huge surge in the popularity of NFL football. The following year, Unitas and the Colts again beat the Giants for the title, winning 31–16.

Bill Curry, the current head football coach at Georgia State University, played center with Johnny Unitas and the Colts from 1967 to 1972. He recalls:

> When I reported to the Baltimore Colts in 1967, there was some question as to whether I would make the team. I was nervous, stressed, and fatigued. At one particularly discouraging moment, John and I started down to the practice field for the afternoon session. Nothing in sport matches football training camp two-a-days for discomfort and disgust, and [Unitas] was happy. I said, "How could you be whistling, old man? It's hot out here!"
>
> He grinned. "You better enjoy today Billy. You're a long time dead."
>
> "What did you say?" I couldn't believe my ears.
>
> "You're a long time dead, so why not enjoy every day, every practice? I love football practice."
>
> I listened, knew I had been challenged, and hustled to

practice with a new attitude. The next six years were the best of my career.[42]

The passion of Johnny Unitas made him impervious to pain—and practically invincible. Longtime L.A. Rams defensive tackle Merlin Olsen would hit Unitas again and again, and after each play he would study Unitas for some sign that he was hurting or intimidated. If Unitas was hurting, he didn't show it. Olsen recalled, "He'd hold the ball one count longer than he had to just so he could take the hit and laugh in your face."[43]

George Weigel offered this assessment of the legendary Colts quarterback:

> It was, of course, a different time and a different ethos in the days when John Unitas walked the playing field like a slope-shouldered, bandy-legged hero out of *High Noon* by way of the Pittsburgh sandlots. Everybody, Unitas included, had an off-season job, selling paint or insurance or cars or whatever, because NFL salaries would not support a family. . . .
>
> Unitas never regarded himself as anything other than an honest craftsman, a professional who was proud to play football and play it well. But in plying his trade, he embodied a set of distinctively American qualities: self-reliance; the work ethic; individual excellence married to a passion for the team.[44]

A passion for the team, a passion for the game, a passion for winning—that's what made Johnny Unitas great. He'd do anything to play football, even for six dollars a game. As long as he was alive, he was going to play—because when your life is over, "you're a long time dead." That's passion talking.

So dream your extreme dreams, my friend, then follow your passion into that wondrous zone where time moves slowly, where thought crackles like lightning, where people levitate in the air, and balls always find their targets.

Magic is within you and all around you, waiting to be unlocked and unleashed—

And passion is the key.

# Extreme *Global Security* Dreams . . .

## *Depend on Teams*

*I've been with the FBI nearly thirty years, and I have never seen a greater priority put on relationships and teamwork. Today, we work more closely than ever with the CIA and other federal partners, with state and local law enforcement, and with our many international colleagues. . . . If you hear about a success against terrorism— whether it's rolling up a sleeper cell here in the States or arresting a top Al Qaeda lieutenant like Khalid Sheikh Mohammed in Pakistan—you know that it was the product of teamwork.*

ROBERT S. MUELLER III, director, FBI
Speech before the San Francisco
Global Trade Council
September 30, 2003[1]

Shortly before D-Day, General George S. Patton Jr. toured bases of the U.S. Third Army west of London. At each stop, "Old Blood and Guts" strode to the microphone dressed in shining boots and helmet, with his Colt .45 holstered at his hip. He launched into a speech that was stirring, unforgettable, and, by all accounts, often profane. It became known simply as "the Speech."

Patton talked about winning. "Americans love a winner," he said, "and cannot tolerate a loser. Americans despise cowards. Americans play to win—all the time. I wouldn't give a hoot for a man who lost and laughed. That's why Americans have never lost and will never lose a war, for the very thought of losing is hateful to an American."[2]

He also talked about teamwork:

*An Army is a team. It lives, sleeps, eats, and fights as a team. This individual heroic stuff is pure [#@%&!]. . . . Every single man in this army plays a vital role. Don't ever let up. Don't ever think that your job is unimportant. Every man has a job to do and he must do it. Every man is a vital link in the great chain. What if every truck driver suddenly decided that he didn't like the whine of those shells overhead, turned yellow, and jumped headlong into a ditch? . . . Every man serves the whole. Every department, every unit, is important in the vast scheme of this war.*[3]

Patton talked about courage. "One of the bravest men I ever saw," he added, "was a fellow on top of a telegraph pole in the midst of a furious fire fight in Tunisia." When Patton saw this man atop the pole while the bullets were flying, he shouted, "What are you doing up there at a time like this?" The man on the pole replied, "Fixing the wire, sir." Patton asked, "Isn't that a little unhealthy right about now?" The man replied that it was indeed, but the wire needed to be fixed. "Don't those planes strafing the road bother you?" asked General Patton. "No, sir," the soldier replied, "but you sure do!" "Now, there was a real man," Patton told the troops, "a real soldier."[4]

Patton talked about the truck drivers who were part of his fighting team in North Africa. The role of driving a supply truck on a desert road might not seem very glorious, yet Patton was bursting with admiration for his drivers. "Those men weren't combat men," he said, "but they were soldiers with a job to do. . . . They were part of a team. Without team effort, the fight would have been lost. All of the links in the chain pulled together and the chain became unbreakable."[5]

Patton knew. Extreme dreams of victory and freedom depend on teams. In this world, tyrants and terrorists continually arise to threaten the security of the globe. When your enemy is bent on destroying your way of life, when he is committing mass murder and crimes against humanity, you can't reason with him. You have to defeat him.

And the only way to defeat him is through teamwork.

## A "SURGE" OF TEAMWORK

Gerard Alexander teaches politics at the University of Virginia and is an expert on the Nazi Holocaust. He cites Human Rights Watch reports that Saddam's regime murdered more than one hundred thousand Kurds during a three-month period in the spring of 1988—a rate of about thirty thousand killed per month, or over a thousand per day. Three years later, the disarray in Iraq after the 1991 Gulf War caused Saddam to respond "with the largest killing spree in its history," in which Saddam targeted the Shiite majority population. Iraqi officials who served under Saddam at the time put the number of slaughtered Shiites as high as two hundred thousand. Saddam's forces also killed an estimated fifty thousand to eighty thousand Kurds that year, plus an unknown number of Ma'dān (or "marsh Arabs") in southern Iraq. Alexander concludes:

> Four months before Saddam's fall, Human Rights Watch estimated that up to 290,000 people had "disappeared" since the late 1970s and were presumed dead. The Coalition Provisional Authority's human rights office estimates that 300,000 bodies are contained in the numerous mass graves. "And that's the lower end of the estimates," said one CPA spokesperson. In fact, the accumulated credible reports make the likely number at least 400,000 to 450,000. So, by a conservative estimate, the regime was killing civilians at an average rate of at least 16,000 a year between 1979 and March 2003.[6]

The terrorist insurgency in Iraq after the fall of Saddam resulted in thousands of deaths, both of Iraqi civilians and of U.S. and Coalition troops—but the toppling of Saddam nevertheless produced a net savings of tens of thousands of lives. Had Saddam remained in power, Alexander reports, his regime would have likely resumed killing at a rate of fifteen thousand to twenty thousand per year. Furthermore, UN economic sanctions were causing the deaths of four thousand to five thousand Iraqi children per month due to lack of food and health care. The fall of Saddam allowed the lifting of sanctions, saving some sixty thousand Iraqi children and adults per year, according to UNICEF estimates. Alexander concludes that our intervention in Iraq has resulted in a net savings of tens of thousands of lives per year, and suggests that those who are "genuinely motivated by a concern for Iraqi civilians have much to be grateful for."[7]

Without question, Iraq once seemed to be sinking toward chaos. But the "Surge" strategy that was conceived and implemented in 2007 by General David Petraeus, commander of the Multi-National Force, produced a dramatic turnaround and placed Iraq on the road to stability and security. In late 2007, Michael E. O'Hanlon and Kenneth M. Pollack of the Brookings Institution went on an intensive eight-day tour of Iraq. On their return, they offered their assessment of the "Surge" in the *New York Times*:

> *Here is the most important thing Americans need to understand: We are finally getting somewhere in Iraq, at least in military terms. As two analysts who have harshly criticized the Bush administration's miserable handling of Iraq, we were surprised by the gains we saw and the potential to produce not necessarily "victory" but a sustainable stability that both we and the Iraqis could live with. . . .*
>
> *Morale is high. The soldiers and marines told us they feel that they now have a superb commander in Gen. David Petraeus; they are confident in his strategy, they see real results, and*

*they feel now they have the numbers needed to make a real difference.*[8]

O'Hanlon and Pollack were impressed by a new spirit of cooperation and teamwork between Americans and Iraqis, and between Sunnis and the Shiites:

> *In Ramadi, for example, we talked with an outstanding Marine captain whose company was living in harmony in a complex with a (largely Sunni) Iraqi police company and a (largely Shiite) Iraqi Army unit. He and his men had built an Arab-style living room, where he met with the local Sunni sheiks—all formerly allies of Al Qaeda and other jihadist groups—who were now competing to secure his friendship. . . .*
>
> *Anbar Province . . . has gone from the worst part of Iraq to the best (outside the Kurdish areas). Today the Sunni sheiks there are close to crippling Al Qaeda and its Salafist allies. Just a few months ago, American marines were fighting for every yard of Ramadi; last week we strolled down its streets without body armor.*[9]

The key to the success of the "Surge" is teamwork. O'Hanlon and Pollack cited the success of the Coalition's new Embedded Provincial Reconstruction Teams—special combined military-civilian units that build cooperation between the U.S. military and the local civilian government to rebuild the war-torn country. The teams combine military advisers, diplomats, bilingual cultural advisers, and reconstruction experts. These teams go out into the towns and villages and help establish city governments and courts, renovate hospitals, promote reconciliation among tribal groups, provide microgrants for small business start-ups, set up agricultural loan banks, open women's centers, and more. O'Hanlon and Pollack gave the Embedded Provincial Reconstruction Teams much of the credit for the success of the "Surge":

> *Wherever we found a fully staffed team, we also found local Iraqi leaders and businessmen cooperating with it to revive the local economy and build new political structures. Although much more needs to be done to create jobs, a new emphasis on microloans and small-scale projects was having some success. . . . We talked to dozens of military officers who before the war had known little about governance or business but were now ably immersing themselves in projects to provide the average Iraqi with a decent life.*[10]

As I write these words, it appears that the Sunnis, Shiites, and Kurds in Iraq are working together more effectively than the Democrats and Republicans in Washington. And once-deadly neighborhoods in Baghdad and Fallujah are now safer than a lot of American inner cities.

It's still too early to say how the situation in Iraq will turn out. It could be that all the reported progress could unravel before this book is off the press—but I don't think so. The Iraqi people have a proud, rich history, and they live in the Cradle of Civilization. Now that they have tasted the benefits of freedom and teamwork, they won't want to let their country slide back into chaos. As U.S. Ambassador to Iraq Ryan Crocker observed, "Iraq has the potential to develop into a stable, secure multiethnic, multi-sectarian democracy under the rule of law. Whether it realizes that potential is ultimately up to the Iraqi people."[11]

## You've Got My Vote

I have two Marine Corps sons. One of them, David, took part in the 2003 invasion, "Operation Iraqi Freedom," which liberated Iraq from Saddam Hussein's rule. After his return, David told me a story about teamwork from the early days of that war:

> *Our lieutenant was leading our motor convoy on a mission when he decided to take a shortcut. We got lost and ended up on a narrow dirt road with a berm on our left and a canal on our right. We had twenty vehicles and forty Marines. The road was so narrow that we couldn't back out or turn around.*
>
> *We reached another canal—and couldn't go forward or back. We knew we needed to move out of there quickly, because the word was being passed along to the enemy that a convoy was stranded at X location like a bunch of sitting ducks. Our lieutenant had a seemingly insoluble problem on his hands, and he started to panic. Iraqi townspeople were standing all around, watching this scene in amazement.*
>
> *At that point, the first sergeant took over. He was calm and organized, and a very quick*

*thinker. He assembled a team and told them, "Dig out that berm so we can get the vehicles moving, then we'll turn around." He had a plan, he gave each Marine an assignment, and he pulled us all together and got us all on the same page. Somehow we made it out of there before any Iraqi troops found us. That first sergeant was calm, confident, and competent to handle the crisis. The lieutenant had the rank, but the sergeant had the leadership, and he understood teamwork. He probably saved our lives.*

This story from my son David's experience in Iraq is, I think, a metaphor for the times in which we live. I believe with all my heart that one important key to a more stable and secure world is teamwork—the ability of people from diverse perspectives, with diverse abilities and backgrounds, to come together behind a common goal.

For several years, following our invasion of Afghanistan and Iraq, it seemed as though our leadership in Washington was like that Marine lieutenant—paralyzed, unable to see a solution. Then someone stepped up, calmly proposed a strategy based on teamwork, and successfully implemented it. That strategy was the "Surge," and the architect was General David H. Petraeus. He provided the plan, and our troops and the Iraqis provided the teamwork.

This is not a political statement. I honestly don't care whether the political party in charge is Republican or Democrat, Libertarian or Green, Rotary or Kiwanis. I simply want our government run by people who place the national interests above the interests of their party.

I want to see our government in the hands of people who practice teamwork instead of partisanship, who are servants of the people, not political bosses.

Let's demand teamwork from the people we put in office. Let's elect those who have a track record of dreaming extreme dreams and assembling teams to make them come true. And what if you don't see any candidates who represent those values? Well, *you* believe in teamwork, don't you? You believe in leading by serving, don't you? Then what are you waiting for? Get involved. Throw your hat in the ring.

You've got my vote.

## 7

# *Principle 5: Thinking* Team *Builds Extreme Dreams*

You rotate eight players, you play seven, you use six and you trust five. I'm very easy to get along with as long as you accept the spirit of the team. The most difficult thing to teach players is how to get away from being themselves and get with the program. You need four or five guys who force the others to comply. When that begins to happen, you're on your way.

> PAT RILEY, former head coach,
> L.A. Lakers, New York Knicks, and
> Miami Heat[1]

DO YOU HAVE WHAT IT TAKES TO BE A CHAMPION? Do you have—

*Ubuntu?*

The Boston Celtics discovered the value of *ubuntu,* and they brought home an NBA Championship—their first in twenty-two years.

From the late 1950s to the late 1980s, the dominant color scheme of the NBA was green and red—Celtic green and Red Auerbach. During the decades when Auerbach led the team as head coach, general manager, or president, the franchise won sixteen NBA Championships. That sixteenth championship capped the 1985–1986 season, when the Celtics won 67 games and went 40-1 at home.

The Celts were not only the best team in the league, but they also had the number two pick in the 1986 NBA Draft. It appeared that Boston's dominance of the NBA would go on and on. The team used its number two pick to draft University of Maryland star forward Len Bias—a young man with superstar potential. Bias was expected to continue the Celtics dynasty after the retirement of Larry Bird. But just forty-eight hours after he was drafted, Len Bias died of cardiac arrhythmia due to a cocaine overdose.

The death of Len Bias was the first of a number of setbacks inflicted on the Celtics over the next few years. Boston's dominance of the NBA ended and would not return until the advent of—

*Ubuntu.*

This African word was introduced to the Celtics by head coach Doc Rivers. Doc, who coached the Orlando Magic for four seasons, took over as head coach of the Celtics in 2004. He discovered the concept of *ubuntu* in, of all places, Milwaukee, Wisconsin. A graduate of Milwaukee's Marquette University, Doc now serves on Marquette's board—and that's how he stumbled onto the concept.

"I was in a board meeting at Marquette," he explained, "and a lady [on the board] had been to South Africa. She asked me if I knew the word. . . . I did not. So she told me about it and sent some information. I loved it. Talk about being in the right place in the right time. It was perfect."[2]

*Ubuntu* is a traditional African concept, rich in meaning, that has no simple equivalent in English. Derived from the Bantu language, *ubuntu* is more than just a word; it's an entire philosophy regarding how people should relate to one another. The closest approximation of the word in English would be "I am, because we are." People with *ubuntu* know they belong to a greater whole.

They believe they themselves are directly diminished if another person is suffering or in need.

The concept of *ubuntu* emphasizes humility and unselfishness, encouragement and empowerment of others, a sense of connectedness with the team, and a recognition that the individual succeeds only when the whole team succeeds. To practice *ubuntu* is to think *team* at all times. *Ubuntu* enables a team of diverse personalities and diversified skills to unite around a common goal and shared values.

Doc Rivers gives much of the credit for the Celtics' NBA Championship to the spirit of *ubuntu* that his players practiced throughout the season. As Celtics shooting guard Ray Allen puts it, *ubuntu* is a way of learning how to "think as a group. You don't think as individuals."[3]

What makes the 2008 Celtics so extraordinary is that they made a complete turnaround in a single season from one of the worst teams in the NBA to the absolute best. The previous season, 2006–2007, began on a gloomy note with the death of Red Auerbach. During the season, the team racked up a dismal record of 24-58, the worst record in the Atlantic division and second-worst in the NBA. That season included an eighteen-game losing streak from January 5 to February 14, 2007—the most dismal streak in Celtics history.

For the 2007–2008 season, the Celtics acquired All-Stars Kevin Garnett and Ray Allen, a change in lineup that gave owner Wyc Grousbeck the confidence to dub his restructured Celtics "Banner Seventeen" in anticipation of a seventeenth NBA Championship. Certainly, the acquisition of stellar talent was a big factor in the Celtics' improvement from a 24-win season to a 66-win season. But talent alone could not explain what the Celtics did to the immensely talented Lakers in the NBA Finals. Such an accomplishment could only be explained in terms of *teamwork* and *ubuntu*.

After winning games one, two, and four, the Celtics demolished the Lakers in game six with a score of 131 to 92. Though the Celtics star trio, Kevin Garnett, Ray Allen, and Paul Pierce, contributed mightily to the point total, role-players James Posey, P.J. Brown, Leon Powe, and Glen "Big Baby" Davis all jumped in and made a crucial difference. In short, the Celtics schooled the Lakers in the precepts of *ubuntu*.

As the game wound down to a close, the Boston crowd chanted, "Seventeen! Seventeen!" In the rafters overhead, sixteen championship banners hung, the last one earned more than two decades earlier. The fans had waited a long time for Banner Seventeen. In the owner's box, Wyc Grousbeck performed a little ceremony that used to be the late Red Auerbach's trademark: he chomped down on an unlit victory cigar. On the floor, Paul Pierce drenched Doc Rivers with red Gatorade. When the final buzzer sounded, the Celtics were NBA champions once more—

A convincing affirmation of the power of *ubuntu*.[4]

## A NEVER-ENDING SALES PITCH

In *Russell Rules*, Celtics legend Bill Russell tells how he learned to live by the principle of *ubuntu* (he used the word *team* instead of *ubuntu*, but the meaning is the same). His breakthrough year as a basketball player came when he was a sophomore at the University of San Francisco. That was the year he joined the varsity team. One of his teammates despised him and told Russell he'd never cut it as a basketball player.

Bill Russell accepted the challenge. He set a goal of becoming the best he could be. In his first three varsity games, Russell focused on his own individual performance—shooting as many buckets as he could without any regard to what his teammates were doing. Russell put on a great one-man show. He was exciting to watch. But his team was crushed again and again. He recalled:

> At the end of the season I realized we had a medio-
> cre 14-7 record, yet we had enough talent to be one of
> the really great college teams in the country. After that
> season, I concluded that "I was wrong. I am part of the
> team and I am not strong enough to change the atmo-
> sphere for the better and the team wasn't strong enough
> to change me, so we feuded." After that season, I vowed
> to never again concentrate on individual goals at the ex-
> pense of the team.[5]

When Bill Russell began playing for the Celtics, he discovered the joy of playing and winning as a team in a whole new way:

> The Celtics were the definition of a genuine team.
> They had been built carefully, player by player, over the
> years. The players had been chosen not only for their spe-
> cific skills but because they complemented each other so
> well. The coach, Red Auerbach, wanted to win as much
> as any of the players. . . . He knew each of the players as
> individuals, respected them, and saw them together as
> a team. That had nothing to do with his being a good
> guy (which he was) but was because he burned to win
> and be seen as the best coach who ever lived (which he
> was)—and the success of his team was the way he could
> get there.[6]

Hall of Fame coach Jim Calhoun is head men's basketball coach at the University of Connecticut. He coached the UConn Huskies to two national championships, the 1999 and 2004 NCAA titles. In *A Passion to Lead*, he explained that his number one challenge every year is to promote a "think *team*" attitude among his players. He wrote:

> At UConn, we work diligently every year at building the concept of team. One idea that I constantly emphasize is this: *When we benefit, I benefit.*
>
> In other words, when the team performs well, everyone on the team will share in its success. I want the players, as a group, to take ownership of the team. And one thing I do to promote team "ownership" is to make sure that every player, whether he is an All-American or a benchwarmer, knows that he is making contributions to the team.
>
> Every player has to know where he fits. And I make a point of telling the team regularly how important everybody is to our success—including and especially the kids who don't get much playing time, and little public recognition of their efforts.[7]

George Karl is the head coach of the Denver Nuggets. From 1969 to 1973, he played college basketball for Dean Smith at the University of North Carolina at Chapel Hill. Many years after leaving UNC and well into his NBA coaching career, Karl received coaching advice from Dean Smith. In 2001, Karl told an interviewer, "I still get letters from Coach Smith. He's taken some clippings and circled the number of times I've used the word *I.* 'Don't we mean *we*, George?' I judge my year on how many times I hear from him on that."[8]

*Ubuntu* is not just for the people out on the playing field. A "think *team*" attitude must be shared by everyone at every level of the organization: owner, executives, managers, coaches, players, secretaries, janitors, interns, and even the fans. Everyone must be imbued with *ubuntu*, fired up with enthusiasm and optimism, and empowered to lift the entire team.

Whitey Herzog, the former MLB outfielder and manager, put it this way:

> The one thing I've decided, after looking at baseball from top to bottom, is that, unless the whole organization is working together for one common purpose . . . you're not going to keep your job. The scouts have to find good players; the coaches have to teach; the minor-league staff has to keep the pipeline full of young players; the manager and the general manager and the front office staff have to keep the players happy and keep the budget in line; and the owner has to find good people and let them do their jobs. It sounds easy but it's not.[9]

Years ago, when I was beginning my research on teamwork, I sent a copy of my outline to Duke basketball coach Mike Krzyzewski. He wrote back and told me he agreed with my outline, and especially the part about the need for unselfishness among players. "It's a paradox," Mike said. "If players would just understand that if they sacrifice some individual stuff on the front end so that the group succeeds on the back end, the individuals will flourish! It's a paradox and most people never get it. For those who do, it makes all of the difference in the world."

## *UBUNTU* IN THE WORKPLACE

The ability to "think *team*" is as important in every other team environment as it is in sports. Wal-Mart founder Sam Walton put it this way: "Exercising your ego in public is definitely not the way to build an effective organization. One person seeking glory doesn't accomplish much. At Wal-Mart, everything we've done has been the result of people pulling together to meet one common goal—teamwork—something I also picked up at an early age."[10]

In *High Five! The Magic of Working Together,* authors Ken Blanchard and Sheldon Bowles relate a parable about teamwork showing that the same "think *team*" principles that produce success in the sports world also promote success in the business world. *High Five!* tells the story of Alan Foster, a manager who runs his office like a one-man band. Unwilling to work in partnership with others, he is fired—and his boss tells him, "Alan, we need good producers who are good team players, too." While trying to come to grips with his failure, he encounters a retired teacher, Miss Weatherby, who once coached a high school girls' basketball team. From Miss Weatherby, Alan learns an *ubuntu*-like appreciation for teamwork. Here's an example of Miss Weatherby's wisdom:

> I happen to believe that a divine spark is the difference between a crowd and a team. . . . At the very instant I lay down my ego and recognize a divine connection, I begin to place others first. When that happens, I'm suddenly transformed. I've gone from being a relatively powerless individual to being part of something far more powerful, productive, and successful than I could be on my own. It all hangs on ten short words. . . . *None of us is as smart as all of us.* . . . Once you accept that none of us is as smart as all of us, you can begin to put your needs, your pride, your agenda on hold and let the team's needs, pride, and agenda become your priority.[11]

Bill Bradley, NBA Hall of Famer and former U.S. senator— believes that the way you play basketball says a lot about the way you think and behave in the "real world":

I can learn more about people by playing a three-on-three game with them for twenty minutes than I can by talking with them for a week. I once hired a new director for my U.S. Senate offices in New Jersey. I liked him, but it wasn't until I played basketball with him that I knew I'd made the right choice. I found out that he was a hard worker (he went for the rebound), competitive with a fierce desire to win (he played close defense), and unselfish (he screened away from the ball).[12]

Are you applying for a job in the corporate world? Then think *team*, my friend. In your interview, make sure you express honest enthusiasm for working in a team environment—or it may be a very short interview! Be positive, optimistic, and supportive of your teammates at all times. The ability to "think *team*" and function productively in a team environment will earn points in your performance reviews—and will position you to grab that next rung on the corporate ladder. Maintain a mind-set of *ubuntu*— "I am, because we are."

## *UBUNTU*—POWERED BY LOVE

Over the years, I've watched Dusty Baker's career in baseball, both as a player (primarily with the Braves and Dodgers) and as a manager (currently with the Cincinnati Reds). I only recently became aware that his philosophy of teamwork was largely shaped by his service with the Marines. He said that, in the Corps, every Marine looks out for every other Marine. A Marine will risk everything to save his buddy's life, Baker said, "even if you don't like him and he doesn't like you. That's teamwork."[13]

Dusty Baker has underscored a profound truth: teamwork is

powered by love. You don't have to *like* your teammate—but you do have to *love* him.

You may think, *How can I love someone I don't even like?* That's the problem with this English word *love*. Unfortunately, we have only one word in our language to describe many different kinds of love. We use the same word to say "I love pizza" as we use to say "I love my children."

The ancient Greeks wisely used three different words for *love*, and each had a distinct shade of meaning. The kind of love I'm talking about here is what the ancient Greeks called *agape* (pronounced *uh-GAW-pay*). *Agape* love is unconditional, a love that is not a feeling or an emotion, but a choice we make. When you choose to do good to people you don't even like, when you choose to affirm them, encourage them, and work in teamwork with them, you are practicing *agape* love.

Vince Lombardi once said: "It's the team! Teamwork is what the Green Bay Packers were all about. They didn't do it for the individual glory. They did it because they loved one another."[14]

In his autobiography, former Chrysler CEO Lee Iacocca recounted a dinner conversation with Lombardi. Coach Lombardi told him:

> If you're going to play together as a team, you've got to care for one another. You've got to *love* each other. Each player has to be thinking about the next guy and saying to himself: "If I don't block that man, Paul is going to get his legs broken. I have to do my job well in order that he can do his." The difference between mediocrity and greatness is the feeling these guys have for each other. Most people call it team spirit. When the players are imbued with that special feeling, you know you've got yourself a winning team.[15]

You can't have teamwork without unconditional love. And loving someone unconditionally has nothing to do with whether you like that person. In fact, it's the unlikable people who need the most love! Highly talented people are often not very likable. Some talented people have big egos and poor people skills. If you choose to love them and practice *ubuntu* toward them, they may not become any more likable—but you may win a championship or two.

## FROM UNDERDOGS TO WONDERDOGS

The Fresno State Bulldogs baseball team had high expectations for their 2008 season—and were even talking about going to the College World Series in Omaha. But after losing twelve of their first twenty games, these Dogs were in the doghouse. They battled their way through the season and finished 47 and 31—a winning record but hardly exceptional.

The unranked Bulldogs went into the NCAA Regionals in Long Beach as a fourth regional seed—the equivalent of being seeded fifteenth or sixteenth in an NCAA basketball tournament. It was a double-elimination tournament—lose twice and you're done. The Bulldogs heard taunts of "two and a barbecue." Opponents expected the Dogs to be eliminated quickly, have a consolation cookout, and slink back home in defeat. Ignoring the taunts, the Dogs shocked nationally ranked Long Beach State and the University of San Diego, advancing to the Super Regionals in Tempe, Arizona.

Fresno State lost the opener against number-three-ranked Arizona State, then bounced back to beat the Sun Devils in two straight elimination games. Defying all expectations, they had won the right to play in the College World Series.

The Bulldogs went to Omaha as the lowest seeded team to ever play in the CWS. No one gave Fresno State a chance against the strong pitching staff of number-five-ranked Rice—but the Bulldogs slammed four homers in a 17–5 victory over Rice.

Next, the Dogs faced the number two Tar Heels of North Carolina. Naysayers said Fresno State had gotten this far on luck alone and would be demolished by the number two team in the nation. But the Bulldogs beat the Tar Heels 5–3 in game one. In game two, the Tar Heels had to come from behind to stave off elimination, winning 4–3. In game three, with both sides facing elimination, the Dogs clobbered North Carolina 6–1 to continue their improbable run.

Next, the unranked Bulldogs from Fresno faced the eighth-ranked Bulldogs from the University of Georgia in the best-of-three finals. They were 6-0 in elimination games and had beaten four nationally seeded teams. But to achieve the most extreme dream in college baseball, they had to beat Georgia—twice. Coach Batesole's Bulldogs were spent—especially the pitching staff.

In game one of the finals, the Dogs used a "pitching-by-committee" approach. Batesole started sophomore Sean Bonesteele (6.75 ERA), and added three relievers to the mix. Georgia's head coach David Perno, by contrast, got seven solid innings out of his top starter, Trevor Holder. Though Fresno State seemed to take over the game, going up 6–3 in the top of the eighth, Georgia scored four runs in the bottom of the eighth to seal the win, 7–6.

Game two: Facing elimination, Fresno State again resorted to "patchwork pitching." And the patchwork quickly came unraveled. After two scoreless innings, Georgia scored five runs in the top of the third. In the press box, reporters phoned their travel agents, seeking early flights home. They were certain Fresno State's run was over.

In the bottom of the third, however, Fresno State responded

with a six-run surge. Every Fresno State player achieved far beyond his normal abilities. Closing pitcher Jake Hower (6.95 ERA)
threw three scoreless innings. In the end, it was a blowout, with
Fresno State winning 19–10. Coach Batesole said, "That's not the
first time this club has answered the bell when they had to."[16]

Game three: Coach Batesole bet the final game on the strong
left arm of his best remaining pitcher, Justin Wilson. Though
Wilson had only three days' rest following a loss to North Carolina, he turned in an eight-inning, nine-strikeout, 129-pitch bra-
vura performance. His final pitch was a called strike clocked at
ninety-one miles an hour.

Wilson's demeanor on the mound was businesslike, almost
emotionless—but I have seen that look before. It's the intense
focus that comes with being "in the zone." When Wilson was in
the dugout, he sat quietly, not talking, with a far-seeing look in
his eye—the look of someone whose mind was in another realm.
Coach Batesole saw it too. He said he knew his Bulldogs would
win the game "when I saw the look in [Justin Wilson's] eye in the
first inning."[17]

Justin Wilson was on his way to pitching a shutout when
Georgia's Gordon Beckham led off the eighth inning with a solo
homer. By then, however, Georgia's dugout was already demoral-
ized, down 6–1.

And where did those six Fresno State runs come from? They
were all driven in by outfielder Steve Detwiler, who had been playing since April with a fully torn tendon in his left thumb. Even
though the pain of that thumb showed plainly on his face every
time he gripped the bat, he homered twice and drove four runners home. He ended up setting a CWS record with four home
runs. After the game he explained, "It's mind over matter. Pain is
temporary. Pride is forever."[18]

Third baseman Tommy Mendonca turned in a brilliant performance, playing with four injured fingers on one hand, two of

them dislocated. He had suffered the injury at the beginning of the postseason, and there had been no time for medical attention. "I've made it this far without a doctor," he said. "Why stop now?"[19]

The emotional spark plug of the team was second baseman Erik Wetzel. While Erik was in high school, his mother, Cathy, was diagnosed with stage-four melanoma. Doctors told her she would not live to see Erik graduate. She not only saw him graduate but got to watch him play college ball. Erik's father, Dave, sold his printing business, bought a motor home, and he and Cathy followed Erik around the country to his away games. Before Cathy Wetzel died in August 2006, Erik told her his dream was to play in the College World Series. Though she didn't live to see Erik's dream fulfilled, Erik told his dad he felt her presence at Rosenblatt Stadium.

Coach Batesole called on closer Brandon Burke to seal the ninth. Burke got one Georgia batter to hit into a double play—but tension mounted as Burke walked Georgia's Ryan Peisel, placing runners at the corners, bringing Matt Olson up to bat. Olson swung on the first pitch—

And lined it right into the glove of Steve Detwiler—game over.

Whooping with joy, Detwiler slipped the game-winning ball into his pocket as he ran to the infield and leaped onto the pile of celebrating Fresno State Bulldogs.[20]

Georgia's coach David Perno was frustrated that his team couldn't find a solution to the Bulldogs from California. His problem: Fresno State had no single star player to defend against—the *entire team as a unit* was the superstar. "We couldn't keep them in the yard," Perno said. "It always seemed to be a different guy. Someone stepped up for them when they needed it most."[21]

Fresno State left fielder Steve Susdorf agreed. "We were all committed to the team," he said. "No one was about himself."[22] That's *ubuntu* talking.

ESPN play-by-play announcer Mike Patrick compared Fresno State's improbable championship win to past sports miracles: the 1968 New York Jets, the 1969 Mets, and the USA hockey team's "miracle on ice" in the 1980 Winter Olympics. ESPN college sports reporter Tim Griffin agreed, writing, "The hyperbole around Fresno State's wild charge to the NCAA baseball championship probably isn't overstated. The Bulldogs' emergence from Underdogs to Wonderdogs will go down in history as one of the most memorable title runs in college sports history, maybe even in all of sports history."[23]

How do you explain it? Personally, I give all the credit to teamwork and *ubuntu*.

Still, I won't argue with Erik Wetzel, who gives the credit to his mom in heaven. Erik, a junior, was drafted by the Colorado Rockies and was tempted to leave school and play pro ball. But before she died, Cathy Wetzel made Erik promise he'd get his college degree. Erik has decided to stay in school and keep his word to his mom.

Good choice.

# Extreme *Elevation* Dreams . . .

## *Depend on Teams*

*When men climb on a great mountain together, the rope between them is more than a mere physical aid to the ascent; it is a symbol of the spirit of the enterprise. It is a symbol of men banded together in a common effort of will and strength against their only true enemies: inertia, cowardice, greed, ignorance, and all weaknesses of the spirit.*

CHARLES SNEAD HOUSTON, American
physician, mountaineer, and former
Peace Corps administrator[1]

British mountaineer George Mallory attempted to conquer Mount Everest on three different occasions in the 1920s. During Mallory's 1923 American speaking tour, a New York journalist asked him, "Why do you wish to climb Everest?" His famous reply: "Because it is there."[2]

On his third attempt in May-June 1924, Mallory and his climbing partner, Andrew Irvine, were spotted just a few hundred yards from the summit. They never returned. Their fate remained a mystery until 1999, when Mallory's frozen body was discovered by climbers.

To this day, no one knows whether George Mallory reached the summit. He died in early June 1924, less than two weeks short of his twenty-eighth birthday.

Climbers from many countries attempted the ascent from the 1920s to the early 1950s, without success. After China closed the borders of Tibet in 1950, expeditions no longer had access to the north face of Everest. Any assault on the summit had to come via the south face through Nepal—and the Nepalese government permitted only one expedition on Everest per year.

A team of Swiss mountaineers made a failed attempt in 1952, coming within eight hundred feet of the summit, only to be defeated by bad weather. So the British prepared an expedition for 1953. The British government was determined to see this attempt succeed. Expeditions from other nations had already reserved the next few years, so 1953 would be Great Britain's last opportunity for a long time.

Another reason the year 1953 was crucial was that the coronation of twenty-seven-year-old Elizabeth II as queen of England was scheduled for June 2, 1953. The goal was that the conquest of Everest would coincide with the coronation—a gift to Her Majesty. It was an extreme dream, not only for the expedition, but for British prestige—a dream that had already taken the lives of at least sixteen climbers.

## A RAZOR'S EDGE

The leader of the Ninth British Expedition to Everest was military mountaineer Colonel John Hunt. He handpicked his team, seeking the most qualified climbers he could find in the British Commonwealth, including two New Zealanders—beekeeper Edmund Hillary and his friend George Lowe. Other team members included deputy leader Charles Evans, twenty-two-year-old George Band, Tom Bourdillon, Alf Gregory, Wilfrid Noyce, Michael Ward, Michael Westmacott, and Charles Wylie. Hunt chose Dr. Griffith Pugh as the team doctor and physiologist because he was a proven expert in survival gear, nutrition, and the use of oxygen tanks. Hunt selected filmmaker Tom Stobart to make a documentary of the expedition. He also invited James Morris, correspondent for the *Times of London*, as journalist-of-record.

In addition to the Britons on the team, Colonel Hunt selected twenty Sherpa guides, whose knowledge of the treacherous Himalayas would be invaluable. The Sherpas are an ethnic group who live in the mountains of Nepal. One of them, Tenzing Norgay, was a highly respected Nepalese-born mountaineer who had moved to Darjeeling, India, and had accompanied Everest expeditions since the 1930s.

When thirty-three-year-old Edmund Hillary and Tenzing Norgay met, they quickly became close friends. Hillary and Norgay were not originally chosen to be the first to reach the summit. That honor was intended for Charles Evans and Tom Bourdillon. The expedition established a base camp in March 1953, then made the ascent over a period of weeks to the South Col (elevation 25,900 feet). The South Col is the doorstep of Everest's "death zone." Climbers can endure this oxygen-deprived altitude for no more than two or three days. If the weather does not cooperate during that brief window of opportunity, the climbers must go back for weeks of recuperation.

When Evans and Bourdillon reached the South Col on May 26, they found that Evans's oxygen system was not working. The two men had to turn back— just one hundred vertical yards short of the summit. When Colonel Hunt received word that Evans and Bourdillon had failed, he sent Hillary and Norgay up the mountain.

Most people think of the conquest of Everest as the accomplishment of two men, Edmund Hillary and Tenzing Norgay. In fact, there were some four hundred people involved in the total effort—and Hillary and Norgay never would have made it without them. A key member of the team was Hillary's close friend, George Lowe.

Hillary later recalled,

> *Everybody would have liked to try to go to the top, but one of the great strengths of our expedition, unquestionably, was that we did have this very strong team spirit. George Lowe led most of the way up to the high camp. He cut lots of steps, trying to reduce the burden on Tenzing and myself. When we said goodbye to the others, I just thanked them for all their help, and they said, "Give it a go."[3]*

Hillary and Norgay made the ascent and camped above the South Col, where they spent a fitful, sleepless night. While waiting for dawn, they lit a cookstove and used it to thaw Hillary's frozen boots and melt ice for drinking water. In the distance below, they could see the lights of Tengboche Monastery where Buddhist monks made offerings for their safety. As the night gave way to morning, Hillary and Norgay strapped on their oxygen packs. Using ice axes to hack steps along the ridge, they made their way toward the summit.

The ascent was difficult and dangerous. In places, the ridge narrowed to a razor's edge. At around 10:00 a.m., they came to a steep barrier—a forty-foot-tall vertical step. They had known of its existence from aerial survey photos, but no one knew whether or not it could be scaled. Standing at its foot, Hillary saw a narrow vertical crack. He found he could wedge himself partway into the crack and use leverage to work his way to the top. Tenzing Norgay followed the same route. Climbers still call that barrier "the Hillary Step" today.

Hillary and Norgay took a zigzag path along the summit ridge until they saw their destination. As Edmund Hillary later described it,

> I was cutting steps in the ice when I noticed that the ridge ahead dropped away. And way off in the distance I could see the barren plateau of Tibet. I looked up to the right about forty or fifty feet up. There was a round snowy dome. So I just cut steps, with Tenzing fairly closely behind. We emerged on the top of the dome and realized we were on the summit.[4]

Standing on the summit, the emotionally reserved New Zealander turned to congratulate his companion with a handshake—but found himself locked in a tight embrace by his exuberant Sherpa friend.

Hillary checked the time. At 11:30 in the morning, May 29, 1953, the first two human beings set foot upon the highest point on Planet Earth.

## Seven Weeks and Fifteen Minutes

Though it had taken Edmund Hillary and Tenzing Norgay seven weeks to reach the top of the world, their limited oxygen supply permitted them to remain there for only fifteen minutes. They spent a couple of minutes looking for evidence that George Mallory had reached the summit in 1924. They found none.

Hillary took a photo of Norgay on the summit, holding his ice ax aloft with the British flag fluttering from its handle. There is no photo of Edmund Hillary on the summit because Norgay didn't know how to operate the camera. "I had my camera," Hillary said, "and I wanted to take photographs of all the leading ridges of the mountain to give absolute proof that we had reached the summit." He never minded that there was no photograph of himself on Everest. His famous photo of Norgay is proof enough. After all, "There must have been someone there to take it."[5]

Hillary recalled that they left only two things behind on the summit. Norgay, a Buddhist, placed some chocolates in a hole in the snow—a gift to the gods. Hillary left a Christian icon. "A priest had asked that we leave this crucifix on the summit," he said, "and I pushed it into the snow."[6]

The return trek was as difficult as the climb. Finally, they saw a human figure climbing toward them as they descended. It was Hillary's friend Lowe, with a thermos of hot soup for them. As soon as correspondent James Morris received the news that Hillary and Norgay were successful, he sent a coded radio message. As planned, the news broke around the world in time for the coronation of Queen Elizabeth II. A few weeks later, the young queen conferred knighthoods on Edmund Hillary and Colonel John Hunt. Tenzing Norgay received the British Empire Medal.

After Everest, Sir Edmund Hillary continued to pursue extreme goals. In 1958, he led a team of New Zealanders on an overland expedition to the South Pole. He also continued exploring the Himalayas, served as a diplomatic emissary to India and Nepal, and founded a nonprofit organization, the Himalayan Trust, to support education, health care, and economic development for the Sherpa people.

He suffered a terrible tragedy in 1975 when his wife, Louise, and teenage daughter Belinda were killed in the crash of a small plane in Nepal. His grief was overwhelming. "In the evenings," he recalled, "I walked alone on the airfield with the great mountains behind and tears running down my cheeks."[7] A few years later, he married June Mulgrew, and she helped him run the Himalayan Trust.

Hillary was pleased to hear that the body of George Mallory was found in 1999. "I had a great admiration for him," he said, "and if they find his camera and prove that he had been to the summit, I would have a great feeling of pleasure for him. For forty-five years I have been regarded as the hero of Everest; I really can't complain."[8] To date, however, no evidence has emerged to prove that Mallory reached the summit.

## "We Were a Team"

The conquest of Everest was a vivid demonstration of the power of teamwork.

Climber Alan Hobson has seen Everest expeditions fail—and he says that, aside from bad weather, the top reason for failure is a lack of teamwork among climbers. As a result, he says, "We choose our climbing team very carefully based on compatibility first . . . and experience second. . . . On Everest, as in life, the most important component, and the one most difficult to manage, is the human one. No family can succeed if its members do not get along."[9]

Colonel John Hunt deserves credit for assembling his team, which included Sir Edmund Hillary and Tenzing Norgay. Historian Audrey Salkeld notes that the Ninth British Expedition was composed of people of extraordinary character and humility. They all chose to use their fame for others rather than for personal gain. Salkeld writes:

> *We can be grateful that Hunt's carefully chosen team was universally aware of its privilege and that all the members, in their own way, have sought to use their prestige in public service. Hunt went on to become The Lord Hunt of Llanvair Warterdine, known for conspicuous work with young people. . . . [Hillary] is best known for his work with The Himalayan Trust, dedicated to improving the lot of the Sherpa community in Nepal. Most notable is his help in establishing the Khumjung School that has served for*

*years in educating Sherpa children throughout the Khumbu. Tenzing founded the Indian Mountaineering Federation with an injunction from President Nehru to "train a thousand Tenzings." Throughout his life he remained a smiling and approachable unofficial ambassador for the Sherpa people. . . .*

*As Lord Hunt has said, the success of his team on Everest was merely the continuation of the effort of all those who had gone before. Yet we can feel ourselves fortunate that in him and his team, the world was blessed with men to match the mountains they climbed.*[10]

Sir Edmund Hillary died in Auckland, New Zealand, on January 11, 2008. He was eighty-eight. He once summed up the conquest of the world's highest peak in these words: "When we climbed Everest, we were a team—and that made a difference."[11]

# 8

# Principle 6: Empowered Individuals Build Extreme Dreams

I've never met anyone who said they left a company because they were recognized too much.

> STEVE FARBER, president of
> Extreme Leadership[1]

I GOT MY START IN SPORTS MANAGEMENT IN SPAR-tanburg, South Carolina, operating a minor-league baseball team in the Philadelphia Phillies farm system. My duties included putting on promotions to attract crowds to the ballpark. Though I was only in my mid-twenties at the time, the team's co-owner, Mr. R. E. Littlejohn, entrusted a great deal of decision-making power to me.

During my third season with the Phillies, I decided to put on the most eye-popping string of promotions that town had ever seen. I paid thousands of dollars to bring sports celebrities to our ballpark to speak and sign autographs—stars like Bart Starr, Paul Hornung, Johnny Unitas, Bob Feller, Satchel Paige, and more.

I spent Mr. Littlejohn's money as if it were trash! He could see I was busting the budget—yet he never said a word. I wondered, *Why doesn't he put on the brakes?* But he didn't try to stop me, so I kept spending and promoting.

The end of the season came, and we'd had a great year. Attendance was way up. We would have cleared an enormous profit—if my promotions hadn't gone way over budget.

Then it hit me: I had a profit-sharing clause in my contract. According to that clause, I was to be paid a bonus at the end of the season—and the bonus was based on a percentage of the profits! That profit-sharing clause was an incentive for me to hold the line on expenses. So when I was on my promotional binge, I wasn't just spending Mr. Littlejohn's money—I was spending my bonus!

I received a bonus of about three thousand dollars, a tidy sum of money, especially for the 1960s. But it was a fraction of the amount I would have collected if I had held the line on the budget.

It was a valuable lesson. Mr. Littlejohn empowered me to make my own decisions so I would learn, grow, and become a better executive. He could have yanked me up short and ordered me to watch the bottom line—but he wasn't interested only in the money. He was interested in my growth.

I learned a lot from that experience—and not just about the baseball business. I learned a big lesson in *empowerment.*

## THE PARADOX OF EMPOWERMENT

Empowerment is the act of increasing the confidence and decision-making ability of the players on a team. It's the act of giving team players full authority to make decisions—including *wrong* decisions—without fear of punishment or retribution.

To empower people is to *trust* them. The leader says to the team members, "I will give you an extreme dream to shoot for. I will coach you and mentor you. But it's up to you to make your own decisions and exercise your own creativity. If you need help or resources, just ask. But you don't need my permission to make decisions. Go for it!"

The word *empowerment* was a buzzword in the 1990s. The problem with a buzzword is that it becomes all buzz and no action. Many employers paid lip service to empowerment but didn't truly *empower* anybody. They might have put in some halfhearted measures to make employees *feel* that their opinions mattered— but actually give employees *real* decision-making power? No way! You can't trust employees with that kind of power! What if they make a mistake?

So bosses remained bosses, maintaining their hierarchical control. They kept their teams on a short leash. Employees still had to ask permission to make meaningful decisions. They had to waste hours and hours filling out bureaucratic paperwork. The few feeble decisions they made were frequently reversed.

Once your team members discover that you don't trust them with decision-making power, *you become the loser.* If you punish mistakes, your players will decide that they have nothing to gain and everything to lose by showing initiative and imagination. They will play it safe and cover up mistakes—and you'll lose the benefit of their creativity.

But when you truly *empower* people, you unleash their potential to achieve unimaginable heights. You make synergy possible. True, you also create opportunities for mistakes. You give players the right to make choices you wouldn't make—and you give up the right to control their actions. Yes, they are still accountable to you—but you have relinquished control. You cannot empower people and control them at the same time, any more than you can shut up a bird in a cage and expect it to soar. When you empower people, you let them out of the cage.

Bosses like to maintain "command and control." But leaders love to see their *players* take control of the situation. You'll never achieve synergy by maintaining "command and control" of the

team. You must let the team control itself. Management guru
Warren Bennis explains empowerment this way:

> Empowerment involves the sense people have that they
> are at the center of things, rather than the periphery. In an
> effectively led organization, everyone feels he or she con-
> tributes to its success. Empowered individuals believe what
> they do has significance and meaning. . . . They live in a
> culture of respect where they can actually do things with-
> out getting permission first from some parent figure. . . .
>
> The organizations that will succeed are those that take
> seriously—and sustain through action—the belief that their
> competitive advantage is based on the development and
> growth of the people in them. And the men and women
> who guide those organizations will be a different kind of
> leader than we've been used to. They will be maestros, not
> masters; coaches, not commanders. . . .
>
> The successful leader will have not the loudest voice,
> but the readiest ear. His or her real genius may well lie not
> in personal achievements, but in unleashing other people's
> talent.[2]

Here's the great paradox of empowerment: the moment you
truly begin to empower your players, *you empower yourself.* As you
relinquish command, you gain respect. As you relinquish control,
you gain influence. As you become less of a boss, you become
more of a leader.

Empowerment is a great tool for recruiting top talent. High-
functioning, creative people enjoy working in an empowering environment. You can't attract great players to a team that is rigid
and bureaucratic. To achieve extreme dreams, you must recruit
the best—and to recruit the best, you must be known as a leader
who empowers people.

The world is constantly changing, and only an organization that empowers people can respond quickly to change. This is true in sports, business, government, education, entertainment, religion, and every other team environment. Your frontline players see change taking place long before you do. If they are empowered to make decisions, your organization will remain nimble and adaptable. If they have to run every decision past you, your approval may come too late.

Bureaucratic, hierarchical organizations are like dinosaurs—too big and too slow to respond to the changing environment. And like dinosaurs, nonempowering organizations are doomed to extinction.

A fully empowered team is made up of people who:

- are confident and optimistic.
- are well-trained and adequately supplied with the resources to do their jobs.
- are recognized and praised for their accomplishments.
- are trusted and expected to exercise initiative and leadership.
- believe their work is meaningful.
- are unafraid to take a reasonable risk for a big payoff.
- are adequately compensated.
- are intensely committed to the extreme dream of the organization.

If your organization is made up of people like that, then you're ready to conquer the world. If not, then your dysfunctional organization is headed for extinction. In time, you may find some of your most talented people drifting away. They may even start their own companies and become your competitors. Would you rather have your best and brightest people utilizing their brilliance *for* you—or would you rather have them competing *against* you?

## PUTTING THE *POW!* IN EMPOWERMENT

An excellent example of empowerment in the business world is the Ritz-Carlton Hotel chain. I've spoken at numerous Ritz-Carlton events, and I've studied the company's culture. The underlying philosophy of every Ritz-Carlton Hotel is distilled into one simple concept: "Ladies and gentlemen serving ladies and gentlemen."

Robert K. Cooper and Ayman Sawaf, in their book *Executive EQ*, observe that the Ritz-Carlton organization "actively promotes trust as the core of its organizational culture. Every Ritz-Carlton employee, including junior bellhops, can spend up to $2,000 on the spot to fix any guest's problem. No questions asked."[3]

Ritz-Carlton employees are immersed in a corporate culture based on twelve "Service Values," which include the following statements:

> I am empowered to create unique, memorable, and personal experiences for our guests. . . . I continuously seek opportunities to innovate and improve The Ritz-Carlton experience. . . . I own and immediately resolve guest problems. . . . I create a work environment of teamwork and lateral service so that the needs of our guests and [my fellow employees] are met.[4]

Think about what that means: Ritz-Carlton employees have not only *permission* but an emphatic *commission* to instantly resolve problems and create memorable experiences for their guests. What's more, employees are instructed to create an environment of teamwork and to provide "lateral service" to meet the needs of fellow employees. Clearly, the Ritz-Carlton does more than merely pay lip service to empowerment. It's an organization that puts the *pow!* in empowerment.

People want their work to have meaning. They want to belong to something greater than themselves. Empowerment enables people to feel that their work is significant, that they themselves are trusted and valued, and that they are connected to something big and important. When you give people an extreme dream to reach for and you empower them to go for it, you unleash their energy and talent in amazing ways.

Al West is the founder of SEI, a NASDAQ-listed asset-management and financial solutions company that administers $423 billion in mutual fund and pooled assets. He founded the company in 1968. West is an enthusiastic believer in empowerment—though he calls it by a different name. "We call it fluid leadership," he said. "People figure out what they're good at, and that shapes what their roles are. There's not just one leader. Different people lead during different parts of the process."[5]

L.A. Lakers head coach Phil Jackson put it succinctly: "The team itself must be the leader of the team."[6] That may seem like double-talk, but it is actually a profound truth. The great NFL coach Marty Schottenheimer offers this insight into what it means for the team itself to be the leader of the team:

> The most successful teams that I've been around were those where the players drove the machine. I'm not talking about during the game. I'm talking about in the locker room, in the meeting room, and on the practice field. Certain conditions were set. And they weren't set by the coaches as much as they were by the players themselves. There was a level of expectation in terms of preparation, effort, and so forth. If certain players fell short, the other guys were quick to say, "Get with it."
>
> That direction is much more effective coming from another player than coming from a coach. Players get tired of listening to coaches. When the guy at the next

locker verbally kicks a player in the butt, it makes an impression. . . .

A coach can scream and holler about teamwork, but the teams that really have it are the ones on which the players live it and demand it every day. It comes with mutual respect and internal leadership.[7]

That's the beauty of empowerment. If you create an environment in which your players feel empowered to take initiative and demonstrate leadership, your job as a leader becomes a lot easier. They will coach one another, motivate one another, confront one another, and bond into that wondrous entity called a *team*.

## HOW TO EMPOWER YOURSELF

In this chapter, I've been talking primarily to leaders—but here's a pointed word of counsel for players and employees:

Whether or not your leader or coach practices the principles of empowerment, *you can empower yourself.* You can take control of your career and magnify your odds of succeeding in an increasingly uncertain economy.

Empowering yourself begins with a recognition that you are in the driver's seat of your career. There may be less job security in today's market than there was a decade or two ago—but so what? You have the power to choose whether or not you will be a desirable and employable player on somebody's team. A career development slogan at Apple Computers states: "Your job security lies in your employability."[8]

Here are some questions to consider: Are you adapting yourself to changing conditions so that you are always in demand? Are your most employable qualities always on display—your talent, attitude, character, and strong work ethic? Are you building a reputation as a team player?

Are you continuing to increase your knowledge base through reading and ongoing education? Are you seeking out mentors and coaches who can continue your growth? Are you learning a new language? Acquiring new computer skills? Are you involved in the arts or charitable work? All these qualities, both your concrete skills and your intangible interests, combine to create an impression about you as a person of substance—a person who adds value to a corporate team.

I'm not suggesting that you should be self-centered or self-absorbed. I'm simply reminding you that *you* are the board chairman, CEO, president, and general manager of Yourself, Incorporated. No one else can decide your future. If you are not investing in your ongoing education, your physical well-being, your exercise program and nutritional habits, your communication and leadership skills, and your spiritual development, then it's hard for you to be of value to anyone else.

So instead of complaining that your boss is too rigid or controlling, why not take a few steps toward empowering yourself?

## HOW TO EMPOWER OTHERS

A decade ago, our daughter Stephanie took a job in the front office of the Tampa Bay Lightning. The team had just been purchased by Art Williams, the billionaire founder of A. L. Williams & Associates. When Stephanie went to the office for her first day of work, she found a handwritten card on her desk. She had not even met Art Williams yet, but he had left her a note of encouragement and empowerment that read: "Dear Stephanie, I'm hearing great things about you. I believe we're going to build something special in Tampa and I also believe you will be one of the key reasons for this success. Stephanie, you are very special. Go, go, go! Art."

When your employer expresses that kind of faith in your future, don't you think you'd feel inspired and motivated? Don't you think you'd be willing to run through brick walls for that leader? Stephanie was! And she had a very successful time working for Art Williams and the Tampa Bay Lightning.

How can you become more effective in empowering the players on your team? Here are some suggestions:

### 1. Tell Your People You Believe in Them

Help your players envision a bright future for themselves. Mike Krzyzewski, head coach of the Duke Blue Devils basketball team, talks about his high school coach:

> He was the first person who taught me not to be afraid of failure. He'd tell me to shoot twenty-five times a game, and I'd say, "No, I can't do that, everyone will hate me." "You do it." And even though I didn't do that all the time, he kept pushing me to be better. If success or talent were on floors, maybe I saw myself on the fifth floor. He always saw me on the twentieth floor. As a result, I climbed more floors when I was with him. I've tried to use that in my way of teaching. He even helped me choose West Point to go to school, where I was afraid of that. He felt that that would give me many more floors in my building, and he was right.[9]

Empower people to believe in themselves—then get out of their way, because they're coming through!

## 2. When Your People Talk, Listen

Are you a good listener? When one of your players or employees wants to talk to you, do you drop what you're doing and give that person your full and undivided attention? Do you *really* listen?

Or do you listen with half an ear while shuffling papers or typing an e-mail? Do you mutter, "Uh-huh, yeah, whatever," while waiting for that person to give up and go away? If so, you should try *really* listening.

A leader who listens is a leader who empowers. It's interesting to notice that the word *listen* is an anagram for *silent*—same letters, different order. Perhaps there's a subliminal message there. If listening doesn't come naturally to you, then remember that you must be silent to listen—you can't be a good listener while you're doing all the talking. When you take the time to look someone in the eye and say, "I'm listening," you empower that person in a way that goes beyond mere words.

## 3. Build People Up; Don't Tear Them Down

One of my favorite words is *edify*. It's not a word we hear much anymore. It means "to build up" and it comes from the same root word as "edifice," a building. Your goal is to "build up" or edify your team so that it can achieve your extreme dreams. Sounds simple enough—yet all too many leaders seem more apt to tear people down than to build them up.

You edify people by encouraging them, cheering for them, building their confidence, and helping them feel good about themselves. Sportswriter Roland Lazenby relates a story about the great Wilt Chamberlain and a word of encouragement Wilt gave to a high school basketball player named Bill Walton. Here's the story in Walton's own words:

The first time I met Wilt I was in high school, and Wilt had just come to the Lakers. Our high school team played the preliminary game to a Lakers/San Diego Rockets game in the San Diego Sports Arena. [I was] sixteen years old and stuttered so badly that I was painfully shy. I'm walking off the court with my head down, and the Lakers are standing there ready to go onto the court. As I walk by, Wilt reaches out his arm and stops me. He steps out of their line and stands in front of me and puts his hand out and says, "Hey, Bill, I'm Wilt. You're doing really well. Keep it up." I was like blown away.[10]

I don't know how much that word of encouragement affected Bill Walton's life, but I do know that Bill went on to a spectacular career playing for Coach John Wooden at UCLA, then professionally with the Trail Blazers, Clippers, and Celtics. Bill overcame that stuttering problem and continues to enjoy a long career in broadcasting. It may well be that those few words, spoken at just the right time, inspired his Hall of Fame career.

Paul "Bear" Bryant, the legendary football coach of the Alabama Crimson Tide, recalled how his football coach at Alabama in the 1930s, Frank Thomas, helped him believe in himself:

I'll never forget, we were going out for the 1935 Rose Bowl game. I went into the men's lounge on the train. Coach Thomas was sitting there with some of the coaches and Red Heard, the athletic director of LSU, and two or three newspapermen. He said, "Red, this is my best football player. This is the best player on my team." Well, shoot, I could have gone right out the top. I mean, he didn't have to say anything else. I know now what he was doing, because I try to do it myself. He was getting me ready. And I was, too. I would have gone out there and killed myself for Alabama that day.[11]

Praise and encouragement are powerful tools for building people up. As leaders, we should always praise our players in public and criticize them only in private. Sometimes constructive criticism is necessary—but it's never necessary to embarrass or shame a player in front of his teammates.

Another thought about praise and encouragement: whenever possible, praise your players in writing. A handwritten note makes a greater impact than e-mail. Why praise people in writing? So that your players can read those positive, uplifting words again and again.

Magic owner Rich DeVos has turned handwritten notes of encouragement into an art form. Why an art form, you ask? Because I have one of his notes framed on my wall like an original Picasso! It reads, "Pat, wherever you go, you knock 'em dead, strike 'em out, score big, win with wonder! You're the best! Love ya a lot . . . Rich." I know for a fact that there are scores, if not hundreds of people around the world who have their notes from Rich DeVos in frames on the wall as well.

### 4. When Tempted to Tear Someone Down, Bite Your Tongue

Sometimes, when we are leading, coaching, or managing, we face situations where the temptation to blast a player is almost overwhelming. We want to say, "No, no, not that way—do it *my* way!" Or "You idiot! What were you thinking?" Or "That's it! You're benched!"

When Chuck Daly coached the Magic, he shared with me a lesson he learned in the 1960s as an assistant to Vic Bubas, head basketball coach at Duke. "Vic taught me to bite my tongue,"

Chuck said. "You have to know when to talk to players and when to keep your peace. I learned to ask myself: Will this player benefit from what I say? Or will he just become less coachable? Sometimes I'd put my knuckles in my mouth or just look someplace else—anything to keep from saying what I was thinking."

### 5. Always Be Truthful

Whitey Herzog has held just about every job there is in baseball. He's a big believer in empowerment and in telling the truth. In *You're Missin' a Great Game*, he explains:

> I don't like to get criticized all the time; you don't like to get criticized all the time. I don't care if he's Ozzie Smith or the last guy on the bench, a player wants to be told how good he is. Pat him on the back when you really mean it. He'll play harder for you and make better decisions later on. . . . Managing is building up, not just tearing down. A positive word can be good for everyone.
>
> On the other hand, like I say, every word you speak has to be honest. If there's one rule you should never violate, it's Always Tell The Truth. . . . You'd be surprised how many managers lie to their players. Maybe a guy asks when he's going to be starting; the manager'll say, "sometime soon," or "just keep working at it, we'll see," when he knows perfectly well that ain't the case. Managers are just like everybody else: They might just be avoiding arguments or confrontation. Or maybe they're worried if they tell a guy he's a benchwarmer, he'll go negative and start causing problems. But players ain't stupid; they'll see the writing on the wall, and if you haven't been honest, you're *really* going to have problems. . . . I never once had a player resent me for telling him the truth.[12]

## 6. Say "Thank You"

You'd be amazed how just a simple word of thanks can profoundly affect a player or employee. Let me share two stories.

During the 1950s and 1960s, six-foot-nine Gene Conley pitched for the Phillies, Braves, and Red Sox—and during the off-season, he played backup center for Bill Russell with the Boston Celtics. In fact, he is the only person to win championships in two different professional sports (the 1957 World Series with the Milwaukee Braves and three NBA Championships with the Celtics, 1959, 1960, and 1961).

Gene now lives in the Orlando area, and I once had the privilege of eating lunch with him. We talked about our mutual fascination with baseball and basketball. At one point, I asked Gene, "Who was the most memorable baseball manager you ever played for?"

Without hesitating, he named Eddie Sawyer, who managed the Phillies in 1948–1952 and 1958–1960. Gene added, "Eddie was the kindest man I ever pitched for."

I said, "Do you have an Eddie Sawyer story you can tell me?"

"Sure," Gene said, "but you'll have to excuse me, because I always get kind of emotional when I tell it."

"Gene," I said, "I'd love to hear it."

"Well," he began, "it was 1959 and the Phillies were playing a doubleheader with the Cardinals. I was in the bull pen and it was the bottom of the ninth. The Cardinals had two on and two out, and Stan Musial came up to bat. Eddie went out on the field, removed the pitcher, and waved me in from the bull pen."

I could hear the emotion in Gene's voice. "What happened?" I asked.

"I struck out Stan Musial and we won the game," Gene replied. "As I walked off the field, Eddie was standing in the dugout. He shook my hand and said, 'Thanks a lot, Gene. I appreciate that.'"

And Gene dabbed at his eyes with the table napkin.

I sat there for a moment, waiting for the rest of the story—but there was none. That was it: a handshake and a thank-you. After all these years, Gene Conley was choked up over a handshake and a thank-you.

Then it hit me: what a powerful story! Forty-five seconds later, Eddie Sawyer probably forgot all about it. But Gene Conley remembered those words *forty-five years* later—and he got all choked up about it! It really doesn't take much to make a lifelong impression on others.

Second story: Paul Wiggin spent eleven years as a defensive end with the Cleveland Browns. He retired in 1967, having never missed a game. He told sportswriter Tony Grossi about his "love-hate relationship" with his coach, Paul Brown:

> I don't know that I ever hated anybody, but if I ever disliked somebody it was Paul Brown. . . . But one time after a game, Paul Brown put his hand on my shoulder and said, "Thanks." I had tears in my eyes. That was one of the most meaningful things. If I live to be a hundred, I'll never forget that. What that told me was he was special in my life. I vividly remember telling my wife that I didn't want to play for anybody else.
>
> He didn't want you to like him when you play for him. Then, when you retire and you're not there anymore and you need anything, Paul Brown was always there for you, like you wouldn't believe.[13]

Did you grasp the incredible thing Paul Wiggin said? His coach put his hand on Wiggin's shoulder and said one word—*one word*! And that word was "Thanks." Not only did that word of thanks bring tears to Wiggin's eyes, but he said, "If I live to be a hundred, I'll never forget that."

So if you want to empower your players to achieve your extreme dream, don't forget to say, "Thanks."

### 7. Don't Dispense Empty Praise

When you encourage and affirm your players, make it meaningful and specific. Avoid generic praise ("Nice job"). Instead, give specific examples of actions or attitudes that impressed you.

Avoid "backhanded compliments." Instead of saying, "I didn't know you had it in you," or "I was pleasantly surprised by the report you turned in" (suggesting that you never had any confidence in that person to begin with), say, "I *knew* you could do great work, but this is even better than I expected!" Pile positives on top of positives.

Encouragement must be sincere. If people get the idea that your praise is insincere flattery, it will lose its impact. Fred Smith Sr. explains:

> Compliments are so valuable they should be used sparingly in order to remain valuable. Nothing was more disturbing to me than to be paired in a round of golf with an overly courteous individual who complimented my every shot—good, bad, and mediocre. He insulted my intelligence, as if I didn't know when I had made a good or bad shot.
>
> Charles Pitts was an excellent golfer who complimented only "a golf shot." I can remember well on the ninth hole when I hit a ball with an eight iron—high over a tree—that landed reasonably close to the pin. He walked across the fairway, shook hands with me, and said, "That's a golf shot." He knew how to keep his compliments valuable.[14]

## 8. Remember—Everybody Needs Encouragement from Time to Time

We never outgrow our need for affirmation. I vividly remember an incident in November 1999. The Magic was playing a home game against Cleveland. Just before game time, I walked by our new coach, Doc Rivers, as he was heading out to the court to coach the very first professional game of his career. He called to me and said, "I saw you and your wife out running the other day."

I said, "Ruth and I are getting ready to run the New York Marathon on Sunday."

"Awesome! Well, have a great time in New York."

"We will," I said. "Have a great game!"

The next day, Saturday, Ruth and I flew to New York. It was a beautiful fall day and we had lunch at Mickey Mantle's Restaurant. Then we walked to the marathon headquarters, then to the NBA store and Barnes & Noble on Fifth Avenue. That night, we had dinner at La Rivista and saw *Annie Get Your Gun* on Broadway. We returned to our hotel room at 11:00 p.m.— and there, in the room, was a fruit basket with a card that read, "Good luck in the marathon. —Doc Rivers."

I hadn't even told him where we were staying—he'd gone to the trouble of finding out. That message of encouragement meant a lot to us both—and it was like the wind in our sails as we ran the marathon the following day.

One of the most fascinating friendships of the nineteenth century was that of novelist Mark Twain and former U.S. president Ulysses S. Grant. Twain co-owned a publishing company, and one of the first projects he acquired was *The Personal Memoirs of Ulysses S. Grant*, which President Grant was writing while dying of throat cancer in 1885.

In *Grant and Twain: The Story of a Friendship That Changed*

*America*, historian Mark Perry tells of Grant's race against time to complete his memoirs. Perry wrote that Twain "believed that Grant's personal resources and deep internal strength would see him through to the end. . . . More important, Grant had proven that he was capable of writing well, even brilliantly"—so brilliantly that Twain didn't edit one word.[15]

Grant sent the chapters to Twain as he wrote them, and Twain had them typeset so Grant could check the proofs for typesetting errors. Twain brought the proofs to Grant's home and the two men talked. "Sometimes I referred to the proofs casually," Twain said, "but entered into no particulars concerning them."[16]

Mark Twain didn't realize that Grant was bothered by Twain's silence. The former president became convinced that the reason Twain made no comment about his writing was that it was not good. Finally, Grant's son, Frederick, went to Twain and confided his father's insecurities.

"Twain was surprised by the comment," Mark Perry writes. "It had never occurred to him that someone as seemingly stolid and self-confident as Grant . . . could remain so uncertain about a task that was nothing as compared to routing Lee's army or running for president. . . . A comment from Twain, Fred suggested, would boost his father's confidence, and it would steel him for the difficult weeks ahead."[17]

So Twain went to Grant and told him what he needed to hear—the truth. Twain honestly believed that Grant's memoirs ranked with the memoirs of Julius Caesar, and he was able to tell Grant in all sincerity that, like Caesar's work, Grant's memoirs were distinguished by their "clarity of statement, directness, simplicity, unpretentiousness, manifest truthfulness, fairness and justice toward friend and foe alike, soldierly candor and frankness and soldierly avoidance of flowery speech."[18]

Though late in coming, that statement of high praise from Mark Twain was a huge encouragement to Grant. It gave the old general the inspiration and energy he needed to complete his memoirs. Grant completed his manuscript on July 18, 1885—five days before his death.

In his own modest way, Twain concluded this experience showed that Grant was "just a man, just a human being, just an author. An author values a compliment even when it comes from a source of doubtful competency."[19] No matter how accomplished or successful, everybody needs the empowerment of encouragement.

## A LESSON IN EMPOWERMENT

Years ago, I received a letter from radio executive John DiPietro of Worcester, Massachusetts. John told me an inspiring story about empowerment. Here, slightly condensed, is what John wrote:

Pat,

Thanks to a talk you gave in Worcester, Massachusetts, I've had the opportunity to uplift the attitudes of ten teenage girls—and I've watched them become champions! Last November, my thirteen-year-old daughter asked me to coach her basketball team. Honored, I accepted.

I remembered a story you told about a college football player who kicked a 52-yard field goal to win the game. Afterwards, his coach said, "You got lucky." The player was devastated and never recovered from that comment. Hearing that story, I thought, "Wow! Coaches and parents have incredible power to affect young lives!" I vowed never to speak a harsh or hurtful word to the kids on my team.

At our first practice, I discovered that some of my players had never even dribbled a basketball before. I told them we were going to focus on being positive. If one player yelled at another for a mistake, the one who yelled would be pulled from the game. We would be a team of encouragers.

The season began and our first game was, well, a character-building experience. We played the strongest team in our league—and they hammered us! It was so bad that two of my players begged me to take them out of the game. We went on to lose four of our first seven games.

In practice, I stressed positive attitude. I taught the players to visualize their free throws going through the hoop. The focus on positive attitude transformed them into believers—and we won the next seven games in a row.

We battled through the playoffs and beat teams that had beaten us in the regular season. Finally, we made it to the championship game against the team that had demolished us in our season opener. Just before the game, two of my players came up to me and their eyes were wide with amazement. They said, "We just talked to some girls from the other team—and they said there's no way *they* can beat *us*!"

Before the game, I gathered our players at the foul line and said, "When we have one minute left to play, we'll be up by twelve points and I'm going to call a timeout. And we'll stand on this spot and give thanks for our effort and for this team."

Then we started the game.

Our opponents scored first—but then our kids took over. At the end of the first quarter, we were up 16-4. At halftime, 23-9. End of the third, up by 20. Some of our kids who had never scored all season were putting up twenty-footers and getting nothing but net!

I called a timeout with 1:22 to go. We gathered at the foul line and I pointed to the scoreboard. I said, "I promised we'd be up by twelve. I was wrong. We're up by twenty-five!" We finished the game, we celebrated, and we went out for pizza.

Thank you, Pat, for reminding me to always encourage and empower my players. There's no doubt in my mind that it was our teamwork, confidence, and positive attitude that made the difference. When you talk to an audience, you never know the effect you'll have. But let me tell you—you sure reached me!

A million thanks!
John DiPietro

I get goose bumps reading those words. That's the power of teamwork—and that's the *power* of empowerment!

# Extreme *Cosmic* Dreams . . .

## *Depend on Teams*

*When you look at the stars and the galaxy, you feel that you are not just from any particular piece of land, but from the solar system.*

KALPANA CHAWLA, space
shuttle astronaut[1]

Friends called her K.C.

Her name, Kalpana Chawla, was not all that easy for her fellow space shuttle astronauts to pronounce. Perhaps a phonetic spelling will help: *CULL-puh-na CHAV-la.*

It's a beautiful name. In the Sanskrit language of ancient India, *kalpana* means "imagination, fantasy, a dream almost too beautiful and impossible to attain."[2] In other words, Kalpana Chawla's name means "Extreme Dream."

On February 1, 2003, she was living out her extreme cosmic dream, returning to earth after a successful mission aboard the space shuttle *Columbia*. It was her second trip aboard *Columbia*, and she had spent sixteen days in space as part of a seven-member crew, helping to carry out some eighty scientific experiments.

But just sixteen minutes from *Columbia*'s scheduled landing at Kennedy Space Center, something went horribly wrong. Flying two hundred thousand feet over Texas at a speed of 12,500 miles per hour, the shuttle broke apart. In its death throes, the disintegrating craft streaked across the sky like a swarm of meteors.

Dr. Kalpana Chawla died, and so did her six teammates—Rick D. Husband, William McCool, Michael P. Anderson, David M. Brown, Laurel Clark, and Ilan Ramon. They joined the crews of Apollo 1 and the space shuttle *Challenger*—courageous teams of astronauts who perished in the pursuit of the extreme dream of human spaceflight.

Who was Kalpana Chawla—this brave soul whose very name spoke of extreme and beautiful dreams?

## "Resign—and Come Back Home"

Kalpana Chawla was born in 1961 in Karnal, Haryana, northern India. Her father settled there in 1947 after fleeing the mass slaughter in Lahore during the Partition, when Muslim Pakistan was carved out of the Hindu nation of India. There were occasional brushfire wars between India and Pakistan during Kalpana's childhood. She recalled air-raid sirens and hiding in ditches near her house until the planes flew away.

Though Kalpana's father had come to Karnal as a refugee, he prospered as the owner of a tire-manufacturing business called Super Tyres. Mr. Chawla had a natural gift for mechanical engineering, and Kalpana inherited her father's engineering aptitude, earning a degree in aeronautical engineering at Punjab Engineering College in Chandigarh. The college offered her a teaching position—but Kalpana dreamed of going into space.

Her problem: how to explain her dreams to her father, who expected her to join him in the family business. She recalled:

> *I don't know why I always liked aerospace engineering. I was in tenth grade when I figured out what I wanted to do. My dad had a rubber tire manufacturing plant and he said, "Oh, you should be a doctor or a teacher, those are much more respectable professions. Why do you want to do this? Mostly guys want to do it." But I said this is what I really want to do. By the time I was in twelfth grade, I applied to engineering schools, and my mom volunteered to go with me for the interviews. The professor said, "Why do you want to do aerospace engineering? Electronics is more ladylike." So again, the same arguments, "This is what I really want to do."*[3]

In 1982, Kalpana applied to a master's program at the University of Texas at Arlington. When her letter of acceptance came, her father was on a two-month business trip in the United States. He had already refused permission for her to attend a flight school in India. What would he think if she told him she wanted to study in the USA? Kalpana could not attend the University of Texas without her father's permission. So, while waiting for him to return from America, she accepted the teaching position at Punjab.

When Mr. Chawla returned home, his wife confronted

him. She told him that his daughter had dreams of going to America, dreams of going into space. It was time he started supporting Kalpana's dreams—and there was no time to lose. It was August 26—and the deadline for admission to the University of Texas was August 31. To his credit, Mr. Chawla—who had always resisted Kalpana's dreams—finally surrendered. He decided to join his daughter's team and help her achieve her dreams.

He went to Chandigarh and found his daughter teaching at the college. He said, "Kalpana, do you want to go to the USA?"

"Yes," Kalpana said. "I'll earn the money myself and pay my own way."

"I will pay your way," Mr. Chawla said.

"It's too late," Kalpana said. "I have no passport, no visa, nothing—and there's not enough time to get them now. I'll have to wait until next year."

"Leave that to me," Mr. Chawla said. "Resign your teaching job and come back home with me."[4]

## From India to the Stars

Kalpana feared that her father's offer was a trick. Once he had her back home in Karnal, she thought, he wouldn't let her leave. But she soon found that he was sincere. Mr. Chawla used his business connections to expedite his daughter's passport and visa applications. He arranged for Kalpana to take a British Airways flight to America, accompanied by her brother Sanjay. If there were no delays, she would arrive at the University of Texas just under the deadline.

But not only was the flight delayed—it was canceled. So Mr. Chawla called some business friends in America, and they contacted the university and arranged a deadline extension. The university even sent a delegation to meet Kalpana and Sanjay at the airport when they arrived.

Kalpana never got over the amazement that her father—who had opposed her dreams for years—suddenly became her teammate in helping her go to America and live out the meaning of that beautiful Sanskrit word *kalpana*. She earned two master of science degrees in 1984 and 1986, then a PhD in aerospace engineering in 1988 from the University of Colorado at Boulder. She went to work at NASA's Ames Research Center and became a certified flight instructor. Kalpana married aviation writer Jean-Pierre Harrison in 1983 and became a naturalized U.S. citizen in 1990. She applied to the astronaut program and was accepted as a member of the shuttle team in 1994.

It was important to Kalpana that she maintain ties with her homeland. At her urging, NASA began an annual tradition of bringing two students from her high school in Karnal to Houston for a summer space experience program. Each year, Dr. Kalpana Chawla would have the students visit for a home-cooked Indian meal. One student, a young woman named Neha Sharma, recalled her advice: "Whatever you believe in, do. Just follow your dreams. Don't worry about whether people encourage you or not."[5]

That's how Kalpana Chawla lived—following her dreams. And that's how she died. Her flight path took her far from a town in northern India to a place among the stars. She was living her extreme dream when she died, part of a NASA team that continues to reach for the stars. And even in death, she continues to inspire the dreams of others.

"Next year I want to do engineering," Neha Sharma said of her college plans, adding that Kalpana Chawla is "a role model" and that she "cannot die."[6]

## When One Teammate Falls . . .

Within hours of the loss of *Columbia*, shuttle program manager Ron Dittemore told reporters that the seven souls who vanished from the skies that day were not just colleagues. They were teammates and family members. Dittemore said:

*Human space flight is a passion. It's an emotional event. And when we work together, we work together as family members. And we treat each other much that way. And whether it's the loss of a crew member or a loss of a member of our ground team or processing teams, it's a sad loss for us. And so we are a very close community. We understand the risks that are involved in human space flight. And we know that these risks are manageable, but we also know that they're serious and can have deadly consequences.*

*And so we are bound together with the threat of disaster all the time, and we know we must count on each other to do what's right. We must count on the ground teams to process correctly. We must count on our suppliers to follow the procedures, just like we have identified to them. And we count on the flight crew members to fly the vehicles within the specifications.*

*We all rely on each other to make each space flight successful. . . . So, when we have an event like today where we lose seven family members, it is devastating to us.*[7]

These words reflect the passion, the daring, and the intense team spirit that have always been a part of the adventure of human space flight. It's a spirit that President John F. Kennedy proclaimed on May 25, 1961, when he committed America to "achieving the goal, before this decade is out, of landing a man on the Moon and returning him safely to the earth." More than two years later, President Kennedy went to San Antonio, Texas, to dedicate NASA's new Aerospace Medical Health Center. The Center represented a major step toward the goal of reaching the moon. In his dedication speech, he said:

*Frank O'Connor, the Irish writer, tells in one of his books how, as a boy, he and his friends would make their way across the countryside, and when they came to an orchard wall that seemed too high and too doubtful to try and too difficult to permit their voyage to continue, they took off their hats and tossed them over the wall—and then they had no choice but to follow them.*

*This nation has tossed its cap over the wall of space, and we have no choice but to follow it. Whatever the difficulties, they will be overcome.*

*Whatever the hazards, they must be guarded against. With the vital help of this Aerospace Medical Center, with the help of all those who labor in the space endeavor, with the help and support of all Americans, we will climb this wall with safety and with speed—and we shall then explore the wonders on the other side.*[8]

On November 22, 1963, the day after President Kennedy spoke those words, he was in a presidential motorcade in Dallas. As his open limousine passed through Dealey Plaza, shots rang out, ending his life— but not his dream.

The NASA team worked steadily on.

Finally, on July 20, 1969, at 4:18 p.m. eastern daylight time, a strange, ungainly spacecraft settled onto the surface of the moon. From that craft, astronaut Neil Armstrong radioed: "Houston, Tranquility Base here. The Eagle has landed." A short time later, in Arlington National Cemetery, an unknown person left a handwritten note next to the eternal flame over President Kennedy's grave. The note read, "Mr. President, the Eagle has landed."[9]

Our dreamers and heroes soar skyward—and sometimes they die. But the passion of human spaceflight remains. When one teammate falls, another steps up, ready to continue the journey to the stars.

The extreme dream of humanity in space goes on.

# 9

# Principle 7: Respect and Trust Build Extreme Dreams

The person on your left or your right might be the person who saves your life. . . . We *must* have mutual respect for each other.

AN UNNAMED COAST GUARD
COMPANY COMMANDER,
Coast Guard training facility,
Cape May, New Jersey[1]

JÜRGEN SCHREMPP, FORMER CEO OF THE CAR conglomerate DaimlerChrysler, has a reputation for going to extremes.

He once climbed the peak known as König Ortler, a 12,812-foot mountain in the Italian Alps. His teammate for that climb was mountaineer Reinhold Messner, who once reached the summit of Mount Everest without oxygen tanks. During their climb together, Schrempp was descending a rock wall when he realized he had no handhold or foothold. The next ledge was a long way down.

Schrempp peered up at Messner, who stood on the ledge above him. "Reinhold," he said, "I'm stuck! What would happen if I fell?" Messner gripped the rope that tethered them together.

"You're tied on to me," the mountaineer said. "I'd catch you and lower you safely down."[2]

Schrempp nodded—then jumped.

Messner hadn't expected such an immediate and trusting response!

But the rope held—and Messner lowered Schrempp safely to the ledge below.

That's trust. That's precisely the level of unquestioning trust that teams must have in order to achieve extreme dreams. Great teams are composed of players who respect and trust one another. Respect leads to trust, and trust produces teamwork.

To respect someone is to show honor or consideration toward that person. It doesn't mean you necessarily *like* that person. You can respect people you dislike and disagree with. You can even respect an opponent.

You can respect the president and other national leaders, even if you disagree with their actions and policies. You can respect the police officer who pulled you over, even if you don't think you deserve the ticket. You can respect your coach, even if you think he's overbearing and unfair and doesn't know his Xs from his Os.

Without a basic level of respect, societies can't function. One of the most corrosive forces in society today is the breakdown of respect between people of opposing viewpoints. Our diversity is our greatest strength—*but only if we maintain a unity of mutual respect*. If respect breaks down, our diversity can destroy us. C. William Pollard, chairman of the ServiceMaster Company, put it this way: "Diversity without unity makes about as much sense as dishing up flour, sugar, water, eggs, shortening, and baking powder on a plate and calling it a cake."[3]

Respect is a kind of unconditional acceptance that we demonstrate to one another in order to turn a heterogeneous collection of individuals into a team. Without respect, teams can't function. The purpose of teamwork is *not* to make everyone on the team think alike. Teamwork respects the differences between people while enabling them to transcend their differences and unite behind a common purpose.

Players can argue with one another and contend long and hard for their points of view. But if the members of a team cannot *respect* one another amid their differences, then teamwork breaks down.

## THE RULES OF RESPECT

We owe a measure of respect to every human being we meet, whether that person is the pope or the president or a panhandler on the street. And let's face it: there are some people who have earned an extra measure of respect—for example, those who have sacrificed to serve in our armed forces. You don't have to like your teammate or socialize with him—but you must respect his right to be on the team with you. By respecting and trusting one another, teammates lift each other up and help each other to achieve heights of success that they could never achieve alone.

UCLA basketball coach John Wooden taught his players to respect themselves and to show respect to others wherever they went. His players demonstrated respect through cleanliness and courtesy. Coach Wooden once told a reporter:

> I like to make spot checks on lockers and see they're not getting slovenly. Wherever we are, we will leave our dressing rooms every bit as neat as when we came in. There will be no gum wrappers on the floor. No tape scattered around. No orange peels. They'll all be placed in a container. And I don't expect our manager to be the pick-up man. Our players understand this.
>
> I help. If I start picking things up, the players soon join

in. We'll have equipment managers around the country tell us no one leaves the dressing room like we do. Well, I think that's part of better basketball. Now I'd have a hard time proving that, but I think it is. I think it gives us a little more unity, a sense of doing things together, of showing consideration for the other fellow. The waitress at the hotel here said this was the finest, best-behaved group of athletes she's had. Our players complimented her on the way she'd been serving them. She could hardly believe it.[4]

Coach Wooden's goal in teaching his players to respect themselves and others was to produce a unified team, with every individual focused on a common goal. Every year, he gave his team a list that he called "Normal Expectations." It was a very short list, consisting of only three rules of respect: "Be on time, do not use profanity at any time, and never criticize a teammate." Coach Wooden concluded:

I make no threats. All I have is a list of expectations. Also, I tell our players, "When you come to practice, you cease to exist as an individual. You're part of a team." Sure, some players might say I'm harsh, but look at it another way. They're looked up to by others and receive a great deal of adulation. Is that a hardship? They're getting a grant-in-aid for their college education. Is that really a hardship?[5]

When Doc Rivers coached the Magic, he had four "Respect Rules" that he preached to the team. Now that he is head coach of the 2008 World Champion Boston Celtics, I'm confident those rules have not changed at all. They are: "Respect your teammates. Respect your coaches. Respect yourself. Respect your family's name."

Those are four simple but powerful rules to live by. If you respect your teammates, you'll have unity on the team. If you respect your coaches, you'll have harmony on the team. If you respect yourself, you'll have dignity wherever you go. And if you respect your family's name, you'll have a reputation to be proud of the rest of your life.

Derek Jeter is a nine-time All-Star shortstop who has spent his entire career with the New York Yankees. He's well known for his polite and respectful manner, addressing coaches and managers as "Mr." or "sir." His father, psychologist Charles Jeter, taught him early in life to be respectful toward others. Once, when young Derek was in Little League and refused to shake hands with his opponents after losing a game, Charles told his son, "It's time to grab a tennis racket, since you don't know how to play a team sport."[6]

That lesson in respect stuck with Derek Jeter and continues to influence his behavior to this day. On one occasion during Jeter's rookie days, retired veteran shortstop Gene "Stick" Michael was chatting with Jeter. Stick suggested that, once the big money started rolling in, Jeter would get a swelled head and become as disrespectful as other young players in the game. "Aww, Stick," Jeter replied, "that'll never happen to me. My dad would kill me!"[7]

## RESPECT THE GAME

There's a phrase commonly heard in the sports world: "Respect the game." This is an important concept in teamwork, and I would love to see teams in other fields of endeavor—business, the military, the government, social service, and so forth—apply this concept to their teamwork situations. Every teamwork arena is a field of competition—a game with its own rules, history, traditions, and code of honor. So it's reasonable and ennobling to consider ourselves as competitors in, say, the game of commerce, or the game of governance, or the game of service to God and humankind. Whatever "game" we're engaged in, we need to respect it.

In 2002, Tom Kelly stepped down as manager of the Minnesota Twins. His replacement was an old friend of mine, Ron Gardenhire. I was president of the Twins AA affiliate in Orlando when Ron managed the club in 1990 and lived in our guesthouse. In an interview with Gardenhire, *USA Today* asked, "What lessons did you learn working under Tom Kelly?" Gardenhire replied,

> Make sure that you always respect the game—and that your players respect the game. You can't believe how many speeches I've heard from Tom Kelly talking about respecting the game. When I first heard it, I said: "Let's think about that. What does he mean, respect the game?" Well, now I know what it means. It's about going out and never leaving anything behind. You go out, don't take the game for granted or it will kick you right in the butt—guaranteed, it will. . . . You give everything you have that day.[8]

Former second baseman Ryne Sandberg spent most of his career with the Chicago Cubs and is one of the best second basemen of all time. His .989 career fielding percentage is a major-league baseball record for second base. When "Ryno" was inducted into the Baseball Hall of Fame, July 31, 2005, the theme of his speech was respect—especially respect for the game. Here are some excerpts:

> The reason I am here, they tell me, is that I played the game a certain way, that I played the game the way it was supposed to be played. I don't know about that, but

I do know this: I had too much respect for the game to play it any other way, and if there was a single reason I am here today, it is because of one word, respect. I love to play baseball. I'm a baseball player. I've always been a baseball player. I'm still a baseball player. That's who I am. . . .

If you played the game the right way, played the game for the team, good things would happen. That's what I loved most about the game, how a ground out to second with a man on second and nobody out was a great thing. Respect.

The fourth major league game I ever saw in person, I was in uniform. Yes, I was in awe. I was in awe every time I walked on to the field. That's respect. I was taught you never, ever disrespect your opponent or your teammates or your organization or your manager and never, ever your uniform. . . .

I wish you all could feel what I feel standing here. This is my last big game. This is my last big at-bat. This is my last time catching the final out. I dreamed of this as a child but I had too much respect for baseball to think this was ever possible. I believe it is because I had so much respect for the game and respect for getting the most out of my ability that I stand here today. I hope others in the future will know this feeling for the same reason: Respect for the game of baseball. When we all played it, it was mandatory. It's something I hope we will one day see again.

Thank you, and go Cubs.[9]

In a 1999 essay, Lakers head coach Phil Jackson reflected on the passing of his former coach, Red Holzman (1920–1998). "Red was my coach with the Knicks," Jackson wrote, "the man who led us to NBA titles in '70 and '73, and a person for whom I had tremendous respect. He was such a great guy, such a great competitor with a true respect for his opponents."[10] Respect for opponents is a major part of respect for the game.

Another aspect of respect for the game is respect for your teammates—whether you like them or not. "I've never felt it was necessary for players to like each other, to be best friends," Jackson reflected. "People are so different. Basketball puts talented players together, not people who are the same. What you must have, though, is respect for the game and trust in each other."[11]

One of Phil Jackson's teammates on the New York Knicks was Walt Frazier, a legendary point guard who enjoyed a long career with the Knicks and Cavaliers. Nicknamed "Clyde" because he wore a hat like that of Clyde Barrow (Warren Beatty) in the movie *Bonnie and Clyde*, Frazier pioneered the art of the steal. In his book *The Game Within the Game*, Frazier agrees with Phil Jackson's view of Red Holzman:

> Discipline and respect were the keys to Red's success as a coach. . . . Red demanded that we respect the team rules, our teammates, and our opponents. Red was old-school all the way.
>
> He didn't want anyone to trash-talk or disrespect the other team in any way. I remember one night and again right before the playoffs, we had already clinched the regular season and I didn't want to play, but Red took me aside and said, "Clyde, you've got to go out there and play for at least a half because the other team expects you to go out there and play. Don't show them up."
>
> Players need to respect themselves first and then give respect to their teammates, coaches, opponents, and referees. They need to respect the fans because without their support, there is no NBA. They need to respect the game and its history. . . . When a player has no respect for himself, his team, or the league, mayhem will certainly follow.[12]

Respect for the game encompasses all other forms of respect. Respect for the game is essential to teamwork.

## HOW TO EARN RESPECT

You can't *demand* respect, but you can *command* respect by earning it. Longtime Ohio State football coach Woody Hayes said: "Lots of people will try to beat you. Make them respect you by what you do."[13] Good advice.

Coaches and other leaders are owed respect, simply because of the position they hold. That's the ideal. Now, here's the reality: leaders probably won't gain the respect of their followers until they have earned it by virtue of their character, their judgment, and their record of results.

Don Shula coached the Miami Dolphins to two Super Bowl victories, including the only undefeated season of the post-AFL/NFL merger era. Shula holds the record for most career wins in the NFL with 347. He once explained the difference between being liked and being respected as a coach:

Lots of leaders want to be popular, but I never cared about that. I want to be respected. Respect is different from popularity. You can't make it happen or demand it from people. The only way you can get it is to earn it. Not by talking, but by doing things that make sense to your team.

They [the players] don't even have to like what you do in order to respect and follow it. The fact that you, as a coach, are asking performers to go beyond themselves, to push their limits, will automatically mean that you'll be doing unpopular things. If what you are after is being liked, that's going to dictate how hard you push; you won't want to offend anybody or get them mad at you. As soon as that happens, there goes your effectiveness—and respect, as well.[14]

One sports leader who commanded respect but couldn't care less about being liked was Leo Durocher (1905–1991). Durocher accumulated 2,009 career victories as a manager by the time he retired. Loud, abrasive, and controversial, "Leo the Lip" also amassed a career record of ninety-five ejections. Some players loved him, a few hated him, but almost all respected him. Bobby Bragan, who played for Durocher with the Brooklyn Dodgers, reported: "He was so knowledgeable and so adept at making the right moves that he just forced you to respect him, which was all he wanted."[15]

And then there's Yogi Berra, probably the most beloved and respected figure in major-league baseball in the past half century. As a catcher with the Yankees, he was named American League MVP three times and is one of only six MLB managers to lead both American and National League teams to the World Series. He is famous far beyond the world of baseball for his entertaining ability to mangle the English language. In his book, *What Time Is It? You Mean Now?* he says, "There's so much to respect in baseball. You have to respect the rules, the traditions, the history, the people dedicated to it."[16] He goes on to lament the breakdown of respect in society and the sports world:

> I don't know if respect is going out of fashion, but sometimes it's not so popular. Look at some of your older people, sometimes they get treated pretty rude. Look at political campaigns—try to remember the last one that wasn't nasty or negative. Even in sports now, guys talk junk or waggle their fingers or strut around like roosters. Where'd the respect go? I don't know. . . .[17]

It does indeed seem that respect is breaking down in our society. Perhaps the key to restoring an old-fashioned sense of respect lies in rebuilding a foundation of teamwork throughout society. Respect is essential to teamwork and to leadership. Sometimes, the ability to command respect is the key to survival in desperate situations.

Richard Winters enlisted in the United States Army in 1941. He attended Officer Candidate School (OCS) at Fort Benning, Georgia, graduating with a commission as a second lieutenant. Assigned to Easy Company of the 101st Airborne Division, he deployed to England in September 1943.

The commanding officer of Easy Company, Captain Sobel, led by bullying and intimidation. "It is impossible to imagine," Winters later reflected, "what would have been the result if we had been led into battle by Sobel. He had driven the men to the point of mutiny, and, more important, he had lost their respect."[18]

So Second Lieutenant Winters was greatly relieved when Captain Sobel was replaced by First Lieutenant Thomas Meehan III shortly before D-Day. Hours before the invasion of Normandy began, C-47 transports and gliders crossed the English Channel at night and dropped paratroopers of the 82nd and 101st Airborne Divisions into France. A combination of darkness and pilot inexperience caused many paratroopers to land far from their drop zones. Many were killed or captured.

One of the first paratroopers killed was Lieutenant Meehan, the commander of Easy Company. Second Lieutenant Winters landed near Sainte-Mère-Église and gathered all the other paratroopers he could find. When he saw that Lieutenant Meehan was not among them, Winters became the de facto commanding officer of Easy Company—a mere handful of men.

Winters led his men to the village of Le Grand-Chemin, where members of the Second Battalion had gathered. A captain from Second Battalion called Winters aside and said, "There's fire along that hedgerow there. Take care of it." Winters later recalled, "That was it. There was no elaborate plan or briefing. . . . I had to quickly develop a plan from there."[19]

Lieutenant Winters and his men scouted the area and found that the "fire along that hedgerow" came from a battery of four 105 mm guns located at a family farm called Brécourt Manor. The guns were connected by trenches and defended by a series of machine-gun nests. The entire emplacement was manned by a platoon of German soldiers—roughly fifty men. Taking out the gun battery looked like a suicide mission. But the guns were raining artillery fire upon the causeway leading away from Utah Beach. The Army's Fourth Infantry Division was pinned down on the beach and couldn't move inland until the guns were taken out.

The captain who ordered Winters to "take care of it" was under the impression that Winters commanded a full company—seventy-five soldiers or more. He had no idea that Easy Company consisted of Winters and a dozen other men. Winters gathered his men and planned the assault.

He ordered two machine guns set up as bases of fire. He sent one man up a tree to reconnoiter. He assigned three men to take out one of the German machine-gun nests with hand grenades. Winters himself would lead a group right into the enemy-occupied trench system. When the order was given, the attack began.

The German soldiers manning the first 105 mm gun were so unnerved when the attack began that they abandoned their position. The Germans retreated through the trenches and some jumped out and ran into the open fields, where they were mowed down by American gunfire. Winters, down in the trench, saw two German soldiers setting up a machine gun. He opened fire, wounding both and knocking out the machine gun.

Leaving three soldiers to hold the first 105, Lieutenant Winters led an assault on the second 105. Winters and his men quickly killed or captured the crew of the second gun. Moments later, soldiers from the Second Battalion arrived, bringing incendiary grenades. The third and fourth guns were captured and, at Winters's orders, all four guns were destroyed with explosives.

Lieutenant Winters lost only one man of his original thirteen-man team—and his unit killed or captured an entire fifty-man platoon. He had silenced the guns of Brécourt Manor. He recalled, "It was only later, much later, that I realized how important knocking out those guns had been to our securing Causeway 2, which became the main causeway for troops coming off Utah Beach."[20]

This incident, now known as the "Brécourt Manor Assault," is studied in textbooks and enacted in training exercises at the United States Military Academy at West Point. It is acclaimed as one of the finest examples of a small, outnumbered team of soldiers overwhelming an entrenched enemy force.

The assault at Brécourt Manor was just the beginning. In the Netherlands in September 1944, Richard Winters—now a captain—led a twenty-man detachment from Easy Company and killed or captured two hundred enemy soldiers. Three months later, the Germans launched a counteroffensive in Belgium. Captain Winters and Easy Company held off several elite divisions of the German army for a full week until the American Third Army broke through the German line. Winters was promoted to major following that battle—now known as the Battle of the Bulge.

Years later, Major Richard Winters was asked what one quality makes a soldier a leader in a time of war. His answer boils down to one word: *respect*. He said:

> Does the individual have the respect of the men? How do you get the respect of the men? By living with them, being a part of it, being able to understand what they are

going through and not to separate yourself from them. You have to know your men. You have to gain their confidence. . . .

If you have character, that means the guy you are dealing with can trust you . . . [and he will] obey right now, no questions asked.

You get it done by making a decision quick, getting to it and getting the thing done. Don't sit back and let the other guy make a decision that will put you on the defensive. Make up your mind quickly and get it done, right or wrong.[21]

After the war, one of Winters's men from Easy Company, Sergeant Floyd Talbert, wrote these respectful words to Winters:

Dick, you are loved and will never be forgotten by any soldier that ever served under you or, I should say, with you, because that is the way you live. You are to me the greatest soldier I could ever hope to meet. . . . Well, you know now why I would follow you into hell. When I was with you, I knew everything was absolutely under control.[22]

Such words mean more than any medal. These are words of respect.

## A MUTUAL BOND OF TRUST

The late broadcasting pioneer Roone Arledge (1931–2002) was a key figure in the rise of the American Broadcasting Company (ABC). In his memoirs, he told how he got his first job in broadcasting. In 1952, after receiving his bachelor's degree in liberal arts at Columbia University, Arledge enrolled in a graduate program at Columbia. Between terms, he worked as a headwaiter at the Wayside Inn in Chatham, Massachusetts.

One Sunday evening, late in the tourist season, Arledge and the staff were closing the dining room at the Wayside Inn. A car pulled up and a tired-looking family piled out. They had spent hours in bumper-to-bumper traffic and the children were hungry. The father asked if the inn staff could reopen the dining room. The hostess refused.

Arledge stepped up and said, "It's okay. I'll wait on them myself." A short time later, the chef set a feast on the table. The family started rushing through dinner. "Relax," Arledge told them. "Take your time and enjoy yourselves."[23]

The father smiled and asked the young man his name. Arledge told him.

Weeks later, Roone Arledge was in New York, looking for employment—preferably something close to the Columbia campus. He learned of an opening at the Manhattan offices of the DuMont Television Network. Now defunct, DuMont was then one of the most powerful broadcasting companies in America.

Arledge applied for a position, and was ushered into the office of DuMont's programming chief, James Cadigan. It was a luxurious suite high in the corporate tower. Mr. Cadigan sat behind his desk, head down, examining Arledge's application for employment. Finally, Cadigan looked up and smiled. "How's everything at the Wayside Inn these days?" he asked. Arledge's jaw dropped when he recognized Mr. Cadigan—the father who had brought his family to the inn several weeks earlier.

"I started work the following Monday," Roone Arledge concluded. "And that was how I began an extraordinary life."[24]

Respect often pays huge dividends. After Roone Arledge went out of his way to show respect to Mr. Cadigan and his family, is it any wonder that Mr. Cadigan wanted this young man on his team?

Respect leads to trust. When you respect your teammates' abilities and character, then you *know* you have teammates you can trust.

Trust leads to loyalty. When you and your teammates earn one another's trust through times of challenge, crisis, adversity, and victory, you forge unbreakable bonds of loyalty. You say to yourself, *I've been through good times and bad times with these teammates. They've never let me down—and I'll never let them down. We're a team.*

Loyalty leads to love. When you and your teammates prove your mutual loyalty to one another, what else can you feel for one another but love?

And love produces team friendships that last a lifetime.

Respect is when we say to our teammates, "You can count on me." Trust is when we say to our teammates, "I can count on you." When players respect one another and trust one another, there is no limit to what they can achieve.

Several years ago, the Dallas Mavericks came to Orlando to play the Magic. Before the game, I ran into Bob Ortegel, the longtime college basketball coach and now a broadcaster for the Mavs. As Bob approached me, his face was alight with excitement, as if he had just discovered the hidden wisdom of the ages. "Pat!" he said. "I've finally figured out basketball!"

"What do you mean, Bob?" I asked.

"If I have the ball and I pass it to you," he said, "I trust you to pass it back to me if I'm more open than you are."

"Okay," I said. "And?"

"That's it!" he said. "That's all there is to basketball!"

I'm sure I must have looked baffled as I walked away—but the more I thought about it, the more I realized that Bob was right. That's really what basketball is all about, in its purest, most essential form. If we as teammates trust one another and play unselfishly, then the one who is open will always take the shot. The teams with the greatest trust usually win. That's the essence of the game of basketball—

And it's the essence of the game of life.

All great teams are made up of people who respect and trust one another. No one goes to the moon unless the team in the spacecraft trusts the team on the ground. No one goes into battle unless the combat team trusts the strategists. No one climbs Everest unless the climbers respect and trust one another.

## TWENTY-FIVE GUYS, TWENTY-FIVE CABS

One of my all-time heroes was Ted Williams (1918–2002). One of the greatest hitters in the history of major-league baseball, Ted spent his entire career with the Boston Red Sox, playing nineteen seasons. He played his first game in 1939 and his last game in 1960. In between, he led the league in batting six times, finished his career with a .344 batting average and 521 home runs, and was the last player to bat over .400 in a season (.406 in 1941). He was a phenomenal talent.

Yet he never won a championship.

In fact, in his entire lifetime, he never even *saw* the Boston Red Sox win the World Series. When he died in 2002, the Red Sox had not won a World Series since 1918, the year of his birth. (Since his death, they have won twice, 2004 and 2007.) Ted Williams played in only one World Series—in 1946, when the Red Sox lost to the St. Louis Cardinals in seven games. How could a team with so much talent on its roster go eighty-six seasons without a championship?

Superstitious souls blamed it on the "Curse of the Bambino," an alleged hex on the Red Sox for having sold Babe Ruth to the New York Yankees in 1919. Well, I don't believe in hexes. Instead, I think the explanation may be found in the words attributed to

Ted Williams many years ago: "twenty-five guys, twenty-five cabs."[25]

What does that mean? It means that the Red Sox were loaded with talent, but lacking in teamwork. Twenty-five talented guys showed up at Fenway Park. They did their jobs, and when the game was over, they left in twenty-five taxicabs. There was no foundation of respect and trust, no loyalty, no love, no friendship, and no sense of *team*.

A similar problem plagued the Red Sox in the 1960s, when Dick O'Connell was the Soxes' general manager. He hired Dick Williams as manager in 1967, and Williams reversed the sliding fortunes of the Red Sox, taking them from a ninth-place finish in 1966 to a pennant in 1967. According to *The Red Sox Encyclopedia*, the players were unhappy with Dick Williams. Chief among the dissidents was outfielder Carl Yastrzemski. Carl and his teammates felt that Williams was disrespectful and overbearing, so they rebelled—and O'Connell was forced to fire Williams. Once more, sportswriters referred to the Red Sox as "twenty-five players who took twenty-five cabs."[26]

In 1973, the Red Sox were again rocked by disharmony. The issue: a lack of respect, leading to a lack of trust. The dispute involved Reggie Smith, who was at odds with his teammates throughout the year. Smith, an African-American, told reporters that the Red Sox had "a code of conduct for white athletes and one for black athletes." He held up a vicious hate letter he received, and talked about the abuse he received from fans, teammates, and the press. "All I ever wanted to do here was my job," Smith said.[27]

Once again, respect and trust had broken down in the Red Sox organization. As Glenn Stout and Richard A. Johnson concluded in their book *Red Sox Century*, "Clubhouse troubles for the team some described as 'twenty-five players who take twenty-five cabs' sank the club."[28]

As late as 1990, *Sports Illustrated* was still bemoaning the Red Sox taxicab woes. Sports columnist Leigh Montville wrote:

> For almost as long as baseball has been played inside the antique, green stadium off Kenmore Square, the knock against this team has been that it is loaded with talent and lacking in certain intestinal virtues. Character? The Red Sox's history has been filled with fat wallets and fatter heads. Twenty-five cabs for twenty-five ballplayers.[29]

When the Red Sox finally ended their eighty-six-year drought, winning the World Series in 2004, many Boston fans said that the "Curse of the Bambino" was finally broken. Nonsense! I think the real reason the Sox finally won a championship was that they learned the meaning of words like *respect* and *trust*.

And maybe, just maybe, they even learned how to carpool.

# Extreme *Healing* Dreams . . .

## *Depend on Teams*

*Just as Kennedy said, "We'll go to the Moon,"
the new president should say, "We'll cure cancer." That's one thing that would not be partisan,
that everybody could get behind.*

KEVIN McCARTHY, congressman
Twenty-second District, California[1]

Jon M. Huntsman stood at the front door of the
Huntsman Cancer Institute at the University of Utah
and welcomed his guest, talk-show host Glenn Beck.
As Beck stepped through the front door of the gleam-
ing, state-of-the-art facility, he gazed in amazement. "I
have never seen a hospital like this!" Beck said.

"This is not just a hospital," Mr. Huntsman replied.
"Hospitals take care of sick people. This place is much
more than that. I'm going to cure cancer—and then I'm
going to turn this building into a Ritz-Carlton Hotel."
Beck laughed, thinking Huntsman was joking. "I'm serious," Jon Huntsman said. "We're going to cure cancer here."[2]

Now, how's *that* for an extreme dream? As Glenn
Beck later said on his radio program, "You know what?
I believe him."[3]

Jon Huntsman has constructed a research center that is second to none—and he's assembled a first-rate team to carry out this mission. The Huntsman Cancer Institute and Hospital is making great strides in identifying the inherited genes that are believed to be responsible for various forms of cancer.

Appearing on Glenn Beck's television talk show on CNN in 2007, Huntsman talked about his cancer research team:

> *We are doubling in size, and we've got to conquer this disease. There are over 200 different types of cancers, and these wonderful people, Dr. Burt, Dr. Beckerle, and their colleagues at other cancer institutes and other places around the country, are working hard to overcome the world's most difficult health problem, which is cancer. . . .*
>
> *I have this great plaque behind my desk, Glenn, and it says: "The greatest exercise for the human heart is to reach down and lift another up." . . . And that's what we're trying to do in cancer [research]. . . . We're going to make a difference.*[4]

The Huntsman Cancer Institute is working to uncover the specific cell mechanisms and individual genes that cause colon cancer, breast cancer, prostate cancer, melanoma, and so forth. Jon Huntsman is personally committed to hunting down and wiping out every form of the disease. You might say that Huntsman has a personal grudge against cancer—and a heart filled with compassion toward those who suffer from the disease. In his book *Winners Never Cheat,* he writes, "My mother, father, and stepmother all died of cancer. I beat the disease twice. It is difficult for me not to become emotional when I greet cancer patients."[5]

Huntsman's mother was diagnosed with cancer when she was in her fifties. Jon administered the shots to control her pain. "I was holding her in my arms when she died," he told Glenn Beck. "She was the sweetest woman. She never said anything negative about anyone, and she died for no reason at all, right in my arms. I said to myself, 'We're going to get rid of this disease. We are going to get rid of this disease no matter what it takes.' "[6]

At the time of his mother's death, Huntsman had never earned more than five hundred dollars a month in his life. He had an extreme dream—but nothing more. He had vowed to put an end to cancer—but without a team to back up his vow, he didn't know where to begin.

### "Jon, You Have Cancer"

Jon Huntsman came from a poor family in rural Idaho. Thanks to the generosity of a wealthy family who invested in his life, he graduated from the Wharton School of Finance in 1959. After service in the U.S. Navy, he pursued a career in the chemical and plastics industry. In 1970, he was appointed by President Nixon to serve in the Department of Health, Education and Welfare and later became a special assistant in the Nixon White House.

He was fifty-four years old in 1991 when his doctor told him he had prostate cancer. He recalls:

> *My bout with cancer left me with greater strength and faith and with an intensified feeling of oneness with my fellow man. It also left me with a vision: I vowed to launch one of the country's preeminent cancer research institutes—a foundation devoted exclusively to helping eradicate the scourge of cancer—all cancers. This was not a fleeting impulse; it was and continues to be a deep passion.*[7]

One year to the day after receiving the diagnosis of prostate cancer, his doctor told him he had a second and unrelated cancer. It was as if cancer were deliberately stalking him, trying to keep him from his mission.

In 1995, Jon Huntsman and the Huntsman family pledged $151 million to construct the Huntsman Cancer Institute, a high-tech cancer research and treatment center. Jon Huntsman's commitment to finding a cure for cancer was severely tested in 2001 when his company faced the threat of bankruptcy, due to the recession. Huntsman decided that bankruptcy was not an option. More important, he had made commitments to charitable organizations, including the Huntsman Cancer Institute. In his interview with Glenn Beck, Huntsman explained:

> *We have the cancer institute. We have centers for abused women and children. We have 5,000 scholarships to underprivileged children. We have*

*programs for the homeless. . . . If we withdrew
these commitments, thousands of people, millions of people would go homeless, would not
have scholarships. So these become vital parts of
our link to integrity and honesty and keeping our
word.*

*So the business was ready to go off the cliff,
and I had to go without a salary and our people
went without bonuses. We had a terrible time
during 2001 and 2002. Energy prices went up.
There was overcapacity. There was a recession,
a perfect storm.*

*The bottom line is that I went to the bank, and
I told Bill Harrison at J. P. Morgan Chase and my
friends at Citibank and my other friends in the
banking business, "I have to take out a loan. I
have to put up my home for collateral. I have
to put up what's left of my company for collateral."*

*They said, "Well, Jon, your business looks
like it might make it. . . ."*

*I said, "No, [this loan] isn't for the business;
this is for charity."*

*They said, "You're crazy! We've never made
a loan to anybody for $50 million, for $75 million, for $100 million so you can turn around and
give it to charity!"*

*I said, "Well, you have to." If people make a
commitment to something as critical as charitable interests, are you going to take away these
scholarships from kids? Are you going to deprive
cancer victims and cancer patients from having
research and proper clinical treatment? I said,*

*"Whatever it takes. Take my business, take my house, but I need the money for charity."*[8]

Jon Huntsman got the loans, kept his word—and paid the loans back.

## A Solemn Duty

Another fan of Jon Huntsman is Fox News business commentator Neil Cavuto. In his book, *More Than Money*, Cavuto writes:

> *A lifelong Republican, Huntsman says he has no problem crossing party lines to fight cancer. The one thing Huntsman wants is more federal matching grants for cancer research, and he'll support anyone, Republican or Democrat, who can deliver the funding. In fact, he's angered some in his own party by saying they are not doing enough in this area of policy, but Huntsman is more interested in his cause than partisanship.*
>
> *That's why this former Nixon White House appointee is happy to work with any Democrat that comes along with a plan to help his cancer efforts. It's Huntsman's not-so-subtle way of pushing both parties to move immediately against what he calls the most lethal scourge in society.*[9]

Neil Cavuto is describing the essence of teamwork: people of diverse viewpoints and backgrounds uniting behind a common goal. That's what the world needs—less party politics and more teamwork. Last time I checked, cancer is pretty much an equal opportunity affliction, attacking liberals and conservatives, Democrats and Republicans, with equal cruelty. Cavuto goes on to say:

> *[Jon Huntsman] doesn't think much of fellow billionaires who wait until they are dead to give their money away. There are too many people in desperate need of help now to justify hoarding vast piles of cash. It's selfish and even unintentionally cruel for billionaires to hang onto their money until death finally loosens their grip. . . .*
>
> *Huntsman hasn't lived his extraordinarily philanthropic life to make a point, but it's there. Anyone, at almost any income level, can give to others—and hopefully they will.*[10]

As Huntsman told Glenn Beck: "Those who are blessed with money have an obligation—no, no, they have a duty. They have a solemn duty in life to give that money back to a better and higher use." Beck asked, "So what's next? Because I know you are donating millions. Are you going to die a broke man?" "I hope so," Jon Huntsman replied. "I came on this earth without a penny, and why not leave that way?"[11]

## "I Will Build You a Shrine"

My friend Dave Thomas, the founder of Wendy's International, had it right when he said, "Teamwork is the starting point for treating people right. . . . The best teams in the world are the ones that help people become better and achieve more than they ever thought they could on their own."[12]

One of Dave Thomas's best friends was a man not unlike Jon Huntsman—a dedicated cancer-fighter named Danny Thomas. Dave Thomas and Danny Thomas were not related, by the way—Danny's original Lebanese name was Amos Alphonsus Muzyad Yaqoob. Danny Thomas, you may recall, was the star of the classic *Make Room for Daddy* TV series and the founder of St. Jude Children's Hospital in Memphis, the most famous research and treatment center in the world for pediatric diseases, especially childhood cancer. After Danny Thomas died in 1991, Dave Thomas paid tribute to him and told his story in an article for *Imprimis* magazine.

In 1943, Danny Thomas was making five dollars a week as a singer and comedian working in small nightclubs. His wife was pregnant, and her uncle urged him to quit show business and join him as a meat-cutter in his butcher shop. Thomas, a devout Catholic, went to church and prayed to Saint Jude for guidance: "Show me my way in life and I will build you a shrine."[13]

A short time later, Danny Thomas got his big break— a booking at Chez Paris in Chicago. Audiences loved him so much that he was held over week after week— for five years. His success at that club led to a career in television. Recalling his promise to Saint Jude, Danny asked a Catholic cardinal what sort of shrine he should build. The cardinal said that the world had plenty of statues, but not enough hospitals for sick children.

So an extreme dream was born. Danny Thomas

made up his mind to build the best children's hospital
the world had ever seen—and he assembled a team
to build his dream. He called upon his entertainer
friends—including Frank Sinatra, Elvis Presley, Dean
Martin, and Milton Berle—to make personal appearances on behalf of the project. He recruited business
leaders around the country to add their fund-raising
efforts to his own. Danny and his wife, Rose Marie
Thomas, got in their car and crisscrossed the country, making personal appearances. Danny began rais-
ing funds and recruiting his research, treatment, and
administrative team in 1957. The hospital opened its
doors in 1962. Dave Thomas described the result of
Danny's efforts:

> *Great names in medicine led the research.*
> *Plenty of impossible things were made pos-*
> *sible because Danny stuck to his mission like a*
> *bulldog. In 1962, only 4 percent of the victims*
> *of acute lymphocytic leukemia survived the dis-*
> *ease; in 1991, 73 percent survived. Only 7 per-*
> *cent of patients with non-Hodgkin lymphoma*
> *recovered; now, about 80 percent do. . . . When*
> *people tell you about the "impossible," just think*
> *of St. Jude's Hospital.*[14]

## A Teamwork Approach

In 1959, Danny visited the Peoria State Hospital for
a meeting with the hospital's superintendent, Dr. Ernest S. Klein, and a St. Jude supporter, Jim Maloof.
The three men stood outside the hospital, posing for

publicity photos, when they heard a boy shout, "Danny Thomas! If you are here, if you're really here, I've got to see you!"[15] Danny looked and saw an eleven-year-old boy in a wheelchair.

He went to the boy and knelt in front of his wheelchair. The boy was blind and trembling due to a form of palsy. His birth name was unknown, but the hospital staff called him Billy Johnson. Abandoned as an infant, blind from birth, Billy had been raised in various institutions.

Billy held an envelope. "Are you really Danny Thomas?" he asked, touching Danny's face. "Yes, son," Danny said. "That's me." The boy pressed the envelope into Danny Thomas's hand. "Take this," he said. "There's seventy-five cents in here. I saved my candy and gum money. I want you to give this to that hospital for the kids." Danny took the envelope and began to cry. Someone who was there said, "Danny Thomas wept as hard as any adult I have ever seen in my life."[16]

Today, Billy Johnson's seventy-five-cent donation is sealed inside the cornerstone of the statue of Saint Jude in front of the hospital. Instead of spending those coins, Danny leveraged that donation. He told the story of Billy Johnson wherever he went, and that story pried open thousands of pocketbooks and checkbooks, helping to raise millions of dollars for St. Jude Hospital. Billy Johnson from Peoria, Illinois, became one of Danny Thomas's teammates in helping to build his extreme dream.

Dave Thomas cited Danny Thomas's example of teamwork as the key to eliminating catastrophic diseases from the human race:

*Danny Thomas's example is worth remembering anytime the temptation arises for "me" to take over "we." Everything that made him a success was based on simple principles:*

*Keep your word. Danny kept his word to God.*

*Let a good cause that's bigger than you take over your life. What is your St. Jude? There ought to be one. Think about it, and support it.*

*Don't get scared by the word impossible. In fact, get together the best talents you can find to tackle the impossible.*

*Do it through people. Danny got people to work together. That's the way it should be, isn't it?*[17]

It is indeed. That's the teamwork approach—and that's how we will one day achieve this extreme dream of ending the scourge of cancer forever.

# 10

# Principle 8: Strong Character Builds Extreme Dreams

Whatever the character traits required for a team to excel, the team leader should be the best example of those traits.

ANTHONY J. LE STORTI, author,
*When You're Asked to Do the Impossible*[1]

IT HAPPENED ON APRIL 8, 1974—AND I WAS THERE!

That was the night of the Braves' home opener with the Dodgers. The great Henry Aaron was making his bid to break Babe Ruth's career home-run record—a record that had stood for thirty-nine years.

In 1973, Hank hit 40 home runs in 392 at-bats, ending the season with 713 homers—one short of Babe Ruth's record. During the off-season, Henry received more than nine hundred thousand letters—and fully one hundred thousand of them were hate letters and death threats. Some small-minded people didn't want to see an African-American surpass Babe Ruth's record. William Leggett of *Sports Illustrated* summed up the situation:

Is this to be the year in which Aaron, at the age of thirty-nine, takes a moon walk above one of the most hallowed individual records in American sport, the 714 home runs hit by George Herman Ruth? Or will it be remembered as the season in which Aaron, the most dignified of athletes, was besieged with hate mail and trapped by the cobwebs and goblins that lurk in baseball's attic? . . .

"It bothers me," says Aaron. "I have seen a President shot and his brother shot. The man who murdered Dr. Martin Luther King is in jail, but that isn't doing Dr. King much good, is it? I have four children and I have to be concerned about their welfare."[2]

The Braves had opened the 1974 season with a three-game road series in Cincinnati. Hank Aaron played in two of those three games, homering in his first at-bat off Reds pitcher Jack Billingham. That home run tied Babe Ruth's record of 714. Now, in the home opener at the Atlanta-Fulton County Stadium, Hank Aaron would need the courage of a Dr. Martin Luther King Jr. just to go out on the diamond and play his game.

I was general manager of the Atlanta Hawks at the time, so I felt fortunate that history would be made right in my own backyard. I was one face in a crowd of 53,775 people, a Braves attendance record. It had rained earlier in the day, so it was muggy and overcast by the time the ump shouted, "Play ball!" Sitting in the stands, I was aware of the tingle of expectation that swept through the crowd—but also a sense of tension.

Hank's first at-bat led off the second inning. He faced Dodgers pitcher Al Downing, a lefthander who claimed this game would be "no different from any other."[3] Downing walked Aaron, drawing a chorus of boos from disgruntled fans who had paid good money to see No. 715 go sailing over the fence.

Aaron's next at-bat came in the fourth inning. After Darrell

Evans got on base due to an error by Dodgers shortstop Bill Russell, Hank stepped up to the plate. Downing tried to keep the ball low—too low. His first pitch kicked up dirt in front of the plate.

Downing's second pitch was a fastball over the middle—higher than he had intended. For Hank, it was a gift.

Aaron took his first swing of the evening—and it was a beauty. I can still hear the sound of Hank Aaron's bat connecting with that ball. In fact, I could feel it in the pit of my stomach. The ball rose, actually seeming to accelerate. It cleared the left-center field fence, over the glove of Dodgers outfielder Bill Buckner—

And the crowd erupted in celebration. Fireworks exploded in midair. Babe Ruth's record was shattered like the sound barrier.

As I watched Hank Aaron round the bases, I saw two young white men jump from the stands and run straight toward Hank. My heart was in my throat. Were these two of the people who had threatened Hank? Then I saw them celebrating and waving him on around the bases.

Aaron's teammates poured onto the field, whooping and cheering. And amid all those big, burly Atlanta ballplayers, I saw one small African-American woman in her late sixties. She ran to the new home-run king, hugged him, and wouldn't let go. Henry Aaron shouted, "Mom! What are *you* doing out here?"

"Baby," Hank's mom replied, "if they're gonna get you, they've gotta get me first!"[4]

Now, *that's* courage and character. You've got to admire a man who ignores a hundred thousand hate letters, steps calmly up to the plate, takes the first good pitch and knocks it into the record books. And you've got to admire Hank's mom, who was shielding him at the most important moment of his career.

It was easy to see where Hank's courage and character came from.

## CHARACTER IN THE CORPS

What is character?

I would define character as the collection of ingrained positive traits that enable a player to compete effectively and ethically, so that he or she sets a positive example to others and helps move the team closer to its goals. Your character is the core of your being, the essence of who you are.

Thomas E. Ricks is a military correspondent for the *Washington Post*. In 1997, he wrote a piece for *Parade* in which he examined the role of character training at the Marine Corps Recruit Depot in Parris Island, South Carolina. The idea for the article originated on a sweltering night in Mogadishu, Somalia, in 1992, when Ricks accompanied a squad of Marines led by a twenty-two-year-old corporal. The central government of Somalia had collapsed, rival militias were shooting anything that moved, yet this young corporal commanded his squad with absolute confidence.[5]

Ricks wanted to know where that Marine corporal's character and confidence came from. To find out, he went to Parris Island in 1995 and followed the recruits of Platoon 3086 for eleven weeks. He continued checking their progress for the next two years. He wrote:

> For the first time in their lives, many [recruits] encountered absolute standards: Tell the truth. Don't give up. Don't whine. Look out for the group before you look out for yourself. Always do your best—even if you are just mopping the floor; you owe it to yourself and your comrades to strive to be the best mopper at this moment in the Corps. Judge others by their actions, not their words or their race. . . .
>
> The drill instructors didn't try to make their recruits

happy. They tried to push members of the platoon harder than they'd ever been pushed, to make them go beyond their own self-imposed limits. Nearly all the members of the platoon cried at one time or another. Yet by the end of eleven weeks almost all had been transformed by the experience—and were more fulfilled than they had ever been. They had subordinated their needs to those of the group, yet almost all emerged with a stronger sense of self. They unembarrassedly used words like "integrity."[6]

Ricks was surprised to learn that Marine Corps character training actually solved problems of racism and intolerance. He described the time a drill instructor, Sergeant Carey, ordered two recruits to share a tent in the woods during a training exercise. One recruit was a white supremacist from Alabama; the other was an African-American former gang member from Washington, D.C. These two Marines had to learn to look out for each other and keep each other alive. They had to practice *teamwork*.

As a result, the two recruits became friends and teammates. Said one, "We stuck up for each other after that." After basic training at Parris Island, the young man from Alabama traveled around the world with the Corps and left his old racist attitudes behind. "You go out and see the world," he told Ricks, "and you see there are cool people in all colors."[7]

Though character training has always been a major emphasis in my role as a parent to nineteen children, I have seen character training taken to a totally new level in the lives of my two Marine Corps sons, Peter and David.

My son David told me that his Marine Corps training has profoundly shaped his character and his life. "There are fourteen leadership traits that all Marines aspire to," he said. "They are, for the most part, character traits: bearing, courage, decisiveness, dependability, endurance, enthusiasm, initiative, integrity, judgment, justice, knowledge, loyalty, tact, and unselfishness. Any person who exemplified those fourteen traits, whether in the Marines or in civilian life would be, by definition, a leader and a person of sterling character."

Peter puts it this way: "Young people grow up fast in the Corps. Every day in the Marines is a lesson in character and leadership. Marines are expected to be rigorously professional in everything they do, to take responsibility and hold themselves accountable, to demonstrate decisiveness and sound judgment, to communicate clearly and work as a team, and to practice absolute integrity at all times. These Marine Corps attitudes and character traits are transferable to the civilian sector. If you want a proven leader with proven character, you want a Marine."

If I were running the country, I would make it a law that, after an eighteen-year-old graduates from high school, he or she must serve two years in the United States Marine Corps—mandatory. We would solve many of the problems in our society in a hurry. (Just a little pontificating from an old Marine dad.)

Let's take a look at some of the character traits that every team needs, both in its leaders and in its players.

## A STRONG WORK ETHIC

Motivational speaker and author Dale Carnegie once advertised in the newspaper for an administrative assistant. Within a couple of days, he received three hundred replies, most beginning with words like these: "I wish to apply for the position you advertised. . . ."

But one woman wrote a letter that stood out from the rest. "You will probably receive two or three hundred letters in reply to your ad," she wrote. "You're a busy man. I'm sure you haven't time to read them all. If you will just reach for your telephone right now and call me at the number below, I will gladly come over, sort through the letters, and place on your desk the ones that are worth your attention. I have fifteen years' experience. . . ."[8]

That was all Dale Carnegie needed to read. He wanted this woman on his team! He picked up the phone and dialed the number. When the woman answered, Carnegie told her he wanted to hire her on the spot. The woman said she was sorry, but right after she had mailed the letter, another employer had offered her a job and she had accepted. Carnegie was too late. The moral of the story: people who are willing to work hard will always be in demand.

In 1999 *People* magazine published a profile of Tom Brokaw, who was then the anchor of the *NBC Nightly News* team. Much of the credit for Brokaw's success goes to what *People* called his "South Dakota work ethic."[9] He once told writer Jill Rosenfeld how he acquired his work ethic:

> My first job was mowing lawns. I had a push mower, and I said to my father, "I could make a lot more money with a power mower." My dad was a Mr. Fix-It type, so he went into the garage and built me one—out of a little old motor, some black plywood, and a few pipes.
>
> I was embarrassed when I saw it. I thought, *I can't be pushing that around. All of my friends are going to have slick-looking machines.* Kids did tease me at first—until they realized that my mower could go through anything. So I got the toughest jobs in town, and suddenly I was making more money than I could count.
>
> The experience was a real lesson for me. It showed me that what counts above all is the excellence of your work.[10]

A strong work ethic is contagious. One hardworking team member can elevate the work ethic of an entire team. As John

Maxwell writes in *The 17 Indisputable Laws of Teamwork*, "When a team member displays a strong work ethic and begins to have a positive impact, others imitate him."[11]


## INTEGRITY IS ABSOLUTE

Arthur Ashe Jr. is remembered as a great tennis player and a great humanitarian. In 1979, he suffered a heart attack and underwent quadruple bypass surgery. He underwent open-heart surgery a second time in 1983, at which time he received an AIDS-tainted blood transfusion. He died of complications from the disease in February 1993, just short of his fiftieth birthday.

Ashe completed the manuscript of his memoirs, *Days of Grace*, just one week before his death, and it was published later that year. In the opening pages of the book, Ashe recalled an incident that took place when he was seventeen years old and playing in the Middle Atlantic Junior Championships in Wheeling, West Virginia. He wrote:

> I was the only black kid in the tournament, at least in the under-eighteen age section. One night, some of the other kids trashed a cabin; they absolutely destroyed it. And then they decided to say that I was responsible, although I had nothing to do with it. The incident even got into the papers. As much as I denied and protested, those white boys would not change their story.
>
> I rode to Washington from West Virginia, . . . silently worrying about what my father would do and say to me. When I reached Washington, where I was to play in another tournament, I telephoned him in Richmond. As I was aware, he already knew about the incident. . . .

"Arthur Junior, all I want to know is, were you mixed up in that mess?"

"No, Daddy, I wasn't."

He never asked about it again. He trusted me. With my father, my reputation was solid.

I have tried to live so that people would trust my character. . . . I want to be seen as fair and honest, trustworthy, kind, calm, and polite. I want no stain on my character, no blemish on my reputation.[12]

Warren Buffett, CEO of Berkshire-Hathaway, was ranked by *Forbes* as the richest person on the planet as of February 2008. He once said, "I look for three things in hiring people. The first is personal integrity, the second is intelligence, and the third is a high energy level. But if you don't have the first, the second two don't matter."[13]

It's important for our young people to learn the value of integrity as early as possible. One young team member who clearly understood the importance of integrity was seven-year-old first baseman Tanner Munsey of Wellington, Florida. The story begins at a T-ball game in 1989.

When Munsey scooped up a grounder and tried to tag a runner heading to second base, umpire Laura Benson called the runner out. Munsey walked up to the umpire and said, "Ma'am, I didn't tag him." The umpire reversed herself and awarded the runner second base. After the game, Tanner Munsey's coach praised him for his honesty and gave him the game ball.[14]

Two weeks later, Laura Benson umpired another T-ball game in which Tanner Munsey played, this time at shortstop. Once again, a batter grounded to Tanner. He scooped up the ball and reached out to tag the runner heading for third. Benson thought Tanner missed the tag and called the runner safe.

Tanner looked at Benson as if something was on his mind—but without a word, he tossed the ball to the catcher and went back to his position. Benson knew something was bothering the boy. She went to him and asked, "Tanner, did you tag the runner?" "Yes, ma'am," he said. Laura Benson reversed herself and called the runner out.[15] The opposing coach protested, and the umpire explained what had taken place at the previous game. "If a player is that honest," she concluded, "I have to give it to him. T-ball is supposed to be for the kids."[16]

Good call.

## HUMBLE AND UNSELFISH

One day in July 2000, I was clearing my voice-mail messages when I heard these words: "Mr. Williams, this is John Wooden, former basketball coach at UCLA." I couldn't help being awestruck at Coach Wooden's humility. He actually felt he needed to identify himself as "former basketball coach at UCLA"!

He went on to give his personal recommendation for a UCLA trainer who was applying for a job with the Orlando Magic. He concluded his message with these words: "I enjoy reading your books very much. Good-bye."

Again and again in my encounters with Coach Wooden, I have been amazed at the depths of his genuine humility, and the way he has been able to instill traits of humility and unselfishness in his players. No question: the character trait of humility is one of the least recognized secrets of success.

True humility doesn't mean that you think less of yourself; it simply means that you think of yourself less. Most humble people have a healthy sense of self-esteem. In fact, it's the dysfunctional and insecure people who tend to be the most arrogant and vain.

People who possess the character trait of humility are always secure in the knowledge that they have nothing to prove.

In a team environment, I equate humility with unselfishness. An unselfish player is just as happy to provide an assist as to get a basket. Richard Stengel, who is now managing editor of *Time*, once wrote about his Princeton basketball coach, the now-retired Pete Carril. Stengel observed:

> I was a scrub, a sophomore backup guard, on the last great Princeton squad, the team that won the National Invitational Tournament in 1975. . . . My coach was the ornery philosopher Pete Carril. . . . [He] saw the 94-foot by 54-foot hard court as a moral playground where the cardinal virtue was unselfishness. The embodiment of unselfishness was the assist, the small act of grace of giving up the ball to a teammate who has a better shot. Check out the box score of a Princeton game: the team gets two-thirds of its baskets off assists, a rarity in this era of run-and-gun shooters who have eyes only for the hoop. . . .
>
> When the leather of the round ball touches your hands, your first thought is, *Who else is open?* Not, *How am I gonna get my shot?* It's not easy to learn, and it goes against the grain of me-first American individualism and the lure of million-dollar sneaker contracts. The highest skill of a Princeton basketball player is not to run, jump or shoot but to *see*. And it is still the rarest basketball skill of all.[17]

Cal Ripken Jr. earned the nickname "Iron Man" by playing in a record 2,632 consecutive games over sixteen seasons. That streak, lasting from May 30, 1982, to September 20, 1998, required that he demonstrate many character traits, from a strong work ethic to perseverance. But when I think of Cal Ripken Jr., the number one character trait I think of is his great humility. In his 1998 book, *The Only Way I Know*, he wrote:

> Some people would label me a "celebrity," but that's a description I'd never be comfortable with. I'm well-known in some circles, but I'm still a regular guy—a profoundly regular guy. . . .
>
> In a restaurant one morning during spring training in Florida the waitress approached halfway through the meal and asked, "Are you a very famous person?"
>
> I suppose the fact that she asked the question proved that I'm not, but I answered, "Depends on what you mean."
>
> "Is your name Carl?"
>
> "Cal."
>
> "Oh, right . . . but you're such a nice person!"
>
> You see, there's an assumption that if you are "famous," you're egotistical and not polite, maybe even arrogant. There's that stereotype, and I suppose some people who become well-known do act more important than they had before, but I hope my actions and words demonstrate that I don't believe I'm different from anyone else.[18]

A few years ago, I attended an induction ceremony at Ted Williams's Hitters Hall of Fame in Florida. I attend the annual induction ceremony every spring, because I love being around my baseball heroes. One morning, Cal was one of a number of major leaguers on hand, signing autographs. The slowest-moving line by far was Cal's line—and the reason was Cal himself.

For every autograph he signed, Cal would look the fan in the eye, engage in conversation, and sign a personalized autograph. Then he'd blow the ink dry—he didn't want the ink to smear. I noticed that Cal's hand was marked with blue ink from rubbing the pen point on his hand so that no blob of ink would ruin the autograph. When he wrote, his signature was clear and legible.

I was reminded that, during the famous streak when Cal was the biggest thing in baseball, he would stay late after every game and sign autographs until they turned the stadium lights out. He did that at home and on the road, and sometimes he wouldn't finish signing until after midnight. He didn't want to disappoint a single fan. That's true humility and unselfishness.

## COURAGE

Eddie Rickenbacker (1890–1973) was an American fighter ace in World War I, a recipient of the Medal of Honor, an Indy race-car driver, and the cofounder of Eastern Airlines. If anyone ever earned the right to define what *courage* means, it was Eddie Rickenbacker. He said, "Courage is doing what you're afraid to do. There can be no courage unless you're scared."[19]

Question: who's the most courageous guy ever to play pro football? My vote goes to Jack Youngblood, defensive end for the Los Angeles Rams from 1971 to 1984. Jack played in 201 consecutive games and missed only one game in his pro career.

On December 30, 1979, Youngblood and the Rams were in Dallas, playing in a divisional playoff game against the Cowboys. Late in the second quarter, a pair of Dallas offensive linemen chop-blocked Youngblood. Pain exploded through his lower leg. The trainers came out, loaded him on a stretcher, and carted him off to the locker room. The team doctor x-rayed his leg and found his calf bone was broken a couple of inches above the ankle.

"Tape up my leg," Youngblood roared, "and bring me some aspirin!"

"Jack," the doctor protested, "your fibula's snapped like a pencil!"

After a heated argument, Youngblood growled, "This is *my* leg! It's *my* career! I'm willing to put it on the line! Why do you keep saying you can't do that?"[20]

Youngblood prevailed. The trainers taped his leg all around the break. "The pain was excruciating," he later recalled. "I can't even describe it. But they couldn't shoot the bone with a pain-killer; that stuff doesn't work on bones."[21]

With effort, he could walk on the broken leg. When halftime was nearly over. Youngblood went to coach Ray Malavasi and told him, "I can play." Surprised, Malavasi said, "Are you sure?"

"If I'm hurting the team, I'll take myself out."[22]

Youngblood told only one teammate, defensive tackle Larry Brooks, that he was playing on a broken leg. He didn't want any-one on the other side of the ball to suspect that he was playing hurt—least of all Cowboys offensive tackle Rayfield "Big Cat" Wright. As Youngblood told *Sports Illustrated*'s Peter King,

> I thought, "How am I going to beat Rayfield like this? Not that I *can't* do it. But how am I *gonna* do it?" When I tried to explode off the ball, I felt the hindrance, so I just tried to push off the other leg. The amazing thing was, at one point, somehow I got around Rayfield Wright, who in my estimation was one of the three or four premier players I ever played against, a Hall of Fame player. I ran Roger Staubach down for a sack.[23]

By the end of the game, the Rams had upset the Cowboys, 21–19. For about an hour after the game, Youngblood felt no pain. "The adrenaline's still going because you're so excited, and you feel okay," he recalled. "Then the pain began. It was just constant. You think you'd get used to it, but not like that."[24]

For the NFC Championship game in Tampa the following week, the team doctors came up with a cast. "It sort of encased my leg in plastic," he said, "and we padded it and taped it for the Tampa game. I took Darvon or Darvocet, something like that, but you can only take so many, or you'd go completely numb."[25] The Rams beat Tampa Bay, 9–0, for the NFC title. Next stop: Super Bowl XIV in Pasadena.

The Rams faced the Pittsburgh Steelers, who featured quarterback Terry Bradshaw, running back Franco Harris, and wide receivers John Stallworth and Lynn Swann. Though the pain in his leg remained intense, Youngblood recalls that it was a "perfect day in Pasadena. Sunny, warm. The fans had these silver flittery boards for the halftime show, and the sun was reflecting off them, and it was just like, 'Woo-hoo! What a day!'"[26]

Though the Steelers were heavily favored, the Rams maintained the lead throughout most of the game. Two minutes into the fourth quarter, the Steelers were deep in their own territory. On third and eight, Bradshaw took the snap, faked a handoff, and went back to throw. Youngblood exploded through the line. There was nothing between Youngblood and Bradshaw but a few wide-open yards of Pasadena real estate. Bradshaw held the ball an extra split second, waiting for his receiver, John Stallworth, to get open down the middle of the field.

"I was right on Terry," Youngblood recalls. "I mean, a half-step away. . . . And he let it go, a beautiful pass." Stallworth caught the ball in stride and took it to the end zone for a seventy-three-yard touchdown. "The difference in me making the play," said Youngblood, "was a half-step. The difference was the broken leg, but that's how it goes. I tried."[27]

Later, the Steelers again faced third and long. Bradshaw completed a pass to Stallworth for forty-five yards. A few plays later, Franco Harris scored on a one-yard run. And that's how the game ended: Steelers 31, Rams 19.

Does Jack Youngblood have any regrets about playing in the Super Bowl on a broken leg? "None," he says. "The only regret

I would have had is if I didn't play. I never would have forgiven myself."[28]

Jack Youngblood retired at the end of that season and received the 1984 Ed Block Courage Award for "representing everything that is positive about professional football."[29] The Courage Award: I can't think of a more fitting honor for a guy who chased down Roger Staubach and Terry Bradshaw on a broken leg.

## PERSEVERANCE

Great teams are made up of leaders and players who never give up. One of the greatest role models of perseverance is the late NCAA basketball coach Jim Valvano—the amazing Jimmy V. Every year, ESPN holds its ESPY Awards show, and one of the annual awards is the Jimmy V Perseverance Award.

I had the privilege of knowing Jim Valvano and having him on my radio show. He coached basketball at North Carolina State University during the 1980s. Basketball fans vividly remember the 1983 NCAA Basketball Tournament when Valvano's underdog Wolfpack beat the top-seeded University of Houston Cougars. North Carolina State's Dereck Whittenburg tossed up a last-second prayer that Lorenzo Charles dunked at the buzzer for a 54–52 victory. Valvano, in total disbelief, ran up and down the court, looking for people to hug.

During a nineteen-year coaching career at Johns Hopkins, Bucknell, Iona, and North Carolina State, Jimmy accumulated a career record of 346-212. He retired from coaching and became a broadcaster for ABC and ESPN, where he often worked alongside veteran basketball commentator Dick Vitale. He was much in demand as a motivational speaker. His favorite topic was perseverance and his best-known line was, "Don't give up, don't ever give up."

In June 1992, Jimmy was diagnosed with an aggressive bone cancer. He was a fighter, but he knew the odds were against him. Determined to make his life and death count for something, he created the V Foundation, an organization devoted to finding a cure for cancer.

On March 4, 1993, Jimmy was honored with the first Arthur Ashe Courage and Humanitarian Award at the inaugural ESPY Awards event. After an introduction by Dick Vitale, Jim got up to give his acceptance speech:

> I'm going to speak longer than anybody else has spoken tonight. That's the way it goes. Time is very precious to me. I don't know how much I have left and I have some things that I would like to say. . . .
>
> To me, there are three things we all should do every day. . . . Number one is *laugh*. You should laugh every day. Number two is *think*. You should spend some time in thought. Number three is, you should have your *emotions* moved to tears. Could be happiness or joy. But think about it. If you laugh, you think, and you cry, that's a full day. That's a heck of a day. You do that seven days a week, you're going to have something special.[30]

Jim talked for a few more minutes, then he saw a notice flashing on the teleprompter—"That screen is flashing up there, 'Thirty seconds,'" he said, "like I care about that screen right now, huh? I got tumors all over my body. I'm worried about some guy in the back going, 'Thirty seconds'?"[31] He talked about the V Foundation and the need to find a cure for cancer.

> ESPN has been so kind to support me in this endeavor and allow me to announce tonight, that with ESPN's support . . . we are starting the Jimmy V Foundation for

Cancer Research. And its motto is "Don't give up, don't ever give up." . . . I'm going to work as hard as I can for cancer research and hopefully, maybe, we'll have some cures and some breakthroughs. . . .

I know, I gotta go, I gotta go. . . . I want to say it again. Cancer can take away all my physical abilities, but it cannot touch my mind, it cannot touch my heart and it cannot touch my soul. And those three things are going to carry on forever. I thank you and God bless you all.[32]

Jim Valvano received a long, thunderous ovation. Less than two months after giving that speech, he passed away. But just as he promised, a part of him lives on—his work in fighting cancer through the V Foundation and his great spirit of perseverance.

As someone once said, you can't control the length of your life, but you can control its width and depth. Jimmy V lived a life that was deep and wide. He lived and died as a man of character.

## CHARACTER IS AN INSIDE JOB

One of the key mentors in my life was Fred Smith Sr. The author of *Learning to Lead* and *Breakfast with Fred*, he was an authority on the importance of character in the business world. He once wrote:

Here are three simple things that I have learned about people.

First, I have learned that I waste time in trying to correct other people's mistakes. I should use the time to utilize their strengths and buttress their weaknesses. A lot of training programs I have seen are geared to overcoming weaknesses—what a waste of time!

Second, I have learned that you can't change anybody else. Each person has to change himself or herself—you can't do it for them. . . . We spend an awful lot of time putting temporary situations in place, thinking that we have changed the person, but in the end it is only a short-term fix.

Third, I have learned that people are the way they are because they want to be that way. . . . We rationalize and give all kinds of reasons that it's not true, but bottom line: You are choosing to be who you are.[33]

What is Fred saying to us?

First, he's telling us we need to recruit people of character to our teams. If we recruit people with strong talents but weak character, those weaknesses will eventually be the undoing of the team. No team ever rises above the limitations of its players, and no individual ever rises above the limitations of his or her character. So we had better recruit people of good character from the outset.

Second, it's useless to try to change people's character. People change only when they want to change. You can preach and cajole all you want, but if they don't want to change, you're wasting your breath. They may tell you what you want to hear and pretend to change—but in the end, they'll do exactly as they please, no more, no less.

Third, people choose their own character. We all become the people we choose to be. There is no end of excuses for why people continue to lie, cheat, steal, slack off, drink, take drugs, abuse their bodies, make babies out of wedlock, and on and on. But the simple fact is that people do these things because they want to. It's their choice.

I joined the Philadelphia 76ers as general manager in 1974. A year or two later, Dick Vermeil arrived in town to take over as head coach of the Philadelphia Eagles. I recall how Dick struggled through a difficult first season. He had constant battles with his players and was continually having to deal with their problems, both on and off the field. At the end of that first season, I saw Dick give a TV interview, and he told the reporter something I'll never forget: "This past season, I spent all my time dealing with the problem guys, and I neglected all the good guys. That's never going to happen again."

If all my years in pro sports have taught me anything, it's that you need talent to win—but if your talent is not backed by a rock-solid, immovable core of character, you're going to fall short every time. I'm not naively suggesting that you should have a roster full of choirboys. I'm just stating what I know to be true: character problems will destroy your team if they get out of control.

If you choose to recruit people who have enormous talent but very little character, if you take them on as "reclamation projects," you are free to do so. But you are probably fooling yourself—and your "reclamation project" may very well disrupt your team and destroy your dreams. Fred Smith's advice is sound: leave the social experiments to the social workers. You have a team to build. The best way to build it is to recruit people who already possess good character.

One final thought from Fred Smith: "Character is an inside job."[34]

Extremely wise words.

This is the question that confronts us as team-builders and extreme dreamers of every kind: What do we have inside us? Do we have a core of character, like tempered steel, at the center of our souls? Have we made character the foundation of our team? Or are we building our lives and our teams on a false foundation?

Extreme dreams depend on high-character teams—

And character is an inside job.

# EPILOGUE

## *Extreme Dreams for Extreme Times*

On the one hand, we possess the technical competence, physical resources, and intellectual capacity to satisfy all the basic needs of mankind. There is little question that we have the wherewithal to provide food, clothing, and shelter for every individual on this planet. . . . On the other hand, we seem to lack the essential ability to work together effectively to solve critical problems.

> CARL E. LARSON and FRANK M. J. LAFASTO, authors,
> *Teamwork: What Must Go Right, What Can Go Wrong*[1]

IT'S THE END OF THE CIVILIZATION, MY FRIEND.

Think I'm kidding? I have it on good authority from no less credible a source than the Associated Press. In a June 2008 wire story, two AP writers offer this bleak assessment of world events:

> Is everything spinning out of control? Midwestern levees are bursting. Polar bears are adrift. Gas prices are skyrocketing. Home values are abysmal. Air fares, college tuition and health care border on unaffordable.

Wars without end rage in Iraq, Afghanistan and against terrorism. . . .

The can-do, bootstrap approach embedded in the American psyche is under assault. Eroding it is a dour powerlessness that is chipping away at the country's sturdy conviction that destiny can be commanded with sheer courage and perseverance. . . .

Maybe this is what the twenty-first century will be about—a great unraveling of some things long taken for granted.[2]

You see? It's official, straight from the Associated Press: We've reached the end of the line. Abandon hope, folks. We're toast.

In fact, just three months after those words were published, the roof *really* fell in, seeming to confirm the AP's proclamation of doom. In mid-September 2008, the seemingly rock-solid financial institutions of Lehman Brothers, Merrill Lynch, and American International Group (AIG) collapsed due to a catastrophic debt and liquidity crisis. A week later, President Bush and Treasury Secretary Henry Paulson proposed a stunning $700 billion bailout program to rescue an American financial system on the verge of implosion. While Congress debated the proposal, two more huge financial institutions failed—Washington Mutual and Wachovia. On September 29, the Dow dropped over 777 points in a single day, and the NASDAQ lost almost 200.

During the congressional debate, the Paulson proposal grew from three pages to more than 450 and finally passed—whereupon stock markets around the world took an even more breathtaking plunge. During a one-hour period of trading on October 10, stock markets across Europe, Asia, and America lost 10 percent of their value *in a single hour of trading*.[3] End of the world? A lot of people thought so. No question, it was the worst stock market crash since the big one in 1929. But it was hardly unprecedented.

As *New York Times* reporter Jennifer 8 Lee observed (and yes, her middle name actually is 8), the American economy experienced a similar panic in 1873. Ulysses S. Grant was the president at the time. Jennifer 8 Lee identified the root causes of that panic: "Rampant real estate speculation culminated in a credit crunch and banking failures that led to broad panic in the stock markets . . . which resulted in a near total collapse of the financial system."[4] Sound familiar?

Bottom line: as Americans, we've been here before—and we survived it.

But, once again, there are those who seem determined to manipulate news consumers with fear and pessimism. For example, the cover of *Time* magazine for the week of October 2, 2008, showed a group of grim-looking men in a soup line from the Great Depression in the 1930s. The caption read "The New Hard Times."

Economic problems, social problems, and political problems come and go. When they come, we have to roll up our sleeves and solve them. And you don't solve problems with fear and pessimism. Those who try to gin up panic and despair when problems arise are not part of the solution. They are part of the problem.

## CHEERLEADERS FOR THE APOCALYPSE

Frankly, all of this gloom-and-doom thinking makes my blood boil. What has pessimism ever accomplished? Not a thing that I can think of. Americans have endured far worse hardships than anything we are suffering today—and we got through it all with a spirit of optimism.

Our nation was ripped apart during the Civil War. We lost 618,000 Americans on both sides of that terrible war—nearly 4 percent of the American male population.[5] But even in the depths of that war, Americans never surrendered to despair.

In the fall of 1918, as World War I drew to a close, something worse than war broke out: a deadly influenza pandemic. It killed 675,000 Americans—ten times the U.S. death toll in WWI. Over a two-year period, the pandemic killed at least 20 million people worldwide—and perhaps as many as 100 million. One-third of the European population died.[6] But even then, humanity never surrendered to despair.

The year 1929 brought the decade-long Great Depression—the deepest, worst, most widespread economic calamity in the history of the world. During the depths of the Depression, unemployment in America rose to between 8 and 15 million—approximately one-third of the non-farm workforce.[7] Still, Americans never surrendered to despair.

During World War II, the entire nation mobilized to fight a totalitarian menace. The United States suffered a million casualties, including nearly 400,000 dead. The war involved almost sixty nations. Entire cities were bombed out of existence. Mass murder became commonplace.[8] Even amid those horrors, Americans never surrendered to despair.

We have persevered through segregation, Vietnam, campus riots, Watergate, the 1973 oil crisis, and the double-digit inflation of the Ford-Carter years. Now here we are in the twenty-first century, with the highest standard of living the world has ever known. We have computers, iPods and iPhones, the Internet, flat-screen TVs with five hundred satellite channels, cars that talk to you, air-conditioned homes, heated swimming pools, theme parks, multiplex theaters, restaurants galore, excellent health care, and on and on—yet the Associated Press tells us it's time for despair.

Do we have problems? Sure we do. Is it time to throw up our hands in despair? Give me a break! Frankly, we don't need any more cheerleaders for the apocalypse—but we could use a few more cheerleaders for Utopia!

I feel sorry for those poor lost souls who huddle in their basements, scared out of their wits, hoping things will get better—and not realizing that *they have the power to change the world*. I feel sorry for folks like these two journalists who live amid the cultural and technological wonders of the twenty-first century and see nothing ahead of them but "a great unraveling." What a failure of vision!

Optimism is contagious—and we should all be in the optimism business. Instead of huddling in the basement, let's work together as a team to solve the problems that face us. Let's dream some extreme dreams, envision a better world, and assemble the teams to get the job done. That's how the human race has always made great strides in the past, and that's how we'll continue to build a better world in the days to come.

## DO SOMETHING SCARY

Don't get me wrong. I'm no Pollyanna. I know that our world is poised on a knife edge between a utopian dream and a dystopian nightmare. I'm just saying that we don't have to surrender to the nightmare. The extreme utopian dream is ours for the taking—

But *we have to dream it* and *we have to build it* through teamwork. We certainly can't build a better world through division and pessimism.

I genuinely, passionately believe that all the problems we face as a nation and as a global society have teamwork solutions. We don't have to wring our hands. We don't have to wait for someone else to do the job. We were placed here on this planet to solve problems, meet needs, and build a better future for our children and our children's children.

We can deal with such towering crises as terrorism, global insecurity, nuclear proliferation, the need for energy independence, the national debt, the environment, and greenhouse gas emissions—if we dream the dreams and build the teams to tackle the challenges. We can solve problems of world poverty and hunger through extreme dreams and teamwork. We can cure AIDS, cancer, Alzheimer's disease, heart disease, and all the other scourges and plagues of humankind—*if* we are willing to dream big dreams and build the teams to make them happen.

What about child abuse, child abduction, child slavery, and child pornography? Or illiteracy, fatherless and motherless children, childhood malnutrition or obesity, homelessness and hopelessness? We can make the world safe for the most innocent and helpless among us—but first we must dream the extreme dreams and build the teams.

We can put an end to crime and drug abuse and gang warfare, along with all the other problems that blight our inner cities and neighborhoods. There was a time in America when people left their windows open and doors unlocked at night—and I believe we could live in such a world again. But it can happen only when we dream that extreme dream and build the teams to make it happen.

I'm sure you have some dreams of your own that I'm not even aware of. What is the urgent crisis you'd like to solve? What are your grand utopian dreams of the future? Wouldn't you like to see those dreams come true?

You may think, *What can one person do?*

Answer: not much.

But a *team of people*, all united behind one extreme dream, can change the world.

Pay no attention to the naysayers. Don't be afraid to attempt the impossible. Don't be afraid of dreaming bold, audacious, extreme dreams. As Eleanor Roosevelt once said, "Do one thing every day that scares you."[9]

Dare to dream a dream so big and brash and bodacious that it brings a lump of terror to your throat! Shoot for the moon, shoot for the stars! Then build a team, lead a team, or join a team, and make your "impossible" dreams come true.

Always remember those eight essential qualities of teamwork, because you've got to have them all: Talent. Leadership. Commitment. Passion. Think *team*! Empowerment. Trust and respect. Good character.

Put those eight teamwork ingredients to work—then *feel the synergy*!

## TWO WHO MADE A DIFFERENCE

In closing, let me tell you a story about the two people who first taught me to dream extreme dreams and build the teams to make them come true—my father and mother, Jim and Ellen Williams.

February 15, 1947, is a day I'll never forget. I was six years old. Dad had been back from service in World War II less than two years. It was a snowy day in Wilmington, Delaware, and my two sisters and I stood outside the hospital, waiting for my mother to give birth. Children weren't allowed inside the hospital, so the three of us stood in the snow. We had nothing to do but wait— and waiting was torture.

In those days, before sonograms, we had no way of knowing if the baby would be a boy or a girl. I desperately wanted a little brother to play ball with. When word came down that my third sister was born, I cried bitter tears.

My parents named the baby Mary Ellen, and we nicknamed her Mimi. After we brought her home, Mom and Dad realized something was wrong with Mimi. Looking back, I believe the doctors must have known right away but didn't have the heart to tell my parents. Nowadays, Mary Ellen's condition could have been detected in early pregnancy by amniocentesis. She had Down syndrome.

In the late 1940s, this condition was known by a different name, and people said such children were "mentally retarded." Back then, there was a sense of shame and tragedy to have a "retarded" child. In most cases, parents had such children institutionalized without any acknowledgment that they existed. The stigma was so great, it was as if such children were a punishment from God.

Today, of course, we know that Down syndrome is a genetic abnormality caused by an irregular number of chromosomes. In those days, however, there was hardly any help for families like ours. There was little research being done.

In the past half century, the situation has changed—thanks in no small part to my parents, Jim and Ellen Williams. They refused to treat Mary Ellen's condition as a secret to be locked away in a closet. They viewed it as a problem to be solved with love, candor, and teamwork. My parents dreamed an extreme dream and they led the way.

Mom and Dad began talking about the problem in community meetings and media interviews. They brainstormed new ideas for fund-raising and consciousness-raising on behalf of treatment and research. As Mom and Dad worked together on this issue, they grew closer together. They felt they were doing something on behalf of Mary Ellen and thousands like her.

My best friend was Ruly Carpenter, the son of Bob Carpenter, owner of the Philadelphia Phillies. One June evening in 1955, Ruly and I were playing sandlot baseball—I was catching, Ruly was pitching. My dad and Ruly's dad were talking behind the backstop while we played ball.

Ruly and I didn't know it, but our dads were dreaming some extreme dreams behind that backstop. Jim Williams and Bob Carpenter had a lot in common. My dad had a daughter with Down syndrome. Bob Carpenter had a son, Kemble, with a similar disability. Together, they laid plans for an event to be called the Delaware All-Star High School Football Game—the Blue-Gold Game.

The purpose of the game was to help children with special needs. The money raised by the game would be administered by a charitable foundation, The Delaware Foundation for Retarded Children (now called the Delaware Foundation Reaching Citizens with Cognitive Disabilities). The first Blue-Gold Game was played the following year, on August 25, 1956, and there were roughly ten thousand fans on hand.

The game became an annual event. In 1958, I helped quarterback the North team and Ruly played tight end. We beat the South, 27–0.

The game is still played annually to this day. In fact, Ruly and I both attended the fiftieth-anniversary game in 2006 and accepted awards honoring our fathers and their extreme dream. Over the years, the Blue-Gold Game has raised millions of dollars for research and assistance programs—and it has been widely emulated around the country. Many Blue-Gold Game players have chosen careers of service to the disabled.

Though the Blue-Gold Game didn't directly benefit my sister Mimi or Ruly's brother Kemble, our families knew that millions of children and their families would be blessed by the new treatments and raised awareness the game would promote. Problems and tragedies are easier to accept when you can see them turned into help and healing for other people.

## AIM HIGH! HIGHER!

It's hard to believe how much the world has changed since Mary Ellen was born. The stigma that once surrounded Down syndrome has largely been erased. There are numerous programs today that help special-needs kids and their families. Many of these changes have come about because Mom and Dad chose to make a difference.

And they did it with teamwork.

My parents were activists who were always involved in one cause or another. When I was a boy, our home was a hub of activity and a meeting place for various committees and organizations. When Mary Ellen was born, her mental health issues became their number one cause. They found other parents who faced the same problems and got them involved. They recruited coaches, teachers, journalists, health-care professionals, and business-people to the team. They involved government officials at every level—including the governor of Delaware.

Looking back, I realize my own passion for teamwork was shaped by the example of my parents. I constantly saw them tackling problems, dreaming big dreams, assembling teams, and having a huge impact on their community and the state. Is it any wonder that I am such a cheerleader for this magical thing called teamwork?

What's your dream, my friend? What is your grand, audacious, scary, extreme dream? You can turn that "impossible dream" into a *reality*—

A reality that is every bit as real as the book you hold in your hands, or the Orlando Magic, or Disneyland, or the Sistine Chapel ceiling, or Neal Armstrong's footprints on the moon. You can do it with teamwork.

Aim high, my friend. Higher! Higher!

Now assemble your team, and make magic happen.

And when you get your extreme dream built, pick up the phone and give me a call, will you? I want to hear *all* about it. . . .

# ACKNOWLEDGMENTS

With deep appreciation I acknowledge the support and guidance of the following people who helped make this book possible:

Special thanks to Bob Vander Weide, Alex Martins, and Rich DeVos of the Orlando Magic.

Hats off to my associates Andrew Herdliska and Latria Leak; my proofreader, Ken Hussar; and my ace typist, Fran Thomas.

Thanks also to my writing partner, Jim Denney, for his superb contributions in shaping this manuscript.

Hearty thanks also go to my friend and publisher Rolf Zettersten, editors Cara Highsmith, Holly Halverson, Bob Castillo, and the rest of the fine staff at Hachette Book Group. Thank you all for believing that we had something important to share, and for providing the support and the forum to say it.

And, finally, special thanks and appreciation go to my wife, Ruth, and to my wonderful and supportive family. They are truly the backbone of my life.

# NOTES

## Foreword by Doc Rivers

1. Desmond Tutu, *No Future Without Forgiveness* (New York: Random House, 2000), 31.

## Introduction: Going to Extremes

1. James Draper Newton, *Uncommon Friends: Life with Thomas Edison, Henry Ford, Harvey Firestone, Alexis Carrel, and Charles Lindbergh* (New York: Harcourt Trade, 1987), 18.

2. "Charles Lindbergh Flies the Atlantic," CharlesLindberg .com, retrieved at http://www.charleslindbergh.com/history/paris .asp; Charles A. Lindbergh, *The Spirit of St. Louis* (New York: Scribner, 2003), 120–21; A. Scott Berg, *Lindbergh* (New York: Berkley, 1999), 57–60.

3. Patrick M. Lencioni, *The Five Dysfunctions of a Team: A Leadership Fable* (San Francisco: Jossey-Bass, 2002), vii.

4. Patrick M. Lencioni, *Overcoming the Five Dysfunctions of a Team: A Field Guide for Leaders, Managers, and Facilitators* (San Francisco: Jossey-Bass, 2005), 3–5.

## Extreme *Sports* Dreams . . . Depend on Teams

1. Warren G. Bennis, *Managing the Dream: Reflections on Leadership and Change* (New York: Perseus, 2000), 7.

2. Bob Griese and Brian Griese, *Undefeated* (Nashville: Thomas Nelson, 2000), 58–81; "Miami's Perfect Season," Pro Football Hall of Fame Web site, retrieved at http://www.profootballhof.com/history/decades/1970s/miami.jsp.

3. Ibid.

4. Ibid.

5. "Legends of Hockey: Induction Showcase—Herb Brooks," LegendsOfHockey.net, retrieved at http://www.legendsofhockey .net/html/ind06Brooks.htm; Associated Press, "Herb Brooks Killed in Car Accident," SI.com, August 11, 2003, retrieved at http://sports-illustrated.cnn.com/hockey/news/2003/08/11/brooks_obit_ap/; Associated Press, "Coach Known Best for 1980 Hockey Gold," ESPN Classic, August 19, 2003, retrieved at http://espn.go.com/classic/obit/ s/2003/0811/1594173.html; Dave Kindred, "Born to Be Players, Born to the Moment," *Washington Post*, February 23, 1980, A1, retrieved at http://www.washingtonpost.com/wp-srv/sports/longterm/olympics 1998/history/memories/80-kindred.htm; Leonard Shapiro, "U.S. Shocks Soviets in Ice Hockey, 4-3," *Washington Post*, February 23, 1980, D1, retrieved at http://www.washingtonpost.com/wp-srv/sports/long-term/olympics1998/history/memories/80-hock.htm.

6. Ibid.

7. Ibid.

8. Ibid.

9. Ibid.

10. Ibid.

## 1. Something Bigger Than Ourselves

1. Charles B. Dygert and Richard A. Jacobs, *Creating a Culture of Success: Fine-tuning the Heart and Soul of Your Organization* (Warwick, NY: Moo Press, 2004), 34.

2. William A. Cohen, *Secrets of Special Ops Leadership* (New York: American Management Association, 2006), 186.

3. "Memorable Quotes from Rocky (1976)," IMDb (Internet Movie Database), retrieved at http://www.imdb.com/title/tt0075148/quotes.

4. Rudyard Kipling, *Songs from Books*, "The Law of the Jungle," retrieved at http://www.gutenberg.org/files/15529/15529-8.txt.

5. John C. Maxwell, *The 17 Indisputable Laws of Teamwork: Embrace Them and Empower Your Team* (Nashville: Thomas Nelson, 2001), 23.

6. Lance Armstrong with Sally Jenkins, *It's Not About the Bike: My Journey Back to Life* (New York: Putnam, 2000), 46–47; David V. Herlihy, *Bicycle: The History* (New Haven: Yale University Press, 2004), 396; Paul Asay, "So Just How Important Is Team Work?," Paul Asay personal Web site, retrieved at http://paulasay.indstate.edu/newsletter/ teamwork.html; "Award-Winning Lance Armstrong Training Series," EnterpriseMedia.com, retrieved at http://www.enterprisemedia.com/ product/00421/awardwinning_lance_armstrong_training_series.html.

7. Ibid.

8. "Leader of the Month for September 2004: Mike Krzyzewski," LeaderNetwork.org, retrieved at http://www.leadernetwork.org/mikekrzyzewskiseptember04.htm.

9. Dave Anderson, "The Knicks' Philosophy Professor," *New York Times*, June 2, 1991, retrieved at http://query.nytimes.com/gst/full page.html?res=9D0CE0D7173CF931A35755C0A967958260.

10. Maureen Mullen, "Courtside with Martina Navratilova," Hall of Fame Network, August 2006, retrieved at http://www.hofmag .com/content/view/372/30/; Bonnie DeSimone, "Act II of Navrati- lova's Career Ends with a Win," ESPN.com, September 11, 2006, retrieved at http://sports.espn.go.com/sports/tennis/usopen06/news/ story?id=2578105.

11. "Winning and Famous Teamwork Quotes," Inspiring-Quotes- and-Stories.com, retrieved at http://www.inspiring-quotes-and-stories. com/index.html.

12. Pat Riley, *The Winner Within: A Life Plan for Team Players* (New York: Berkley Trade, 1994), 15–16.

13. Leonard E. Read, "I, Pencil: My Family Tree, as told to Leon- ard E. Read," retrieved at http://www.econlib.org/LIBRARY/Essays/ rdPncl1.html.

14. Ibid.

15. From "When You Wish upon a Star," lyrics by Ned Washing- ton, music by Leigh Harline, from Walt Disney's motion picture *Pinoc- chio* (1940).

16. Video Clip: "The Miracle of the Huddle," viewed at http://bill curry.net/video06.html.

## Extreme *Entrepreneurial* Dreams . . . Depend on Teams

1. Kep Sweeney, *The New Restaurant Entrepreneur* (Chicago: Dear- born Trade Publishing, 2004), 208.

2. Jill Rosenfeld, "Training to Work: Charles Katz," FastCompany .com, retrieved at http://www.fastcompany.com/magazine/37/one .html?page=0%2C5; "Mr. Charles R. Katz," ZoomInfo.com, retrieved at http://www.zoominfo.com/people/Katz_Charles_1025654.aspx; Editors, "1stUp.com Surpasses 5.5 Million Subscriber Mark," *Busi- ness Wire*, September 25, 2000, retrieved at http://findarticles.com/p/ articles/mi_m0EIN/is_2000_Sept_25/ai_65456992.

3. "Trilogy History," Trilogy.com, retrieved at http://www.trilogy .com/newsite/aboutus.htm/; Chuck Salter, "Insanity, Inc.," FastCom-

pany.com, December 1998, retrieved at http://www.fastcompany
.com/node/36161/print; "Trilogy Enterprises: Company Description,"
Hoovers.com, retrieved at http://www.hoovers.com/trilogy-enter-
prises/--ID__51391--/free-co-profile.xhtml; "Trilogy Software: High
Performance Company of the Future?," Wiley Publishers, retrieved
at http://www.wiley.com/college/man/schermerhorn332879/site/stu-
dent/ic/page00.htm.

4. Ibid.

5. Ibid.

6. Ibid.

7. Ibid.

8. Ibid.

9. George Labovitz, Yu Sang Chang, Victor Rosansky, *Making
Quality Work: A Leadership Guide for the Results-Driven Manager* (Hoboken, NJ: John Wiley & Sons. 1995), 34–41.

10. Ibid.

11. Ben Cohen and Jerry Greenfield, "You Have the Power and
Responsibility to Build a Better World," address to DePauw Univer-
sity (Indiana) students, November 18, 2002, retrieved at http://www
.depauw.edu/news/index.asp?id=12357; David Gage, *The Partnership
Charter: How to Start Out Right with Your New Business Partnership (or
Fix the One You're In)* (New York: Basic Books, 2004), 93.

12. Laura Rich, *The Accidental Zillionaire: Demystifying Paul Allen*
(Hoboken, NJ: John Wiley & Sons, 2003), 39–41.

13. Charlene O'Hanlon, "David Packard: High-Tech Visionary,"
IT Channel News by CRN and VARBusiness, November 8, 2000, retrieved at http://www.crn.com/it-channel/18812197.

14. Pat Williams with Jim Denney, *How to Be Like Walt: Capturing
the Disney Magic Every Day of Your Life* (Deerfield Beach, FL: Health
Communications, 2004), 90, 295.

15. Pat Williams with Jim Denney, *How to Be Like Rich DeVos: Succeeding with Integrity in Business and Life* (Deerfield Beach, FL: Health
Communications, 2004), 14.

16. Cheryl Dahle, "The Agenda—Social Justice," FastCompany
.com, January 1, 2001, retrieved at http://www.fastcompany.com/
node/36697/print; Megan Lindow, "Moguls & Entrepreneurs: Kristine Pearson and Rory Stear," *Time*, October 25, 2007, retrieved at
http://www.time.com/time/specials/2007/article/0,28804,1663317_
1663322_1669935,00.html; "Welcome to Freeplay," Freeplay.com, retrieved at http://www.freeplayenergy.com/; "Self-Powered Progress,"

FreeplayFoundation.org, retrieved at http://www.freeplayfoundation
.org/.

17. Ibid.

18. Ibid.

19. Ibid.

20. Ibid.

21. Ibid.

22. Ibid.

23. Ibid.

24. Ibid.

## 2. Principle 1: Top Talent Builds Extreme Dreams

1. Loral Langemeier, *The Millionaire Maker* (New York: McGraw-Hill Professional. 2006), 233.

2. Eric Zweig, *Gentlemen, This Is a Football: Football's Best Quotes and Quips* (Richmond Hill, Ontario: Firefly Books, 2006), 99.

3. Donald T. Phillips, *Run to Win: Vince Lombardi on Coaching and Leadership* (New York: St. Martin's, 2002), 14–23.

4. Ibid.

5. Ibid.

6. Ibid.

7. "Knute Rockne," Coaching Quotes, retrieved at http://www
.coachqte.com/rockne.html.

8. "Leadership Profile: Coach Mike Krzyzewski," American Leaders Organization, September 2, 2007, retrieved at http://theamericanlead-ersorganization.blogspot.com/2007/09/leadership-profile-coach-mike
.html.

9. Pat Summitt, *Reach for the Summit* (New York: Broadway, 1999), 146.

10. Sam Deep, Lyle Sussman, *Smart Moves for People in Charge* (New York: Basic Books, 1995), 171.

11. Lencioni, *The Five Dysfunctions*, 91–92.

12. Michael Lewis, *The Blind Side: Evolution of a Game* (New York: W. W. Norton, 2006), 13–24; Leonard Shapiro, "The Hit That Changed a Career," *Washington Post*, November 18, 2005; E01.

13. Dave Anderson, "The Knicks' Philosophy Professor," *New York Times*, June 2, 1991, retrieved at http://query.nytimes.com/gst/fullpage
.html?res=9D0CE0D7173CF931A35755C0A967958260.

14. John Wooden, *Wooden on Leadership* (New York: McGraw-Hill, 2005), 182–83.

15. John Wooden, *Wooden* (New York: McGraw-Hill, 1997), 75–76.

16. Maggie Rauch, "A Will to Win: Rick Pitino on Motivation," AllBusiness.com, retrieved at http://www.allbusiness.com/marketing-advertising/4290829-1.html.

17. Whitey Herzog, *You're Missin' a Great Game* (New York: Berkley, 2000), 166–67.

18. Joe Torre with Henry Dreher, *Joe Torre's Ground Rules for Winners: 12 Keys to Managing Team Players* (New York: Hyperion, 2000), 21.

19. Judy Battista, "Pro Football: Bledsoe Accepts His Backup Role with Class," *New York Times*, February 1, 2002, retrieved at http://query.nytimes.com/gst/fullpage.html?res=9C05E2D8163DF932A35751C0A9649C8B63; Associated Press, "My Future Right Now Is One Game: Bledsoe Could Be Playing Final Game with Patriots," CNN/Sports Illustrated, January 31, 2002, retrieved at http://sportsillustrated.cnn.com/football/2002/playoffs/news/2002/01/31/bledsoe_future_ap/.

20. Bruce Markusen, "The First All-Black Lineup," BaseballGuru.com, retrieved at http://baseballguru.com/markusen/analysismarkusen01.html; Ed Gebhart, "Murtaugh Fielded First All-Minority Team, and He Didn't Even Know It," *Delco Times* (Delaware County, PA), September 11, 2006, retrieved at http://www.zwire.com/site/news.cfm?newsid=17179891&BRD=1675&PAG=461&dept_id=18168&rfi=6; Earl Bugaile, "The Night Clemente Broke the Record . . . and Other Memories from Three Rivers Stadium," Peters Township Magazine online, retrieved at http://ptm.cmpublishing.com/0606/0606threerivers_eb.htm.

21. Ibid.

22. Ibid.

23. Ibid.

## Extreme *American* Dreams . . . Depend on Teams

1. Reader's Digest Association, *Reader's Digest Quotable Quotes: Wit and Wisdom for All Occasions* (Pleasantville, NY: Reader's Digest Association, 1997), 184.

2. Walter Isaacson, *Benjamin Franklin: An American Life* (New York: Simon & Schuster, 2003), 313; remarks of Gerald R. Ford at Naturalization Ceremonies at Monticello, Virginia, July 5, 1976, retrieved at http://www.ford.utexas.edu/library/speeches/760649.htm; "Jefferson, Thomas," *Encyclopedia Americana*, retrieved at http://ap.grolier

.com/article?assetid=0221870-00; "Thomas Jefferson, First Inaugural Address," Bartleby.com, retrieved at http://www.bartleby.com/124/pres16.html; Trudy J. Kuehner, "New Perspectives on the Genesis of the U.S.: A Report of FPRI's History Institute for Teachers," *Newsletter of FPRI's Wachman Center for International Education*, Foreign Policy Research Institute, September 2004, retrieved at http://www.fpri.org/footnotes/092.200409.kuehner.earlyamericanhistory.html; United States Information Agency (USIA), "Chapter 3: The Road to Independence," *Outline of U.S. History*, retrieved at http://usinfo.state.gov/products/pubs/histryotln/road.htm.

3. Ibid.

4. "The Murder of Crispus Attucks," American Treasures of the Library of Congress, retrieved at http://www.loc.gov/exhibits/treasures/trr046.html.

5. Chester Hearn, *Army: An Illustrated History* (Osceola, WI: Zenith Press, 2006), 20.

6. Arthur Schlesinger Jr., "The Cult of Ethnicity, Good and Bad," *Time*, July 8, 1991, retrieved at http://www.time.com/time/magazine/article/0,9171,973355,00.html.

7. Neil A Hamilton, *Rebels and Renegades: A Chronology of Social and Political Dissent in the United States* (New York: Routledge, 2002), 339.

### 3. Principle 2: Great Leaders Build Extreme Dreams (Part 1)

1. Geoffrey Colvin, "How One CEO Learned to Fly," *Money* magazine, October 16, 2006, retrieved at http://money.cnn.com/2006/10/16/magazines/fortune/Secrets_greatness_McNerney_Boeing.fortune/index.htm.

2. John C. Maxwell, *The 21 Indispensable Qualities of a Leader: Becoming the Person Others Will Want to Follow* (Nashville: Thomas Nelson, 1999), 150.

3. Ronald Reagan, "Remarks at the Brandenburg Gate," West Berlin, Germany, June 12, 1987, Ronald Reagan Presidential Foundation and Library, retrieved at http://www.reaganlibrary.com/reagan/speeches/wall.asp; Michael Reagan with Jim Denney, *Twice Adopted* (Nashville: Broadman & Holman, 2004), 258–59.

4. Lain Hughes (University of Georgia), "CNN," *New Georgia Encyclopedia*, January 30, 2004, retrieved at http://www.newgeorgia encyclopedia.org/nge/Article.jsp?id=h-2643&pid=s-55.

5. Larry King, quoted in "Larry King," MyWordSmith.com, retrieved at http://www.truthteacher.com/mywordsmith/larry_king.htm.

6. Mike Sigers, "27 Secrets to Interviewing Like Larry King," February 6, 2008, retrieved at http://www.simplenomics.com/27-secrets-to-interviewing-like-larry-king-part-one/.

7. T. Boone Pickens, "T. Boone Pickens: His Life, His Legacy," BoonePickens.com, retrieved at http://www.boonepickens.com/boone-isms/default.asp.

8. Agatha Gilmore, "Smart Entertainment: How Tricks from Showbiz Can Help You Succeed," StoryFocus Communications, November 2007, retrieved at http://www.storyfocus.com/resources/2007_1202_clo.html.

9. Denis Waitley, *The New Dynamics of Winning: Gain the Mindset of a Champion for Unlimited Success in Business and Life* (New York: HarperCollins, 1995) 78.

10. Mike Krzyzewski with Jamie K. Spatola, *Beyond Basketball: Coach K's Keywords for Success* (New York: Warner Business Books, 2006), 33–34.

11. Mary Schmitt Boyer, "Boston Celtics Coach Doc Rivers Reveals Source of Inspiration," *Cleveland Plain Dealer*, May 15, 2008, retrieved at http://www.cleveland.com/sports/plaindealer/index.ssf?/base/sports/1210840297106190.xml&coll=2.

12. Andy Stanley, "Why I'm a One-Point Preacher," Rick Warren's Ministry Toolbox, retrieved at http://www.pastors.com/RWMT/article.asp?ArtID=9806.

13. Rick Pitino, *Success Is a Choice: Ten Steps to Overachieving in Business and Life* (New York: Broadway, 1997), 33–35.

14. Ibid.

15. Ibid.

16. Dale Carnegie, *How to Win Friends and Influence People* (New York: Simon & Schuster, 1998), xvi.

17. Jack and Suzy Welch, "The Leadership Mindset," The Welch Way: The Official Website of Jack and Suzy Welch, retrieved at http://welchway.com/Management/Career-Management/You-re-a-Leader-Now/The-Leadership-Mindset.aspx.

18. Danny Litwhiler, *Living the Baseball Dream* (Philadelphia: Temple University Press, 2007), 130.

19. Ibid.

20. Chad Lewis with Doug Robinson, "Reflections: Memories Include a Friendship with President Bush," *Desert News* (Salt Lake City), July 31, 2006, retrieved at http://findarticles.com/p/articles/mi_qn4188/is_20060731/ai_n16649966.

21. Ibid.

22. Ibid.

## 4. Principle 2: Great Leaders Build Extreme Dreams (Part 2)

1. Jill Ewert, "In-value-able," Sharing the Victory, retrieved at http:// www.sharingthevictory.com/vsItemDisplay.lsp?method=display &objectid=67821149-65D6-4D97-9FEBAD590F783CCC.

2. Ed Ruggero, *Duty First: A Year in the Life of West Point and the Making of American Leaders* (New York: HarperCollins, 2002), 243–44.

3. Charles W. Colson, "Personal Character: Does It Matter for Civil Society?," Geneva College Commencement Address, May 1998, Geneva College, Beaver Falls, PA, retrieved at http://www.american-rhetoric.com/speeches/charleswcolsongeneva.htm.

4. Thomas Jefferson, "A Personal View of Washington," the Prayer at Valley Forge, retrieved at http://www.prayer-at-valley-forge.com/personal_view.html.

5. David McCullough, "The Glorious Cause of America," assembly address at Brigham Young University, September 27, 2005, Speeches Web site, retrieved at http://speeches.byu.edu/reader/reader .php?id=10804.

6. Ibid.

7. Stephen E. Ambrose, "Excerpt from *To America: Personal Reflections of an Historian*," eReader.com, retrieved at http://www.ereader .com/servlet/mw?t=book_excerpt&bookid=8030&si=59.

8. Ibid.

9. Peter R. Henriques, *George Washington*, text retrieved at http:// chnm.gmu.edu/courses/henriques/hist615/gwnpsbio.htm.

10. Ibid.

11. Ibid.

12. Thomas Sowell, "What Kind of 'Experience'?," National Review Online, February 5, 2008, retrieved at http://article.national review.com/?q=YWExNTI0YjcxNjExZGJiY2MwZTcyYm JhZWI2NTczOGE=.

13. Colson, "Personal Character."

14. Hal Bodley, "More Visible Steinbrenner Going Strong at 75," *USA Today*, February 27, 2006, retrieved at http://www.usatoday.com/ sports/baseball/al/yankees/2006-02-27-steinbrenner_x.htm.

15. Dave Anderson, "Sports of the Times; The Gehrig, Showalter Connection," *New York Times*, September 23, 1993, retrieved at http://

query.nytimes.com/gst/fullpage.html?res=9F0CE1DD1430F930A157
5AC0A965958260.

16. Gerardo R. Ungson and John D. Trudel, *Engines of Prosperity: Templates for the Information Age* (London: Imperial College Press, 1998), 282.

17. Corporate Profile: "Past Leaders: John F. Welch, Jr.'s Biography," GE.com, retrieved at http://www.ge.com/company/history/bios/john_welch.html.

18. "Etcetera," University of Bahrain, retrieved at http://staff.uob.bh/eng/show.asp?user=VB2x9pTG4s5pPJm3ole4dre3Lo7rm3ole4dYe
fvb3FXxla8wdG4s5pPJDFFEg27&subo=274.

19. Margaret Thatcher, *The Downing Street Years: First Volume of the Memoirs of Margaret Thatcher* (New York: Harper Collins, 1993), 23.

20. Theodore Roosevelt, "Citizenship in a Republic," Speech at the Sorbonne, Paris, April 23, 1910, Theodore Roosevelt Association Web page, retrieved at http://www.theodoreroosevelt.org/life/quotes.htm.

21. Ward Hill Lamon, *Recollections of Abraham Lincoln, 1847–1865* (Washington, D.C.: Dorothy Lamon Teillard, 1911), 202; Isaac W. Heysinger, *Antietam and the Maryland and Virginia Campaigns of 1862* (New York: Neil Publishing Co., 1912), 285; Jonathan M. Beagle, "George Brinton McClellan," *Encyclopedia of the American Civil War: A Political, Social, and Military History* (New York: W. W. Norton & Company, 2000), 1277; David J. Eicher, *The Longest Night: A Military History of the Civil War* (New York: Simon & Schuster, 2001), 216–18.

22. Ibid.

23. Ibid.

24. Noel M. Tichy and Eli B. Cohen, *The Leadership Engine: How Winning Companies Build Leaders at Every Level* (New York: Harper-Collins, 2002), 189–91.

25. Ibid.

26. Ibid.

27. Ibid.

28. Venkata Ramana, *The Book of Uncommon Quips and Quotations* (Delhi: Pustak Mahal, 2004), 17.

29. Michael Bergdahl, *What I Learned from Sam Walton: How to Compete and Thrive in a Wal-Mart World* (Hoboken, NJ: John Wiley & Sons, 2004), 71–72.

30. Ibid.

31. Ibid.

32. Jill Ewert, "In-value-able," Sharing the Victory, retrieved at

http://www.sharingthevictory.com/vsItemDisplay.lsp?method=displa
y&objectid=67821149-65D6-4D97-9FEBAD590F783CCC.

33. Tom Osborne, *Faith in the Game: Lessons on Football, Work, and Life* (New York: Broadway Books, 1999), 15, 19, 126.

34. Peggy Noonan, "'Get It Done': Gen. Petraeus Is a Man of 'Straightforward Decisiveness' Who Values 'Action with Results,'" *Wall Street Journal*, August 10, 2007, retrieved at http://www.opinionjournal.com/columnists/pnoonan/?id=110010448.

## Extreme *Exploratory* Dreams . . . Depend on Teams

1. Dante Alighieri, *The Divine Comedy of Dante Alighieri*, trans. Henry Wadsworth Longfellow (Boston: Houghton, Mifflin and Company, 1895), 84.

2. Dennis N. T. Perkins, with Margaret P. Holtman, Paul R. Kessler, and Catherine McCarthy, *Leading at the Edge: Leadership Lessons from the Extraordinary Saga of Shackleton's Antarctic Expedition* (New York: American Management Associates, 2000), 61.

3. Ibid., 1–151; Alfred Lansing, *Endurance: Shackleton's Incredible Voyage* (New York: Carroll & Graf, 2002), 1–262; Sir Ernest Shackleton C.V.O., *South! The Story of Shackleton's Last Expedition 1914–1917*, full text retrieved at http://www.gutenberg.org/files/5199/5199-h/5199-h.htm.

## 5. Principle 3: Commitment Builds Extreme Dreams

1. John Cook, *The Book of Positive Quotations*, 2nd ed. (Minneapolis: Fairview Press, 2007), 266.

2. L. Jon Wertheim, "Sleight of Hands: With Doc Rivers Manipulating the NBA's Lowest-Paid Roster, the Magic Is Poised to Pull a Playoff Berth Out of Its Hat," *Sports Illustrated*, April 10, 2000, retrieved at http://vault.sportsillustrated.cnn.com/vault/article/magazine/MAG1018889/index.htm.

3. Riley, *Winner Within*, 66.

4. Jackie MacMullan, "The NBA: Feeling the Heat," *Sports Illustrated*, February 28, 2000, retrieved at http://vault.sportsillustrated.cnn.com/vault/article/magazine/MAG1018409/index.htm.

5. Nate Carter, *God Never Panics: He Is the Anchor of Your Soul* (Shippensburg, PA: Destiny Image Publishers, 2005), 100.

6. David H. Freedman, *Corps Business: The 30 Management Principles of the U.S. Marines* (New York: HarperCollins, 2000), 141.

7. Jack Canfield and Mark Victor Hansen, *A 5th Portion of Chicken Soup for the Soul: 101 More Stories to Open the Heart and Rekindle the Spirit* (Deerfield Beach, FL: Health Communications, 1998), 302.

8. Zig Ziglar, *Over the Top* (Nashville: Thomas Nelson, 1997), 234.

9. Jeff Keller, *Attitude Is Everything* (Tampa, FL: INTI Publishing, 1999), 41.

10. Patricia D. Galloway, *The 21st-Century Engineer: A Proposal for Engineering Education Reform* (Reston, VA: ASCE Publications, 2007), 72.

11. John C. Maxwell, *The 17 Essential Qualities of a Team Player: Becoming the Kind of Person Every Team Wants* (Nashville: Thomas Nelson, 2002), 19.

12. Ray Didinger, *Game Plans for Success: Winning Strategies for Business and Life from 10 Top NFL Head Coaches* (New York: McGraw-Hill Professional, 1996), 78.

13. Phillips, *Run to Win*, 104.

14. Ibid.

15. Ibid.

16. Donald R. Glover and Daniel W. Midura, *Team Building Through Physical Challenges*, (Champaign, IL: Human Kinetics, 1992), 33.

17. Vince Lombardi Jr., *What It Takes to Be #1: Vince Lombardi on Leadership* (New York: McGraw-Hill, 2001), 255.

18. Thom Loverro, *Hail Victory: An Oral History of the Washington Redskins* (Hoboken, NJ: John Wiley & Sons, 2006), 78.

19. "Inspirational Quotations," Climb Back Inc., retrieved at http://www.climbback.com/master.php?BPID=7.

20. John C. Maxwell, *Talent Is Never Enough: Discover the Choices That Will Take You Beyond Your Talent* (Nashville: Thomas Nelson, 2007), 263.

21. Brian Landman, "College Football: Bowden Exudes Tranquility While Talking of Family Loss," *St. Petersburg Times*, September 9, 2004, retrieved at http://www.sptimes.com/2004/09/09/Sports/Bowden_exudes_tranqui.shtml; Hubert Mizell, "Football Takes Backseat for Bowden Family," *St. Petersburg Times*, September 9, 2004, retrieved at http://www.sptimes.com/2004/09/09/Columns/Football_takes_backse.shtml; Mark Long, AP, "No. 5 Miami Defeats No. 4 Florida State in Overtime, 16-10," HurricaneSports.com, September 12, 2004, retrieved at http://hurricanesports.cstv.com/sports/m-footbl/recaps/091104aaa.html#; Joe Henderson, "It Was Hard for My Mind

Not to Be Somewhere Else," Tampa Bay Online, September 12, 2004, retrieved at http://sports.tbo.com/sports/MGBH9J7G0ZD.html.

22. Ibid.

23. Ibid.

24. Ibid.

25. Ibid.

26. Ibid.

## Extreme *Creative* Dreams . . . Depend on Teams

1. Annie Dillard, *An American Childhood* (New York: Harper & Row, 1987), 159.

2. Rona Goffen, *Renaissance Rivals: Michelangelo, Leonardo, Raphael, Titian* (New Haven, CT: Yale University Press, 2004), 440; Benjamin Blech and Roy Doliner, *The Sistine Secrets: Michelangelo's Forbidden Messages in the Heart of the Vatican* (New York: HarperCollins, 2008), 101–20; Diane Stanley, *Michelangelo* (New York: HarperTrophy, 2003), 6, 26–27; Giorgio Vasari, "Michael Angelo, Part 2," *Giorgio Vasari's Lives of the Artists*, retrieved at http://www.efn.org/~acd/vite/VasariMA2.html; Bernadine Barnes, "Michelangelo On and Off the Sistine Ceiling," *Art Bulletin*, December 1995, retrieved at http://findarticles.com/p/articles/mi_m0422/is_n4_v77/ai_17846073/pg_2; Joshua Korenblat, "Rethinking the Renaissance," Ekphrasis.net, retrieved at http://www.ekphrasis.net/arthistory.html.

3. Warren Bennis, "Interview: Organizing Genius—The Secrets of Creative Collaboration," *NewsHour with Jim Lehrer*, March 26, 1997, retrieved at http://www.pbs.org/newshour/gergen/march97/bennis_3-26.html.

4. Williams and Denney, *How to Be Like Walt*, 215.

5. Ibid., 177–214.

6. Ibid., 289.

7. Ibid., 296.

8. Ibid., 87.

9. Ibid., 96.

10. Ibid., 103.

## 6. Principle 4: Passion Builds Extreme Dreams

1. Mike Kilduff, "Passion Play: Athletes Describe Their Love for Playing Sports," *Sporting News*, August 27, 2001, retrieved at http://findarticles.com/p/articles/mi_m1208/is_35_225/ai_77811426.

2. Steve Addy, *The Detroit Pistons: Four Decades of Motor City Memories* (Champaign, IL: Sports Publishing, 1997), 132–34; Eric Neel, "The Big Score," ESPN.com, December 13, 2005, retrieved at http://sports.espn.go.com/espn/page2/story?page=neel/051213; "That 80s Show," NBA Encyclopedia Playoff Edition, retrieved at http://www.nba.com/history/highest_scoring_game_021107.html; John Maxwell, "Highest Scoring Game Ever," Motor City History, retrieved at http://www.nba.com/pistons/news/highest_score_071211.html.

3. Ibid.

4. Ibid.

5. Ibid.

6. Ibid.

7. Bill Russell, *Second Wind: The Memoirs of an Opinionated Man* (New York: Random House, 1979), 155–56.

8. Ibid., 156–57.

9. Mike Kilduff, "Passion Play: Athletes Describe Their Love for Playing Sports," *Sporting News*, August 27, 2001, retrieved at http://findarticles.com/p/articles/mi_m1208/is_35_225/ai_77811426.

10. Ibid.

11. Lawrence Shainberg, " Finding 'The Zone,' " *New York Times*, April 9, 1989, retrieved at http://query.nytimes.com/gst/fullpage.html?res=950DE0DD1E3FF93AA35757C0A96F948260&sec=&spon=&pagewanted=print; Andrew Cooper, "In the Zone: The Zen of Sports," Shambhala Sun, March 1995, retrieved at http://www.shambhalasun.com/index.php?option=com_content&task=view&id=2098; Mychael Urban, "Taking a trip to 'The Zone,'" April 27, 2007, MLB.com, retrieved at http://mlb.mlb.com/news/article.jsp?ymd=20070426&content_id=1932055&vkey=news_mlb&fext=.jsp&c_id=mlb; Rob Reheuser, "A Stroll Down Memory Lane," NBA Encyclopedia Playoff Edition, retrieved at http://www.nba.com/encyclopedia/finals/Memory_Lane.html.

12. Ibid.

13. Ibid.

14. Ibid.

15. Ibid.

16. Ibid.

17. Gene N. Landrum, *Empowerment: The Competitive Edge in Sports, Business, and Life* (Burlington, Ontario: Brendan Kelly Publishing, 2006), 390.

18. Stuart Hameroff, "Time, Consciousness and Quantum Events

in Fundamental Spacetime Geometry," retrieved at http://www.quan-tumconsciousness.org/Time.htm.

19. Ibid.

20. Ibid.

21. Shainberg, "Finding 'The Zone'"; Andrew Cooper, "In the Zone: The Zen of Sports," *Shambhala Sun*, March 1995, retrieved at http://www.shambhalasun.com/index.php?option=com_content&task=view&id=2098; Mychael Urban, "Taking a trip to 'The Zone,'" April 27, 2007, MLB.com, retrieved at http://mlb.mlb.com/news/article.jsp?ymd=20070426&content_id=1932055&vkey=news_mlb&fext=.jsp&c_id=mlb; Rob Reheuser, "A Stroll Down Memory Lane," NBA Encyclopedia Playoff Edition, retrieved at http://www.nba.com/encyclopedia/finals/Memory_Lane.html.

22. Ibid.

23. Ibid.

24. Kirsten A. Holmstedt, *Band of Sisters: American Women at War in Iraq* (Mechanicsburg, PA: Stackpole Books, 2007), 27–34.

25. Ibid.

26. Eugene G. D'Aquili and Andrew B. Newberg, *The Mystical Mind: Probing the Biology of Religious Experience* (Minneapolis: Fortress Press, 1999), 142.

27. Ibid.

28. Michael Cassutt, "The Cassutt Files: In the Zone," *Sci Fi Weekly*, October 23, 2006, retrieved at http://www.scifi.com/sfw/column/sfw13949.html.

29. Mike Krzyzewski with Donald T. Phillips, *Five-Point Play: The Story of Duke's Amazing 2000-2001 Championship Season* (New York: Warner Books, 2001), 89–91.

30. Ibid.

31. Ibid.

32. Ibid.

33. Mike Vaccaro, *Emperors and Idiots: The Hundred Year Rivalry between the Yankees and Red Sox, From the Very Beginning to the End of the Curse* (New York: Doubleday, 2005), 235.

34. Jim Prime and Bill Nowlin, *Ted Williams: The Pursuit of Perfection* (Champaign, IL: Sports Publishing, 2002), 185.

35. Sam Amico, "Around the NBA Playoffs: The Amico Report," InsideHoops.com, April 26, 2004, retrieved at http://www.inside-hoops.com/amico-042604.shtml.

36. Mike Kilduff, "Passion Play: Athletes Describe Their Love for

Playing Sports," *Sporting News*, August 27, 2001, retrieved at http://findarticles.com/p/articles/mi_m1208/is_35_225/ai_77811426.

37. Andy Russell, *A Steeler Odyssey* (Champagne, IL: Sports Publishing, 1998), 153–54; Mike Kilduff, "Passion Play: Athletes Describe Their Love for Playing Sports," *Sporting News*, August 27, 2001, retrieved at http://findarticles.com/p/articles/mi_m1208/is_35_225/ai_77811426.

38. Ibid.

39. Ibid.

40. Ibid.

41. "Johnny Unitas," ExplorePAHistory.com, retrieved at http://www.explorepahistory.com/hmarker.php?markerId=1005; Bill Curry, "Unitas, the Teammate, Was Larger Than Life," ESPN.com, September 11, 2002, retrieved at http://espn.go.com/nfl/columns/curry_bill/1430697.html; Rick Johnson, "The Making of Johnny U," Baltimore24x7.com, September 29, 2006, retrieved at http://www.baltimore24x7.com/column_view.php?cid=88&id=573&view=archive.

42. Ibid.

43. Ibid.

44. George Weigel, "Review: Johnny U by Tom Callahan," *Commentary*, January 2007, retrieved at https://www.commentarymagazine.com/viewarticle.cfm/johnny-u-by-tom-callahan-10822?page=2.

## Extreme *Global Security* Dreams . . . Depend on Teams

1. Robert S. Mueller III, "San Francisco Global Trade Council, San Francisco, California, September 30, 2003," Federal Bureau of Investigation, Major Executive Speeches, retrieved at http://www.fbi.gov/pressrel/speeches/gebhardt093003.htm.

2. Stanley P. Hirshson, *General Patton: A Soldier's Life* (New York: HarperCollins, 2002), 474–76; Robert G. Torricelli and Andrew Carroll, *In Our Own Words: Extraordinary Speeches of the American Century* (New York: Kodansha America, 1999), 140–46.

3. Ibid.

4. Ibid.

5. Ibid.

6. Gerard Alexander, "A Lifesaving War: The Death Toll in Iraq Would Have Been Vastly Higher over the Last Year If Saddam Had Remained in Power," *Weekly Standard*, March 29, 2004, vol. 009, no. 28, retrieved at http://www.weeklystandard.com/Utilities/printer_preview.asp?idArticle=3889; CNN, "Hussein Was Symbol of Autocracy,

Cruelty in Iraq," CNN.com, December 30, 2006, retrieved at http://www.cnn.com/2006/WORLD/meast/12/29/hussein.obit/index.html.

7. Ibid.

8. Michael E. O'Hanlon and Kenneth M. Pollack, "A War We Just Might Win," *New York Times*, July 30, 2007, retrieved at http://www.nytimes.com/2007/07/30/opinion/30pollack.html?_r=2&page wanted=1&oref=slogin; Robert Perito, "USIPeace Briefing: Embedded Provincial Reconstruction Teams," United States Institute of Peace, March 2008, retrieved at http://www.usip.org/pubs/usipeace_brief-ings/2008/0305_prt.html.

9. Ibid.

10. Ibid.

11. Anne Flaherty, "New Iraq Report: Fifteen of Eighteen Bench-marks Satisfactory," Associated Press, July 1, 2008, retrieved at http://ap.google.com/article/ALeqM5j2KfQBk9ZhPhOJZ7biQo-Ikmd-JoAD91LA8P80; Karen DeYoung, "U.S. Embassy Cites Progress in Iraq: Most Congressionally Set Benchmarks Met, Report Finds," *Washington Post*, July 2, 2008, A08.

## 7. Principle 5: Thinking *Team* Builds Extreme Dreams

1. Dave Anderson, "The Knicks' Philosophy Professor," *New York Times*, June 2, 1991, retrieved at http://query.nytimes.com/gst/fullpage .html?res=9D0CE0D7173CF931A35755C0A967958260.

2. Steve Bulpett, "Celts Unite, Word Has It: New Motto Promotes Team Success," *Boston Herald*, October 4, 2007, retrieved at http://www.bostonherald.com/sports/basketball/celtics/view.bg?articleid= 1035964; Mary Schmitt, "Boston Celtics Coach Doc Rivers Reveals Source of Inspiration," *Cleveland Plain Dealer*, May 15, 2008, retrieved at http://www.cleveland.com/sports/plaindealer/index.ssf?/base/sports/ 1210840297106190.xml&coll=2; CBS Sports, "Boston vs. Los Ange-les: Celtics Can Hang 17th Title Banner after Destroying Lakers in Game 6," CBSSports.com Wire Reports, June 18, 2008, retrieved at http://www.sportsline.com/nba/gamecenter/recap/NBA_20080617_ LAL@BOS.

3. Ibid.

4. Ibid.

5. Bill Russell with Alan Hilburg and David Falkner, *Russell Rules: 11 Lessons on Leadership from the Twentieth Century's Greatest Winner* (New York: New American Library, 2001), 41–44.

6. Ibid.

7. Jim Calhoun, *A Passion to Lead: Seven Leadership Secrets for Success in Business, Sports, and Life* (New York: Macmillan, 2007), 208.

8. Ken Rappoport, *Tales from the Tar Heel Locker Room* (Champagne, IL: Sports Publishing, 2005), 95.

9. Don Martin, *TeamThink* (New York: Dutton, 1993), 219.

10. Sam Walton with John Huey, *Sam Walton: Made in America* (New York: Bantam, 1993), 16.

11. Ken Blanchard and Sheldon Bowles, *High Five!: The Magic of Working Together* (New York: HarperCollins, 2001), 58–60.

12. Bill Bradley, *Values of the Game* (New York: Broadway, 2000), 19.

13. Steve Jacobson, *Carrying Jackie's Torch: The Players Who Integrated Baseball—and America* (Chicago: Lawrence Hill Books, 2007), 217.

14. Phillips, *Run to Win*, 23.

15. Lee Iacocca with William Novak, *Iacocca: an Autobiography* (New York: Bantam, 1984), 44.

16. Kevin C. Cox, "Dogged pursuit of a title marks Fresno State's Cinderella run," *Sports Illustrated*, June 25, 2008, retrieved at http://sportsillustrated.cnn.com/2008/writers/luke_winn/06/25/winn.fresnostate/index.html; Kevin C. Cox, " Improbable Fresno State Wins CWS," *Sports Illustrated*, June 26, 2008, retrieved at http://sportsillustrated.cnn.com/2008/writers/luke_winn/06/26/cws.title.game/index.html; Associated Press, "Fresno State Shocks Georgia for First CWS championship," June 26, 2008, ESPN.com, retrieved at http://sports.espn.go.com/ncaa/baseball/recap?gameId=2817700611; Tim Griffin, "Bulldogs Overcome Deficits, Injuries to Shock College Baseball World," ESPN.com, retrieved at http://sports.espn.go.com/ncaa/news/story?id=3462143; Fresno State University, "Postgame Quotes," Bulldogs.com, June 25, 2008, retrieved at http://www.bulldogs.com/fresno/item/postgame_quotes/; Jennifer Iannone, "Fresno State Infielder Fueled by Memory of His Late Mother," *Athens (GA) Banner-Herald*, June 25, 2008, retrieved at http://www.onlineathens.com/stories/062508/baseball_20080625054.shtml; BarkBoard.com Staff, "Fresno State— 2008 National Champs!," WarriorSportsNetwork.com, June 25, 2008, retrieved at http://hawaii.scout.com/a.z?s=219&p=2&c=764981.

17. Ibid.

18. Ibid.

19. Ibid.

20. Ibid.

21. Ibid.

22. Ibid.

23. Ibid.

## Extreme *Elevation* Dreams . . . Depend on Teams

1. John Gookin, *NOLS Wilderness Wisdom: Quotes for Inspirational Exploration* (Mechanicsburg, PA: Stackpole Books, 2003), 11.

2. Sir Edmund Hillary, "Climber: Everest's First Conqueror Reflects on the Changing Face of the Highest Adventure," *People*, June 14, 1999, vol. 51, no. 22, retrieved at http://www.people.com/people/archive/article/0,,20128487,00.html; Brian Sweeney, ed., "Sir Edmund Hillary: King of the World," NZEdge.com, retrieved at http://www.nzedge.com/heroes/hillary.html; Audrey Salkeld, "First to Summit," NOVA Online Adventure, November 2000, retrieved at http://www.pbs.org/wgbh/nova/everest/history/firstsummit.html; Alan Hobson, *From Everest to Enlightenment: An Adventure of the Soul* (Calgary, Alberta: Inner Everests, 1999), 71; Lindsay Taylor, "Mountaineer Sir Edmund Hillary Dies," January 11, 2008, retrieved at http://www.channel4.com/news/articles/society/environment/mountaineer+sir+edmund+hillary+dies+/1316247.

3. Ibid.

4. Ibid.

5. Ibid.

6. Ibid.

7. Ibid.

8. Ibid.

9. Ibid.

10. Ibid.

11. Ibid.

## 8. Principle 6: Empowered Individuals Build Extreme Dreams

1. Steve Farber, "How to Get the Story Learner's Edge," My ArticleArchive.com, retrieved at http://www.myarticlearchive.com/articles/6/219.htm.

2. Warren Bennis, *Managing the Dream: Reflections on Leadership and Change* (New York: Da Capo Press, 2000), 29–30.

3. Robert K. Cooper and Ayman Sawaf, *Executive EQ: Emotional Intelligence in Leadership and Organizations* (New York: Perigee, 1998), 87.

4. Mark DeCocinis: Regional Vice President (Asia Pacific), Ritz-Carlton Hotel Company, "The Portman Ritz-Carlton: Setting Up Our Ladies and Gentlemen for Success," Exhibit 1: "The Ritz Carlton: Credo, Employee Promise, Motto, and 12 Service Values," 9, retrieved at http://media.ft.com/cms/5aa22940-74a7-11db-bc76-0000779e2340.pdf.

5. Fast Company staff, "Is Your Company up to Speed?" *Fast Company*, May 2003, retrieved at http://www.fastcompany.com/magazine/71/uptospeed.html.

6. "The Importance of Teamwork," QuoteDoctor.com, retrieved at http://www.quotedoctor.com/teamwork.htm.

7. Marty Schottenheimer, "Creating a Winning Environment," from Ray Didinger, *Game Plans for Success: Winning Strategies for Business and Life from 10 Top NFL Head Coaches* (New York: McGraw-Hill Professional, 1996), 17–18.

8. Philip Holden, *The Excellent Manager's Companion* (Aldershot, UK: Gower Publishing, 1998), 185.

9. Mike Krzyzewski, quoted in "Academy of Achievement: The Hall of Preparation," Achievement.org, retrieved at http://www.achievement.org/autodoc/steps/prp?target=krz0-004.

10. Roland Lazenby, "Big Norman," HoopsHype.com Articles, August 24, 2006, retrieved at http://hoopshype.com/articles/wilt_lazenby.htm.

11. Paul Bryant with John Underwood, "Part I: I'll Tell You About Football," *Sports Illustrated*, August 15, 1966, retrieved at http://vault.sportsillustrated.cnn.com/vault/article/magazine/MAG1078879/7/index.htm.

12. Herzog, *You're Missin' a Great Game*, 172.

13. Tony Grossi, *Tales from the Browns Sideline* (Champagne, IL: Sports Publishing, 2004), 64.

14. Fred Smith Sr., "Essays on Competence: Maintain the Value of Compliments," ChristianityTodayLibrary.com, retrieved at http://ctlibrary.com/lebooks/thepastorssoul/soulintegrity/pstsoul5-11.html.

15. Mark Perry, *Grant and Twain: The Story of a Friendship That Changed America* (New York: Random House, 2004), 174–76.

16. Ibid.

17. Ibid.

18. Ibid.

19. Ibid.

## Extreme *Cosmic* Dreams . . . Depend on Teams

1. Lance Secretan, *Inspire! What Great Leaders Do* (Hoboken, NJ: John Wiley & Sons, 2004), 28.

2. K. P. Nayar, "Missing Out on the Glory," *Telegraph* (Calcutta), February 5, 2003, retrieved at http://www.telegraphindia.com/1030205/asp/opinion/story_1638008.asp.

3. Philip Chien, *Columbia, Final Voyage: The Last Voyage of NASA's First Space Shuttle* (Boston: Birkhäuser, 2006), 49–50; Nancy Gibbs, "Seven Astronauts, One Fate," *Time*, February 2, 2003, retrieved at http://www.time.com/time/magazine/article/0,9171,1101030210-418517,00.html; Todd S. Purdum, "Loss of the Shuttle: The Trauma; Another Blow and More Loss for an Already Anxious Nation," *New York Times*, February 2, 2003, retrieved at http://query.nytimes.com/gst/fullpage.html?res=9904E1DE1238F931A35751C0A9659C8B63; Amy Waldman "Loss of the Shuttle: The Call of Space; For Resolute Girl, the Traditions of India Imposed No Limits," *New York Times*, February 3, 2003, retrieved at http://query.nytimes.com/gst/fullpage.html?res=9A0DE0D61338F930A35751C0A9659C8B63; K. P. Nayar, "Missing Out on the Glory," *Telegraph* (Calcutta), February 5, 2003, retrieved at http://www.telegraphindia.com/1030205/asp/opinion/story_1638008.asp; Josy Joseph, "The Chawlas' Odyssey," *Rediff India Abroad*, February 7, 2003, retrieved at http://www.rediff.com/news/2003/feb/01spec.htm.

4. Ibid.

5. Ibid.

6. Ibid.

7. CNN, "Dittemore: 'Bound Together with the Threat of Disaster,'" CNN, February 2, 2003, retrieved at http://www.cnn.com/2003/US/02/01/sprj.colu.dittemore.cnna/.

8. President John F. Kennedy, "Remarks at the Dedication of the Aerospace Medical Health Center," San Antonio, Texas, November 21, 1963, retrieved at http://www.jfklibrary.org/Historical+Resources/Archives/Reference+Desk/Speeches/JFK/003POF03AerospaceMedicalCenter11211963.htm.

9. David Whitehouse, "The Eagle Has Landed," July 16, 1999, BBC News, retrieved at http://news.bbc.co.uk/2/hi/special_report/1999/07/99/the_moon_landing/394481.stm.

## 9. Principle 7: Respect and Trust Build Extreme Dreams

1. Donald T. Phillips with Adm. James M. Loy, USCG, Ret., *Character in Action: The U.S. Coast Guard on Leadership* (Annapolis, MD: Naval Institute Press, 2003), 14.

2. Karen Lowry Miller with Joann Muller, "Jurgen Schrempp: The Auto Baron," *BusinessWeek*, November 16, 1998, retrieved at http://www.businessweek.com/1998/46/b3604044.htm.

3. C. William Pollard, *The Soul of the Firm* (Grand Rapids: Zondervan, 2000), 35.

4. Neville L. Johnson, *The John Wooden Pyramid of Success: The Authorized Biography* (Los Angeles: Cool Titles, 2003), 122–23.

5. Ibid.

6. Harvey Araton, "Sports of the Times; Jeter Lays Off His Pal's Bait, Saying Plenty," *New York Times*, March 6, 2001, retrieved at http://query.nytimes.com/gst/fullpage.html?res=9F06E2DF103BF93 5A35750C0A9679C8B63&sec=&spon=&pagewanted=all.

7. Ibid.

8. Seth Livingstone, "Gardenhire Teaches Respect for the Game," *USA Today Baseball Weekly*, May 14, 2002, retrieved at http://www.usa today.com/sports/bbw/2002-05-15/extra.htm.

9. Ryne Sandberg, "Induction Speech," Baseball Hall of Fame, Cooperstown, New York, July 31, 2005, Community High School District 155 Web site, retrieved at http://www.d155.org/cls/Athletics/baseball/documents/sandberg_speech.doc.

10. Phil Jackson, "Pacific Phil," ESPN.com, 1999, retrieved at http://sports.espn.go.com/espnmag/story?id=3244734.

11. Ibid.

12. Walt Frazier, *The Game Within the Game* (New York: Hyperion, 2007), 17–19.

13. John Lombardo, *A Fire to Win: The Life and Times of Woody Hayes* (New York: Macmillan, 2005), 248.

14. Brad Adler, *Coaching Matters: Leadership and Tactics of the NFL's Ten Greatest Coaches* (Herndon, VA: Brassey's, 2003), 110.

15. Donald Honig, *The Man in the Dugout: Fifteen Big League Managers Speak Their Minds* (Lincoln: University of Nebraska Press, 1995), 4.

16. Yogi Berra with Dave Kaplan, *What Time Is It? You Mean Now? Advice for Life from the Zennest Master of Them All* (New York: Simon & Schuster, 2003), 111.

17. Ibid., 108–10.

18. Christopher J. Anderson, "Dick Winters' Reflections on His Band of Brothers, D-Day and Leadership," HistoryNet.com, retrieved at http://historynet.com/ah/blwinters/index.html; John C. McManus, *The Americans at D-Day: The American Experience at the Normandy Invasion* (New York: Macmillan, 2004), 216–24.

19. Ibid.

20. Ibid.

21. Ibid.

22. Cole C. Kingseed, *Old Glory Stories: American Combat Leadership* (Annapolis, MD: Naval Institute Press, 2006), 261.

23. Roone Arledge, *Roone: A Memoir* (New York: HarperCollins, 2004), 6–7.

24. Ibid.

25. Andrew Halcro (President, Avis/Alaska), "Hope Springs Eternal for Red Sox Fans," Article on Teamwork, AndrewHalcro.com, retrieve at http://www.andrewhalcro.com/hope_springs_eternal_for_red_sox_fans.

26. Robert Redmount, *The Red Sox Encyclopedia* (Champaign, IL: Sports Publishing, 1998), 201.

27. Glenn Stout and Richard A. Johnson, *Red Sox Century: The Definitive History of Baseball's Most Storied Franchise* (New York: Houghton Mifflin Books, 2004), 350–51.

28. Ibid.

29. Leigh Montville, "Long Gone," *Sports Illustrated*, July 2, 1990, retrieved at http://vault.sportsillustrated.cnn.com/vault/article/magazine/MAG1136735/index.htm.

## Extreme *Healing* Dreams ... Depend on Teams

1. Steve Davis, Larry Elin, and Grant Reeher, *Click on Democracy: The Internet's Power to Change Political Apathy into Civic Action* (Boulder CO: Westview Press, 2002), 214.

2. "Honest Questions with Jon Huntsman," *Glenn Beck Show* (Encore Presentation) December 25, 2007, transcript retrieved at http://transcripts.cnn.com/TRANSCRIPTS/0712/25/gb.01.html.

3. Ibid.

4. Ibid.

5. Jon M. Huntsman, *Winners Never Cheat: Everyday Values We Learned as Children (But May Have Forgotten)* (Upper Saddle River, NJ: Wharton School Publishing, 2005), 163.

6. "Honest Questions with Jon Huntsman."

7. Jon Huntsman, "Foreword," *Prostate Cancer: Portraits of Empowerment* by Nadine Jelsing (Boulder, CO: Westview Press, 1999), ix–xi.

8. "Honest Questions with Jon Huntsman."

9. Neil Cavuto, *More Than Money: True Stories of People Who Learned Life's Ultimate Lesson* (New York: HarperCollins, 2004), 239.

10. Ibid., 243–44.

11. "Honest Questions with Jon Huntsman."

12. Dave Thomas, founder, Wendy's International, "What Makes for Success?," July 1996, Hillsdale College *Imprimis*, retrieved at http://www.hillsdale.edu/news/imprimis/archive/issue.asp?year=1996&month=07; St. Jude Children's Research Hospital, "Danny's Promise," StJude.org, retrieved at http://www.stjude.org/stjude/v/index.jsp?vgnextoid=576 bfa2454e70110VgnVCM1000001e0215acRCRD&vgnextchannel=5 af213c016118010VgnVCM1000000e2015acRCRD; Abny Santicola, "Star Power: When Newly Successful Actor Danny Thomas Founded ALSAC/St. Jude Children's Research Hospital 50 Years Ago, He Started a Hollywood Fundraising Connection That Still Shines Today," FundRaisingSuccessMag.com, June 1, 2007, retrieved at http://www.fundraisingsuccessmag.com/story/story.bsp?sid=56707&var=story; Gary L. Lisman and Arlene Parr, *Bittersweet Memories: A History of the Peoria State Hospital* (Victoria, BC: Trafford Publishing, 2005), 241–42.

13. Ibid.

14. Ibid.

15. Ibid.

16. Ibid.

17. Ibid.

## 10. Principle 8: Strong Character Builds Extreme Dreams

1. Anthony J. Le Storti, *When You're Asked to Do the Impossible: Principles of Business Teamwork and Leadership from the U.S. Army's Elite Rangers* (Guilford, CT: Globe Pequot, 2003), 153.

2. William Leggett, "A Tortured Road to 715," *Sports Illustrated*, May 28, 1973, retrieved at http://vault.sportsillustrated.cnn.com/vault/article/magazine/MAG1087387/index.htm.

3. Ron Fimrite, "End of the Glorious Ordeal," *Sports Illustrated*, April 15, 1974, retrieved at http://sportsillustrated.cnn.com/baseball/mlb/features/1999/aaron/aaron_story/.

4. Ibid.

5. Thomas E. Ricks, "We Can Learn from Them," *Parade*, November 9, 1997, reprinted with permission by Sgt. Grit Marine Special-

ties, Grunt.com, retrieved at http://www.grunt.com/scuttlebutt/corps -stories/bootcamp/corpsvalues.asp.

6. Ibid.

7. Ibid.

8. Dale Carnegie and Associates, Inc., Oliver Crom and Michael Crom, *The Sales Advantage: How to Get It, Keep It, and Sell More Than Ever* (New York: Simon & Schuster, 2003), 59.

9. *People* staff, "Tom Brokaw: News Anchor," *People*, May 10, 1999, retrieved at http://www.people.com/people/archive/article/0,,20128165,00.html.

10. Jill Rosenfeld, "Training to Work: Tom Brokaw," *Fast Company*, July 2000, retrieved at http://www.fastcompany.com/magazine/37/one.html?page=0%2C6.

11. Maxwell, *The 17 Indisputable Laws*, 108.

12. Arthur Ashe with Arnold Rampersad, *Days of Grace* (New York: Ballantine, 1993), 4.

13. Stephen Covey, "The Thirteen Behaviors of a High Trust Leader," retrieved at http://www.coveylink.com/documents/13%20Behaviors%20Handout%20(wtihout%20contact).pdf.

14. Craig Neff, "Scorecard: An Honest Kid," *Sports Illustrated*, July 10, 1989, retrieved at http://vault.sportsillustrated.cnn.com/vault/article/magazine/MAG1068563/3/index.htm.

15. Ibid.

16. Ibid.

17. Richard Stengel, "Stardom? They'd Rather Pass," *Time*, March 16, 1998, retrieved at http://www.time.com/time/magazine/article/0,9171,987992,00.html.

18. Cal Ripken Jr. with Mike Bryan, *The Only Way I Know* (New York: Penguin, 1998), 289.

19. W. David Lewis, *Eddie Rickenbacker: An American Hero in the Twentieth Century* (Baltimore: Johns Hopkins University Press, 2005), 124.

20. Peter King, "At All Cost: T.O.'s Super Bowl Saga Can't Compare to Youngblood's," *Sports Illustrated*, January 31, 2005, retrieved at http://sportsillustrated.cnn.com/2005/writers/peter_king/01/30/mmqb.sboffweek/index.html; Wayne Drehs, "Wait over for Hall-bound Youngblood," November 19, 2003, ESPN.com, retrieved at http://espn.go.com/classic/s/2001/0127/1044351.html; Larry Harris, "What We're About," Ed Block Courage Award, retrieved at http://www.edblock.org/about.htm; Tom Danyluk, Paul Zimmerman, *The*

*Super '70s: Memories from Pro Football's Greatest Era* (Chicago: Mad Uke Publishing, 2005), 213.

21. Ibid.

22. Ibid.

23. Ibid.

24. Ibid.

25. Ibid.

26. Ibid.

27. Ibid.

28. Ibid.

29. Ibid.

30. Mike Towle, *I Remember Jim Valvano: Personal Reflections and Anecdotes About College Basketball's Most Exuberant Final Four Coach, as Told by the People and Players Who Knew Him* (Nashville: Cumberland House Publishing, 2001), 139; "Jim Valvano, 1946–1993," the V Foundation for Cancer Research Web site, retrieved at http://jimmyv.org/rememberingjim/timeline.cfm; Jim Valvano, "Espy Awards Acceptance Speech," March 4, 1993, the V Foundation for Cancer Research Web site, retrieved at http://jimmyv.org/rememberingjim/espy.cfm.

31. Ibid.

32. Ibid.

33. Fred Smith Sr., *Breakfast with Fred* (Ventura, CA: Regal Books, 2007), 105–6.

34. Fred Smith, "Fred Smith Urges Us to Consider the True Meaning of Ethical Living," SAWorship.com (San Antonio's Online Christian Magazine), retrieved at http://www.saworship.com/article-page.php?ID=1369&Page=index.php.

## Epilogue: Extreme Dreams for Extreme Times

1. Carl E. Larson, Frank M. J. LaFasto, *Teamwork: What Must Go Right, What Can Go Wrong* (Thousand Oaks, CA: Sage Publications, 1989), 13.

2. Alan Fram and Eileen Putman, "Everything Seemingly Is Spinning Out of Control," Associated Press, June 22, 2008, retrieved at http://ap.google.com/article/ALeqM5gFmTVpBYsENBOX-9wQvY ZGzhk-xQD91F0KMO0.

3. Edmund L. Andrews, "Vast Bailout by U.S. Proposed in Bid to Stem Financial Crisis," *New York Times*, September 18, 2008, retrieved at http://www.nytimes.com/2008/09/19/business/19fed.html; Michael Gray, "Almost Armageddon: Markets were 500 Trades From

a Meltdown," *New York Post*, September 21, 2008, retrieved at http://www.nypost.com/seven/09212008/business/almost_armageddon_130110.htm; Vikas Bajaj, "Whiplash Ends a Roller Coaster Week," *New York Times*, October 10, 2008, retrieved at http://www.nytimes.com/2008/10/11/business/11markets.html.

4. Jennifer 8. Lee, "New York and the Panic of 1873," *New York Times*, October 14, 2008, retrieved at http://cityroom.blogs.nytimes.com/2008/10/14/learning-lessons-from-the-panic-of-1873/?scp=4&sq=crash&st=cse.

5. William J. Bernstein, *The Birth of Plenty: How the Prosperity of the Modern World Was Created* (New York: McGraw-Hill Professional, 2004), 364.

6. Molly Billings, "The Influenza Pandemic of 1918," Stanford.edu, June 1997 (modified February 2005), retrieved at http://virus.stanford.edu/uda/.

7. The Eleanor Roosevelt Papers, "The Great Depression (1929–1939)," *Teaching Eleanor Roosevelt*, ed. Allida Black, June Hopkins, et al. (Hyde Park, NY: Eleanor Roosevelt National Historic Site, 2003), retrieved at http://www.nps.gov/archive/elro/glossary/great-depression.htm.

8. The Gilder Lerhman Institute of American History, "Module: World War II," retrieved at http://www.gilderlehrman.org/teachers/module19/index.html.

9. Maria Shriver, *And One More Thing Before You Go . . .* (New York: Simon & Schuster, 2008), 18.

You can contact Pat Williams at:
Pat Williams
c/o Orlando Magic
8701 Maitland Summit Boulevard
Orlando, FL 32810
phone: 407-916-2404
pwilliams@orlandomagic.com

Visit Pat Williams's Web site at:
www.PatWilliamsMotivate.com

If you would like to set up a speaking engagement for Pat Williams, please call or write his assistant, Andrew Herdliska, at the above address, or call him at 407-916-2401. Requests can also be faxed to 407-916-2986 or e-mailed to aherdliska@orlandomagic .com.

We would love to hear from you. Please send your comments about this book to Pat Williams at the above address. Thank you.